PENGUIN HANDBOOKS

Left Over for Tomorrow

Marika Hanbury Tenison was born during the Munich crisis and educated at a London day school, which she left when she was fifteen. Until her marriage to the explorer Robin Hanbury Tenison in 1959 she lived in Chelsea. Now her time is divided between their remote farm on Bodmin Moor in Cornwall (where she writes and cooks, and breeds Tibetan dogs) and their mews house in Paddington, where she has built a streamlined mini test-kitchen. She has recently accompanied her husband on an expedition to the Amazon jungle.

Although never taught to cook professionally, she has been interested in the subject since she was ten, and has collected cookery books for as long as she can remember. Her love for entertaining dates back to her childhood, when she helped her mother, who is Swedish and herself a brilliant cook, to prepare dinner parties. Since she began writing a few years ago her articles on cookery, travel and other subjects have appeared in various magazines including *Nova*, the *Observer*, *Vogue* and *Homes and Gardens*, and she is frequently to be seen on Westward Television. She is at present cookery editor of the *Sunday Telegraph* and cookery adviser of the 'Magpie' programme on Thames Television. Her first cookery book, *Soups and Hors d'Oeuvres*, has been published in Penguins, and she has recently written *Deep Freeze Cookery*

Robin and Marika Hanbury Tenison have a daughter who is studying at a ballet school and a small son who does nothing much yet.

Left Over for Tomorrow

MARIKA HANBURY TENISON

PENGUIN BOOKS

Penguin Books Ltd, Harmondsworth,
Middlesex, England
Penguin Books Inc., 7110 Ambassador Road,
Baltimore, Maryland 21207, U.S.A.
Penguin Books Australia Ltd, Ringwood,
Victoria, Australia

First published 1971
Reprinted 1972, 1973
Copyright © Marika Hanbury Tenison, 1971

Made and printed in Great Britain by
Cox & Wyman Ltd,
London, Reading and Fakenham
Set in Monotype Bembo

To Lucy with my love and with thanks to Mary Holborow who did so much to make this book possible

Contents

Foreword

In praise of leftover dishes

Since first starting to write this book I've met a number of
Philistines who've said things like, 'But I thought efficient
housekeepers shopped to *avoid* having leftovers.' I've also read
a number of cookery books which maintain that, whenever
possible, only just enough meat for one meal should be bought
at a time.

What a lot these people miss, and how empty their culinary
experiences must be!

Leftovers for me form the backbone of my daily family
cooking and also the basis for many of my favourite dinner
party dishes. Without leftovers my housekeeping bills would
soar and I would lose a large portion of the fun and satisfaction
I get from cooking and experimenting with food.

What counts as a leftover?

Anything that has been cooked and remains uneaten at the
end of a meal; carcases and bones; the trimmings of meat;
the outside leaves and peelings of vegetables; egg whites when
the yolks have been used for mayonnaise; those crumbs of
stale cake and the last bit of jelly which no one had room for.
The scope is enormous and the uses to which they can be put
are as many as they are varied.

Even the most mundane and humble of ingredients can add
flavour to some other recipe or be transformed into a really
delicious dish in its own right. Onion skin, for instance – those
shiny brown leaves which are so often chucked in the waste bin
– give not only colour but also a strong rich flavour to stocks
and soups; those thick white stalks of cauliflower leaves,
usually thrown away without a second glance, can become a

vegetable on a par with asparagus, and a few ounces of cooked fish can be reinstated as a classy first course.

The great cooks are the ones who use their imagination and their initiative to produce great things from small beginnings, and in the field of leftovers both these talents can be given full rein. In this book I have given my own ideas and the recipes I most frequently use for leftovers of every sort, but I could go on for ever and I hope, sincerely, that the book will not only give ideas for the basis of leftover dishes but encourage the reader to improve and expand on my ideas.

All cooking should be fun; cooking with leftovers should not only provide enjoyment but also the satisfaction of knowing that great dishes are being created from the most humble of origins at a minimum cost.

Introduction

Kitchen Equipment

In nearly all these recipes the chief ingredient is either chopped, minced, or puréed, and a few pointers on kitchen equipment especially designed to cope with these functions may be a help.

Knives

Sharp knives are a *must*. Cheap knives blunt quickly and never really cut as well as they might, so I feel this is one case where it's worth spending more and getting the best. Keep a collection of at least five knives in a convenient place in the kitchen; a large thick bladed one for cutting and chopping meat; a long thin one for cutting and chopping vegetables; and at least two all-purpose short, sharp, stubby ones for doing a multitude of jobs.

Invest in a good solid wall or table knife sharpener and try to sharpen all your knives at least twice a week. Keeping them in tip-top condition will make all the fiddly jobs in the kitchen much easier and far less of a chore.

Chopping Boards

Dual purpose as they both protect your working surfaces and your knife blades. Avoid the fancy formica boards and stick to a large (at least 18 inches square) old-fashioned wooden kind.

Electric Liquidizers, Food Mills and Sieves

All these will perform the same function in the end, the only difference is in price. A good electric liquidizer is a boon when making soups and purées of all kinds, but if you cannot afford one, a metal food mill (the best are made by the French firm

Mouli) with a selection of sieves, does the job equally well and is relatively inexpensive.

Well-equipped kitchens should have at least two sieves for straining and puréeing. Here again, it's worth while buying one of the more expensive brands as it will last longer and prove to be more efficient. Have both a slightly coarse metal sieve and one of the fine-haired varieties.

Keep a piece of clean muslin in the kitchen for straining soups and stocks.

Choppers and Cutters

Most gimmicky choppers fail dismally to be of any real use. For all coarse chopping I use one of my sharp knives and for fine chopping that invaluable French tool, an hachoir or mezzaluna, a curved-bladed, two-handled knife which chops with a see-saw motion and quickly reduces such things as onions to the size of breadcrumbs.

Well-sharpened kitchen scissors serve a number of useful purposes from cutting parsley to trimming off bacon rinds.

Mixing, Beating, and Whisking

No kitchen can have too many wooden spoons, they get used for everything from mixing to beating and blending. Buy a selection of all sizes and shapes and keep them as near to the stove as you can.

A hand electric mixer is useful for all mixing and beating but a rotary whisk does the job just as well if not so fast (also good for developing the arm muscles).

A small wire whisk is invaluable for making all sauces, especially those liable to curdle.

Storing Leftover Foods

As a general rule all cooked food and leftovers should be cooked and used up as soon as possible. Perishable foods are well known for being subject to the effects of bacteria and micro-organisms causing the growth of germs which can cause upset stomachs and, on occasions, extreme illness. To prevent this, all cooked food should be treated, packaged and stored correctly.

Cooked meat and poultry which has been roasted and is left hanging around the warm kitchen before being stored in a larder or refrigerator is particularly susceptible to attack from flies, bacteria and other organisms. Because the food is warm these will multiply with amazing rapidity and although refrigeration will check their growth it will not kill them. All cooked food should be cooled as quickly as possible, be kept lightly covered with a clean cloth, aluminium foil, Saranwrap or greaseproof paper. As soon as it has cooled, store the leftover in a refrigerator or really cold larder.

One of the problems with leftovers is that they tend to dry out after the original cooking. To prevent this lightly wrap meat, poultry or fish before storing it in a refrigerator or larder, making sure that enough air is left to circulate inside the wrapping to allow the food to 'breathe'. Wrapping food which is to be kept in a refrigerator for more than twenty-four hours also helps to prevent the penetration of smells from one item to another.

Never cut, slice, or mince leftovers until just before you require them.

Cooked meat	leave in one piece cover lightly	centre of refrigerator or cool larder	2-3 days
Cooked poultry	cover lightly	centre of refrigerator or cool larder	2-3 days
Cooked game	cover lightly	centre of refrigerator or cool larder	2-3 days

Cooked fish	cover lightly	near the top of the refrigerator	1–2 days
Cooked vegetables	cover lightly or keep in a polythene box	bottom of refrigerator or cool larder	3–5 days
Stocks and soups:			
meat	cover with foil	bottom of refrigerator	4–5 days
vegetable	cover with foil	bottom of refrigerator	2–3 days
Cooked casseroles, stews, etc.	cover with foil	centre of refrigerator or cool larder	2–4 days
Milk puddings, custards, etc.	cover with foil	bottom of refrigerator or cool larder	2–3 days
Cooked fruit, jellies etc.	cover lightly	bottom of refrigerator or cool larder	3–4 days
Raw fruit salads, etc.	cover lightly	bottom of refrigerator or cool larder	3–4 days
Grated cheese	tightly covered container	refrigerator or dry cool place	10–14 days
Eggs:			
whites	covered container	refrigerator	4–5 days
yolks	covered with water to prevent hardening	refrigerator	3–4 days
Breadcrumbs:			
soft	tightly covered container	cool dry place	4–8 days
dried	tightly covered container	cool dry place	indefinitely
Pancakes	lightly covered	refrigerator or cool place	4–8 days
Raw pastry	well wrapped	bottom of refrigerator or cool larder	2–3 days

Preparing and Cooking Leftovers

Like any other food, leftovers must be fresh. Cooked meat or vegetables which have been left to dry out and go stale are never going to be turned into anything worth eating, and whenever possible all leftover food, be it vegetable peelings or the remains of a sirloin of beef, should be used as quickly as is convenient.

Vegetable trimmings and peelings should be washed, dried and kept in a cool place until they can be used to make stock or soup.

Meat carcases and poultry bones should be broken up and made into stock for soup within 24 hours.

Leftover meat, poultry, fish, and puddings should be carefully stored and used up within the shortest possible time.

Whenever feasible it is best to keep one leftover ingredient as the backbone of a dish; a combination of remains from the last few meals may seem like a good idea but all too often results in a woolly flavoured and textured nonentity. Since food which has already been cooked tends to lack flavour and taste, these must be provided by outside ingredients and great care should be taken to ensure that seasoning, herbs and spices are sharp and intense enough to give the extra lift which may be needed.

All cooked food should be re-heated rather than re-cooked so that as much goodness is retained as possible. Re-heated food should be brought up to at least the temperature of 375°F. in order to prevent any spread of bacteria and, in most cases, this should be done as quickly as possible. To aid this re-heating process, cooked meat or poultry should be thinly sliced, finely chopped, or minced. Presentation, as always, is of paramount importance; slices should be uniform, meat and vegetables should be evenly cut into strips or cubes and care should be taken with the colour and garnishing of each dish.

Trim off all fat from cold meat which is to be used in a made-up dish – it doesn't taste any better the second time round. Always trim discoloured parts or tough fibres from cooked vegetables before re-heating them.

Cooked meat and vegetables lose some of their nutritional value in the first cooking, and a fresh vegetable or crisp salad should be served with most made-up dishes.

Deepfreezing Leftover Dishes

I find one of the greatest boons of the twentieth century is my deep freeze, and I keep a special corner for made-up dishes from leftovers which can be quickly thawed and heated to serve for lunch or supper. Often there is enough cold meat to make two rather than one dish such as Shepherd's or Cottage Pie, and both time and heating costs will be saved by doubling up the quantities, cooking one for only half the time, and storing it in the deep freeze.

Soups and made-up dishes for freezing should be cooled quickly, carefully packaged in polythene bags or suitable containers, and frozen at once. Most dishes can be thawed in the oven or over boiling water.

Made-up dishes should not be kept for longer than 8–12 weeks in the deep freeze and should be carefully labelled with the date and number of servings.

Recipes suitable for freezing are marked with a *.

Oven Temperatures

Every oven varies in temperature, even if it is the most modern standard make. They are affected by their position, by the pressure of gas or the voltage of electricity which reaches them at any given time and, in the case of solid fuel cookers, by the direction of the wind.

The following table and indeed the oven temperatures and settings in the recipes should not be considered infallible. Always check the maker's temperature chart when possible, and remember that most ovens need a little time to warm through before they reach the desired heat.

Very cool	225–250 degrees F.		Reg 0–½
Cool	250–275	,, ,,	Reg ½–1
Warm	275–300	,, ,,	Reg 1–2
Moderate	300–350	,, ,,	Reg 2–3
Medium	375	,, ,,	Reg 4
Medium Hot	400	,, ,,	Reg 5
Hot	425–450	,, ,,	Reg 6–7
Very Hot	475–500	,, ,,	Reg 8–9

Weights and Measures

Throughout this book I have used only teaspoon, tablespoon, gill, pint, lb. and oz. for the recipes, and all measures are level.

For your information:

4 teaspoons = 1 tablespoon.
8 tablespoons = 1 gill.
2 gills = ½ pint.
½ pint = 10 fluid oz. = 1 British Standard cup.
1 British Standard cup = 1¼ American cups.
1 British Imperial pint = 20 fluid oz.
1 American pint = 16 fluid oz.
16 oz. = 1 lb.
1 tablespoon gelatine = ½ oz. gelatine – enough to set 1 pint liquid.
The juice of 1 lemon = 2–3 tablespoons and will give more juice if the lemon is softened for a few minutes in a warm oven before squeezing.
1 egg white = approx. 1 fluid oz.

For those who are already converting to the metric system:

1 kilogramme = approx. 2 lb. 3 oz.
28 grammes = approx. 1 oz.

1 litre = 35 fluid oz. = 1¾ pints.
1 decilitre = 3½ fluid oz. = about 6 tablespoons.

Useful Tips

BROWN BREADCRUMBS: Golden breadcrumbs can be bought ready prepared in packets or can be made at home by finely grating stale white bread and frying the crumbs in butter or fat. When the crumbs are a golden brown, drain them well on crumpled kitchen paper and leave in a cool place to dry out. Home-made browned breadcrumbs can be stored in an airtight jar, in a dry place, for up to a month.

PEELING TOMATOES: Tomatoes are almost impossible to peel if you attack them raw, but drop them for a minute or two into boiling water and you will find the skins slide off with no trouble at all – use the tomato peelings to flavour stocks.

PARSLEY: The quickest way to deal with parsley when a recipe calls for it 'finely chopped' is to cut it into a mug with kitchen scissors. Snip, snip, snip and in only a couple of minutes the sprigs are as fine as you want them.

MASHING POTATOES: If you have a Mouli food mill now is the time to use it. These useful machines turn potatoes into soft light squiggles in no time at all.

SQUEEZING LEMONS: Warm lemons produce more juice than cold ones, so pop them into a warm oven for a minute or two before squeezing.

ORANGE AND LEMON PEEL: When a recipe calls for orange or lemon peel cut into thin julienne strips, cut off the peel with a sharp potato peeler: in this way you will get the outside skin only with no pith or membrane to make that bitter taste.

WHIPPING EGG WHITES: Take the whites out of the refrigerator for half an hour before whipping them; this will increase their bulk.

SEASONING: Instead of straight salt and pepper try out a tip from the Chinese. They fry a mixture of salt and pepper, without fat, until the salt begins to turn brown. This brings out the full flavour of the seasoning.

Budget-stretching Ingredients

So often one seems to be faced with the prospect of a quantity of leftover meat, fish or poultry which, however ingenious one tries to be, just does not look as if it will be adequate for the number of servings it needs to stretch to. There is of course a limit to how far ingredients can be increased by the addition of sauces, chopped vegetables, etc. Don't despair, there are a few tricks which can help with this problem.

1. Increase the quantity of meat by adding a small tin of corned beef, luncheon meat or spam, etc.

2. Increase the amount of fish or chicken by the addition of a small tin of tuna fish (this may seem a bit strange in the case of chicken but surprisingly their texture is so similar and tuna is so meaty that they blend remarkably well).

3. Sauces will become richer and more bulky if an egg yolk or two, beaten with a little cream, is stirred into the sauce before pouring it over meat, poultry, or fish.

4. The addition of a tin of thick cream of chicken soup can be added to chicken dishes served in a white sauce. A small tin

of stewed steak can be added to meat dishes served in a brown sauce.

5. All meat, chicken, and fish dishes look more adequate if they are surrounded with a ring of boiled rice or of creamy mashed potatoes. In the same way cold meat, poultry, and fish salad dishes will stretch further if they are surrounded by some shredded lettuce or watercress and well garnished with hard-boiled eggs, tomatoes, cucumber, etc.

6. Poultry and fish in cream sauces can be increased by the addition of some chopped or quartered hardboiled eggs.

Finally: Remember that small quantities of meat, poultry, fish and vegetables can often make an interesting first course, see Chicken and Egg Cocottes, page 32, etc.

Seasonings – Herbs and Spices

Meat, poultry, and fish that has been cooked and is then re-cooked in a made-up dish, tends to lose some of its flavour in the process. As a result dishes made from leftovers often need the sparkle of added flavourings to give them taste and excitement. Seasoning, herbs, and spices all help but the addition of one or two unusual ingredients can often make all the difference between a rather dreary dish and one that is something special. Keep a good selection of these extra ingredients in your larder or store cupboard, and try experimenting with these assets.

Basic seasonings, herbs and spices

SALT: Use fine salt for cold dishes and sea salt for cooked dishes.

PEPPER: I seldom use ground white pepper as I find it very lacking in flavour. Use freshly ground black pepper for all dark coloured soups, stews, and casseroles etc. Use freshly ground white pepper for all light coloured dishes. This, by the way, isn't imperative but I personally think it makes a lot of difference. I keep a pair of large pepper mills near my stove and would be most unhappy without them.

BASIL: Add to vegetable soups and dishes with tomato flavouring.

BAY LEAVES: Indispensable in a bouquet garni, and gives flavour to sauces and casseroles.

BOUQUET GARNI: Mixed herbs which give a necessary taste to soups and stocks. The standard combination is a bay leaf, 2 sprigs of parsley, and a sprig of thyme. Bouquets garnis can be bought, ready made up and tied in little muslin bags, from many good grocery shops.

CELERY SALT: A useful flavouring for soups and made-up dishes – can be used in place of celery when this is out of season.

CURRY POWDER OR PASTE: A teaspoon or two added to soups or réchauffés gives additional taste when it's really needed. Curry flavouring must be well cooked (at least 15–20 minutes) or it tends to give a gritty texture to the dish.

DILL: A popular Scandinavian herb. Add dried dill to fish dishes.

JUNIPER BERRIES: Use ground or crushed berries in pâtés.

MACE: Ground mace or a blade of mace has a wonderful old-fashioned taste and smell – use it sparingly (it has a strong determined flavour) in sauces, potted meats, pâtés, etc.

MINT: Another old-fashioned herb; the perfect partner to young peas and lamb.

NUTMEG: Add a little ground nutmeg to some soups and to vegetables.

PARSLEY: Dried parsley is on the tasteless side. Use fresh, finely chopped parsley, in soups, sauces and as a colourful garnish.

ROSEMARY: A strongly flavoured herb that is popular in the East. Use sparingly in soups, sauces and with lamb and pork dishes.

SAFFRON: A yellow spice with a strong colour mostly used for flavouring cooked rice dishes.

SAGE: Use a pinch or two in soups and tomato dishes.

TARRAGON: One of the best herbs, and one which I use frequently. Add a little tarragon to salad dressings, chicken, and fish dishes.

THYME: One of the ingredients of a bouquet garni.

Other flavourings

Seasoning isn't always all that is needed to make a dish taste exciting. Often an extra ingredient or flavouring can make all the difference.

On the whole these extra ingredients tend to be rather on the strong side, so treat them with deference, adding only a little at a time until the perfect taste has been attained. Many of them will also help to give colour and strength to soups, stews, and made-up dishes thereby not only improving the taste but the appearance as well.

ANCHOVY ESSENCE: Although anchovies are, of course, fishes, they have a curious taste which I find can be used to give pep to meat and poultry dishes as well as to those made from fish. Any product made from anchovies is heavily salted so care should be taken with seasoning. Add a few drops of anchovy essence to soups, stews, made-up dishes and sauces for both hot and cold dishes.

ANCHOVY FILLETS: Like the essence, these can add flavour to a great many dishes. Chop three or four fillets very finely and add them before cooking begins.

APPLE PURÉE: Tinned apple purée can be a boon to the store cupboard. It goes well with many pork, bacon, ham, and sausage dishes and a tablespoon or two will often add that 'something special' to an otherwise uninteresting dish. The purée can also be used to supplement other fruit in puddings.

CHUTNEY: Most chutneys and pickles are mainly used as an accompaniment for curries and cold meat but both sweet and sharp varieties can be chopped up and added to hot and cold dishes to give an interesting taste.

GARLIC: One thing that I would not be without in my kitchen. Those people who turn up their noses at 'foreign type' food just don't know what they're missing; perhaps they might be converted if they knew that (a) it has been proved that garlic keeps you healthy, and (b) it's not necessary to go around with one's mouth tightly shut for twenty-four hours after eating garlic – munching on a sprig of fresh parsley quickly dispels all the leftover smell.

Garlic adds pep and zip to almost any dish or sauce. To obtain the full flavour, the cloves should be minced, finely chopped, crushed, or squeezed through a garlic press, and although there are substitutes (like garlic salt and garlic juice) I myself don't feel that these are nearly as good as the real thing.

Since this book is written with a wide readership in mind, I have been fairly conservative in my use of garlic when using it in the recipes. If you like the taste, double the quantity and use it frequently.

HORSERADISH: Grate fresh horseradish and mix with vinegar and cream. Soak dried horseradish in a little warm water before using. Add whipped cream and seasoning to ready-made horseradish sauce. Use as a flavouring in sandwiches, sauces, and mayonnaise.

MUSHROOMS: Fresh, dried, and tinned mushrooms can be of great use in adding richness and variety to almost all leftover dishes. Dried mushrooms have the strongest flavour (very rich and meaty); they should be soaked in warm water until soft, and the water can be used to add to soups, gravy and sauces. Drain tinned mushrooms, and use the liquid in soups, gravy and sauces, etc. Wash fresh mushrooms (avoid peeling them if possible as the peel contains a lot of the goodness) and cook them in melted butter or boiling water with seasoning and lemon juice.

MUSHROOM KETCHUP: Highly concentrated essence of mushroom which adds colour and flavour to soups, gravy, sauces, etc. Use sparingly.

MUSTARD (English): Use in sauces and salad dressings.

MUSTARD (French): Throughout this book I have used French Dijon mustard which has a faint tinge of tarragon and a bright yellow colour. Use in sauces and salad dressings, and with cold meats.

STOCK CUBES: Don't be afraid (or ashamed) to use them. Both beef and chicken cubes can give flavour to a dish. Stock cubes are also invaluable on many occasions when making home-made stock. Stocks made from cooked bones *can* turn out to be a little on the colourless side and one, or even half, a stock cube can give them the strength which may be needed.

SOY SAUCE: A popular Chinese flavouring which can now be bought from most grocery shops or delicatessens. The sauce adds a good brown colour to dishes, but should be used sparingly as it's definitely on the salty side. Use in soups, sauces, and all Chinese dishes.

TABASCO: Very, very hot. Made from searing red chilis, and capable of blowing the roof of your mouth off if not used with great caution. A few drops only are enough to zip up soups, sauces, salad dressings, etc.

TOMATO PURÉE: Concentrated tomato which adds taste, richness, and colouring to soups, sauces, and tomato dishes. It comes in tins and tubes, and a tablespoon or two is usually ample to give a good flavour to the dish.

TOMATO KETCHUP AND CHUTNEY: Again the tomato taste which makes a good addition to almost any dish. Tomato ketchup has a vinegary and rather pronounced flavour, and should be used carefully. Tomato chutney makes a good 'extra' in cold mousses and moulds.

VINEGAR: Use wine vinegar whenever possible as it's less harsh and more subtle than other kinds. On the whole I find that white wine vinegar is most frequently used in my kitchen.

WORCESTER SAUCE: Another strong sauce with its own

particular zest. Use sparingly in soups, sauces, sea food dressings, and in devilled or barbecued dishes.

Cooking Lubricants

Nearly all dishes call for some kind of fat or oil in the cooking process and a recipe can often be ruined by using the wrong kind. White sauces and their variations, for instance, must be made with butter as this is an essential taste in the sauce itself; using dripping or other fat in the place of butter would change the whole essence of the sauce. Lard, bacon fat, or dripping, on the other hand, can all be used for frying, and indeed a good meat dripping will often give a special and delicious flavour to a made-up dish.

BUTTER: For everything except sweet dishes and sweet sauces I use the cheapest brand of salted butter and find it quite adequate. For sandwiches or butter for the table, I use a more expensive brand.

MARGARINE: Animal fats are often prohibited for people on diets, and margarine can be used in the place of butter in any of the recipes in this book. I have yet to find a margarine which tastes exactly the same as butter (whatever the advertisements say) and personally I only use it as an economy when making cakes or buns.

OIL: Here I feel very strongly as I use oil at the rate at which some people drink beer. Always use olive oil (it's good for your skin apart from anything else) and be wary of the cheaper brands as they sometimes tend to have a rancid taste. I buy mine in bulk from Boots the Chemists. Use for frying fish, meat and vegetables, for marinades and for making mayonnaise.

LARD: If good use is made of dripping from roast meat and from rendering down bacon rinds and raw fat, it shouldn't really be necessary to buy extra lard (refined pig fat). Use for frying vegetables or meat *but not for fish*.

DRIPPING AND RENDERED FAT: Use for frying meat, poultry and vegetables *but not for fish*.

Leftover Wine

The odd inch or so of wine left in the bottom of a bottle after a dinner party is like gold dust to the cook. I keep a bottle for red wine and one for white, and drain off any leftover dregs into the respective container. Ideally the wine should not be kept for too long or it will get vinegar overtones; this can be prevented by sealing the wine in the bottle by pouring a little olive oil over the surface.

Use *red wine* in meat stocks, stews, casseroles and rich sauces.

Use *white wine* in fish and vegetable stocks, in fish dishes, egg dishes, and white sauces.

Both *red* and *white wine* can be used for marinading meat and fish.

The use of other wines and spirits in cooking leftovers

A tablespoon or two of a wine or spirit can make all the difference to what might perhaps have turned out to be a rather uninteresting dish. Don't however go berserk with the bottle as a little goes a long way, and nothing is more obvious or more unpalatable than a dish one has tried to disguise by the addition of great quantities of alcohol.

DRY SHERRY: Add to soups, fish, egg, and poultry dishes, sauces for fish, poultry, tongue, and ham.

SWEET SHERRY: Custards and puddings.

PORT: Some rich stews and casseroles, Cumberland sauce, and puddings.

MADEIRA: Aspics and puddings.

VERMOUTH: Soups, sauces, and fish dishes.

BEER AND CIDER: For marinading and tenderizing meat, and in some stews and casseroles.

BRANDY: A touch of brandy (it need not be the best five-star) adds flavour and piquancy to many leftover meat and fish dishes – in the case of meat it can also help tenderize it. Brandy can also improve sauces and many puddings.

LIQUEURS: Although these are expensive, even a teaspoon or two can give a lift to puddings with a fruit base. Kirsch, Grand Marnier, and Orange Curaçao are particularly good for this purpose.

Finishing Touches

The appearance of leftover food is of special importance; a really well presented dish made from the remains of a cold roast and some cooked vegetables can be made to look just as appetizing as any dish produced from fresh ingredients. Because once-cooked meat, vegetables, and fish which have been kept overnight tend to lose some of their colour and bloom, it is all the more important to give them a lift by a little decoration and garnish.

Here are some ideas for quickly made garnishes for both hot and cold dishes.

1. SLICED MEAT IN A SAUCE

Sprinkle the meat with some finely chopped parsley just before serving.

Decorate the meat with thin strips of tinned red pimento.

Arrange a pattern of thin strips of green pepper (blanched in boiling water for 2 minutes) over the surface of the dish.

2. MADE UP MEAT DISHES IN A DARK SAUCE

Sprinkle the dish with finely chopped parsley just before serving.

Sprinkle with brown breadcrumbs, dot with butter, and brown quickly under a hot grill before serving.

Decorate with triangles or crescents of baked pastry, see page 328.

Sprinkle with finely chopped red pimento (or green pepper, blanched for 2 minutes in boiling water).

Decorate with small triangles of crisply fried bread.

3. MADE UP MEAT, POULTRY OR FISH DISHES IN A WHITE SAUCE

Sprinkle with finely chopped parsley.

Sprinkle with finely chopped fresh tarragon, chervil or chives.

Cover with grated cheese and brown under a hot grill.

Sprinkle with hardboiled egg whites, finely chopped and with hardboiled yolks pushed through a sieve to give a mimosa effect.

Decorate with chopped, or strips of, red pimento or green pepper (blanched for 2 minutes in boiling water).

Garnish with thin slices of black olives.

Make a pattern on the surface of the dish with thin strips of anchovy fillets.

4. COLD POULTRY, MEAT, OR FISH DISHES

Surround with finely shredded lettuce leaves.

Garnish with thin slices of lemon.

Decorate with thin slices of, or chopped, peeled tomato or cucumber.

Add colour with quartered, sliced, or chopped hardboiled eggs.

Garnish with diced beetroot, chopped pimento, or chopped green pepper.

Decorate with thin strips of anchovy.

Add extra taste by sprinkling with chopped or crumbled, crisply fried bacon.

The freshness of chopped aspic or tomato aspic jelly can give a sparkle to cold dishes and to cold sliced meat or poultry.

Finally: One point to bear in mind: all food must be interesting or appetites fade. One of the worst offences is to produce a meal consisting of two or more courses which have a marked similarity in both taste and colour. Tomato soup, followed by meat in a tomato sauce, and ending in a scarlet-coloured jelly, will be a disaster. In the same way, three courses with cream or cheese bases will also dull the taste senses.

Starters

The idea of a first course is not to fill you up before the main course arrives, but rather to whet the appetite for what lies ahead. The first course should be light, exciting, and attractive to look at and, since the ingredients are usually used in small quantities only, leftovers can be put to good use for this purpose.

The number of recipes included in this section are not many, but you will find a wide variety of suitable dishes in the sections on fish and cold dishes which can happily be served as an appetizer at the beginning of a meal. In general I would recommend cutting down the ingredients of a main dish to about half if you wish to serve it as a starter.

Heat, or lack of it, is important in this first course as it will set the trend for the rest of the meal. If dishes are to be served chilled, serve them on cold plates; if it's to be a hot dish to start with, make sure the plates are really piping hot, and the dish is served straight from the oven. Such small touches can make or mar a meal.

Plan meals with care and make sure that the first course provides a contrast to the rest of the food. One creamy dish followed by another never proves to be a success.

Savoury Stuffed Eggs

SERVES 4.   No cooking.

   6 hardboiled eggs
   6 tablespoons cooked finely minced turkey, chicken, or ham
   ½ pint mayonnaise

1½ tablespoons tomato ketchup
salt and pepper
lettuce leaves

Cut each egg in half and remove yolks. Mash yolks and mix with the minced meat. Bind the mixture with tomato ketchup and enough mayonnaise to make a thick, firm consistency, season with salt and pepper and pack into the egg whites.

Place the eggs, flat side down, on a bed of lettuce leaves, spoon over the remaining mayonnaise and garnish with tomato slices.

Serve as a first course or as a summer salad.

Chicken and Egg Cocottes

SERVES 4.   Cooking time: about 10 minutes.

4 eggs	salt and freshly ground black
4 oz. cooked chicken	pepper
4 tablespoons cream	fireproof cocottes or ramekin
½ oz. butter	dishes

Butter the cocottes and place them in a roasting-tin half full of boiling water. Finely chop the chicken and divide between the bottom of the four dishes. Break eggs over the chicken and cover with a spoonful of cream. Sprinkle with salt and pepper and dot with a little butter. Bake in a moderate oven (350°F., Reg. 3) for 6–10 minutes until eggs are just set.

Serve at once.

Variations: Replace the chicken with

4 oz. chopped tongue
a spoonful of pâté
4 oz. cooked meat or fish mixed with a little cream
4 oz. cooked ham moistened with a little tomato ketchup
4 oz. cooked smoked fish, mixed with lemon juice and herbs

Add flavourings of ketchup, chutney, Worcester sauce.

For a more substantial dish place a thin slice of tomato sprinkled with grated cheese on the top of each ramekin.

Potted Salmon*

If you fish yourself or if some kind friend happens to present you with one of his spoils, the chances are that after serving it for one or even two meals, you are likely to have some remains or trimmings left over. This method of potting fish makes the best of small quantities of cooked salmon and can be successfully kept in a very cool place or refrigerator for up to 10 days.

SERVES 4.   Cooking time: 5–7 minutes.

½ lb. cooked salmon or sea trout	3 oz. butter
salt and freshly ground black pepper	½ teaspoon ground mace
	½ teaspoon lemon juice

Flake the fish with a fork. Melt 2 oz. butter in a heavy pan, add the fish as soon as the butter has melted, season with salt, pepper and mace and cook over a low heat for 5 minutes without browning. Mix in lemon juice and pack the fish with the juices into a small jar or terrine.

Heat remaining butter until foaming, strain through a muslin cloth and pour over the fish.

Serve potted fish as a first course with wedges of lemon and freshly made hot toast.

Fish Cocktail

Why is it that so many people are hung up on prawn cocktails? Those rather uninteresting concoctions of tired lettuce, tasteless prawns, and synthetic dressing, appear again and again in restaurants throughout the country, ruining the reputation of both prawns and the seafood sauce which accompanies them.

This is a book about 'leftovers', so it is not the place to start giving my opinions on how a really good prawn cocktail *should* be made, but the same idea can be adapted for using up small quantities of any white fish, salmon, shellfish, tinned salmon, or tuna you may happen to have in your larder. If well made and prettily presented, a fish cocktail made with the most humble of ingredients can make a most delicious start to a meal.

SERVES 4.   No cooking.

6–8 oz. cooked white fish,
  shellfish (lobster, crab, etc.) or
  tinned salmon or tuna
1 teaspoon lemon juice
few drops Tabasco sauce
freshly ground black pepper

1 lettuce heart
½ pint mayonnaise (see page 265)
1½ tablespoons tomato ketchup
1 tablespoon cream
few drops Worcester sauce
lemon slices

Flake the fish with a fork, sprinkle it with lemon juice, a few drops Tabasco, and some freshly ground black pepper, and leave to marinade in a cold place for ½ hour. Shred the lettuce and arrange it in the bottom of four glass goblets or dishes. Blend mayonnaise with tomato ketchup, cream, and a few drops Worcester sauce.

Place the fish on the lettuce, pour over the sauce and decorate each glass with very thin slices of lemon.

Serve the fish cocktail chilled with thin slices of buttered brown bread.

Fish Salad with Avocado Sauce

SERVES 4 as a first course. No cooking.

8–10 oz. cooked white fish or shellfish	salt and pepper
2 ripe avocados	pinch of cayenne
1 tablespoon lemon juice	lettuce leaves
1 teaspoon grated onion	lemon slices
1 tablespoon olive oil	tomato or cucumber slices

Cut fish into thin strips and arrange on a small serving dish on a bed of lettuce leaves.

Peel avocados and mash the flesh with a fork until smooth, add lemon juice and grated onion and gradually blend in oil, beating until the sauce is thick and all the oil has been absorbed. Season with salt, pepper and cayenne and spoon sauce over the fish. Chill before serving and garnish with thin slices of lemon, tomato or cucumber.

Fish and Anchovy Ramekins

These make a good starter for an evening meal and have the great asset of sharpening the appetite rather than dulling it. It is, however, rather an oily dish and should not be served to anyone on a fat-free diet.

SERVES 4 as a first course. Cooking time: about 10 minutes.

8 oz. cooked fish (use any white fish, salmon or shellfish but not smoked fish)	½ tablespoon finely chopped chives or spring onion tops
1 oz. butter	1 teaspoon lemon juice
8 anchovy fillets	¼ teaspoon grated lemon rind
2 tablespoons sherry	freshly ground black pepper
½ tablespoon finely chopped parsley	

Divide fish into four and arrange each portion in a ramekin dish. Drain and finely chop anchovy fillets.

Heat butter, add anchovy fillets, sherry, parsley, chives, lemon juice and rind, season with pepper and cook for 3 minutes.

Pour the sauce over the fish and bake ramekins in a moderately hot oven (400°F., Reg. 5) until hot through and bubbling, about 8–10 minutes.

Fish Florentine

SERVES 4.   Cooking time: 25 minutes.

Individual dishes of fish, spinach, and tomatoes with a cheese sauce make a good starter to a meal and are a good way of using up cooked fish.

1¼ lb. cooked fish (almost any fresh or smoked fish can be used)	1 small onion, finely chopped
	½ pint double cream
	4 oz. grated cheese
1 packet frozen spinach	1 large tomato, sliced
salt and pepper	pinch of paprika

Cook spinach until tender in a little boiling salted water. Drain well and chop finely. Flake the fish into small pieces.

Place alternate layers of spinach and fish in 4 buttered ramekin dishes, seasoning each layer with salt and pepper.

Mix the cream and chopped onion together, season lightly with salt and pepper, pour over the fish and spinach, and top with slices of tomato.

Cover the dishes with grated cheese and sprinkle with paprika. Bake them in a moderate oven (350°F., Reg. 3) for 20 minutes and brown under a grill for 5 minutes.

Note: 1–2 teaspoons lemon juice and a pinch of ground nutmeg can be added to the spinach.

Avocados with Chicken

Even the smallest leftovers of chicken can be put to good use. This recipe makes a really sensational start to a dinner party, but it is rich and should be followed by a rather light main course.

SERVES 4.   No cooking.

2 large ripe avocados
juice of ½ lemon
2 oz. cooked chicken
1 tablespoon finely chopped
  celery

2 tablespoons double cream
1 tablespoon chopped almonds
salt and pepper
paprika

Cut each avocado in half, discard the stone and scoop out the flesh. Cut the avocado flesh into small dice and sprinkle with lemon juice to prevent browning.

Cut the cooked chicken into very small dice. Roast the chopped almonds in a hot oven until golden brown, about 3 minutes, leave to cool.

Lightly mix together the avocado flesh, chicken, celery, almonds and cream. Season with salt and pepper and spoon the mixture into the avocado shells. Sprinkle over a little paprika and chill before serving.

Potted Beef *

As an alternative to pâtés, old-fashioned potted meats make a cheap and quickly made first course, and can be made from a variety of leftover ingredients.

SERVES 4.   Cooking time: about 5 minutes.

8–12 oz. cooked beef
2½ oz. butter
pinch marjoram

pinch mace
salt and pepper
1–3 teaspoons brandy (optional)

Mince the meat through the coarse blades of a mincer. Melt three-quarters of the butter, add the meat, season with salt, pepper, and the herbs, and cook over a fairly low heat for 3 minutes. Add brandy.

Pack meat and butter into small jars or pots. Melt remaining butter until foaming and strain it through muslin over the meat, and leave to cool.

Note: Potted meats can be kept for up to 10 days if they are kept in a cold place and protected by this butter seal.

Chicken Pâté made from Cooked Chicken*

As a first course these quantities should be enough to serve 4, but the pâté can also be used as a spread for sandwiches or canapés. It is quickly made and delicious.

4 oz. cooked chicken	1 teaspoon mixed finely
1 chicken liver	chopped herbs
1 clove garlic	small pinch mace
2 oz. butter (or dripping from	salt and freshly ground black
a roast chicken)	pepper

If the chicken liver is not already cooked, fry it gently in a little butter for about 5 minutes.

Mince and re-mince chicken and chicken liver through the fine blades of a mincing machine. Finely chop or mince the garlic.

Heat butter in a saucepan, add garlic, and cook gently until it becomes transparent (do not brown). Add chicken, chicken liver, and herbs, mix well, and season with salt and plenty of freshly ground black pepper. Cook gently for 5 minutes, then pack in a small pot or terrine and chill for at least 1 hour.

Serve the pâté with wedges of lemon and freshly made toast.

Chicken or Turkey Cocottes

SERVES 4.   Cooking time: 20 minutes.

4 hardboiled eggs	salt, pepper and pinch cayenne
4 oz. cooked chicken or turkey	2 oz. mushrooms
1 oz. butter	½ oz. butter
1 oz. flour	1 tablespoon cream
½ pint milk	1 oz. grated cheese
1 tablespoon sherry	
2 teaspoons French Dijon mustard	

Chop hardboiled eggs and chicken or turkey meat. Melt butter, add flour and mix well. Gradually blend in ½ pint milk stirring continually until the sauce comes to the boil and is thick and smooth. Add sherry and mustard. Season with salt, pepper, and a pinch of cayenne.

Chop mushrooms and cook for 1 minute in ½ oz. melted butter. Fold eggs, chicken or turkey, and mushrooms into the sauce and spoon mixture into 4 cocottes or baking dishes. Top with cream and grated cheese and bake in a hot oven for 10 minutes until golden brown and bubbling.

Potted Chicken*

SERVES 4.   Cooking time: about 5 minutes.

10–12 oz. cooked chicken	salt
1 oz. cooked bacon	paprika
2½ oz. butter	pinch dried mixed herbs
1 teaspoon lemon juice	

Coarsely mince or finely chop the chicken and bacon. Heat three-quarters of the butter, add chicken, bacon, and lemon juice, season with salt, paprika, and a pinch of mixed dried herbs. Cook gently for 3 minutes. Pack meat into small pots, jars, or in a small terrine.

Heat remaining butter until foaming and strain through muslin over the meat.

Ham and Mushroom Custard

'Custard' always sounds like a sweet dish but savoury custards can be delicious, and make a useful first course with a difference.

SERVES 4.   Cooking time: 30 minutes.

1 onion, finely chopped
4 oz. button mushrooms, sliced (or small tin mushrooms)
1 oz. butter
4 oz. *ham or boiled bacon*

2 tablespoons tomato purée
$\frac{1}{4}$ pint stock or gravy
salt and pepper
3 eggs
$\frac{1}{2}$ pint single cream

Cut the ham into small dice.

Melt the butter, add onion and mushrooms, and cook over a medium heat for about 3 minutes until the onion is soft. Add the diced ham and tomato purée and mix well. Blend in stock or gravy, season with salt and pepper and cook gently for a further five minutes. Spoon the mixture into a greased baking dish.

Beat the eggs with $\frac{1}{2}$ pint single cream, season with a little salt and pepper, and pour over the ham mixture. Bake in a moderate oven (350°F., Reg. 3) for about 20 minutes until set.

Serve as a first course or as a light lunch or supper dish.

Potted Ham*

SERVES 4.   Cooking time: about 5 minutes.

10–12 oz. ham or boiled bacon   pinch mace
2½ oz. butter   salt and pepper
pinch marjoram

Coarsely mince or finely chop the ham. Melt three quarters of the butter, add meat, season with salt, pepper, and herbs, and cook gently for 3 minutes. Pack the meat into small jars, pots, or in a small terrine.

Melt remaining butter until foaming and strain through muslin over the meat. Leave to cool and serve with hot toast.

Mediterranean Chicken or Ham Salad

This makes a good sharp starter in hot weather.

SERVES 4.   No cooking.

6 oz. cooked chicken or ham   1 tablespoon finely chopped
6 oz. cooked French beans   parsley
½ cucumber   pinch dried mixed herbs
4 large ripe tomatoes   3 tablespoons olive oil
8 anchovies   1 tablespoon white wine
10 black olives   vinegar
1 tablespoon finely chopped   salt and freshly ground black
   chives or spring onion tops   pepper

Cut meat into thin matchstick strips. Chop beans. Peel and thinly slice cucumber. Peel and thinly slice tomatoes. Cut anchovies into thin strips. Stone and thinly slice olives.

Arrange a layer of beans, cucumber slices and tomato slices in the bottom of a shallow dish. Sprinkle with a little chives and parsley, cover with a layer of meat, and finish with a second layer of beans, cucumber, tomato, parsley, and chives.

Combine olive oil, vinegar, and herbs, mix well and season generously with salt and freshly ground black pepper. Pour the dressing over the meat and vegetables and garnish the surface with a pattern of anchovies and black olive slices. Chill for at least an hour before serving.

Note: A more substantial dish may be made by adding thin slices of cooked potato or hardboiled eggs to the dish.

Potted Liver*

SERVES 4. Cooking time: about 5 minutes.

10-12 *oz. cooked liver*	pinch sage
1 *oz. cooked bacon or ham*	salt and pepper
2½ *oz. butter*	1-3 teaspoons brandy
pinch marjoram	(optional)
pinch mace	

Coarsely mince or finely chop the liver and bacon or ham. Melt three-quarters of the butter, add liver and bacon, season with salt, pepper, and the herbs, and cook gently for 3 minutes. Add brandy and pack the meat into small jars, pots, or in a small terrine.

Melt remaining butter until foaming and strain through muslin over the meat. Leave to cool and serve with hot toast.

Insalata di Patate (see also p. 218)

SERVES 4. No cooking.

½-¾ *lb. boiled potatoes*	1 tablespoon chopped pimento,
8 anchovy fillets	or chopped green or red
	pepper

1 tablespoon finely chopped
 spring onion tops or chives
6 black olives
2 ripe tomatoes

½ pint mayonnaise
1 tablespoon cream
freshly ground black pepper

Cut the potatoes into small dice; drain and finely chop the anchovies; stone and chop the olives; peel, remove the core and seeds and finely chop the flesh of the tomato.

Lightly mix together the potatoes, anchovies, pimento, onion or chives, olives and chopped tomatoes.

Blend the mayonnaise with the cream and season with freshly ground black pepper, add this to the potato mixture and stir gently with a wooden spoon.

Chill before serving and decorate with thin strips of pimento.

A clove of garlic, crushed or put through a garlic press can be added to the mayonnaise.

Soups

Small amounts of leftover fish, meat, poultry and vegetables can quickly be made into a satisfactory soup with a little imagination and the addition of a good strong stock or some additional flavourings. A few ounces of meat or poultry, cut into thin strips, added to a rich meat stock can provide a hearty beginning to a meal, and some leftover vegetables can be combined to make a colourful, light start to a summer meal.

The appearance and texture of soups is of great importance and care should be taken to ensure that a clear consommé really is crystal clear, that a cream soup is bland and velvety, and that a rich meat soup has a strong true colour and not the muddy tones of dreaded 'Brown Windsor'.

A tablespoon of tomato purée, gravy, meat juices, or clear pan drippings can all add colour and flavour to meat soups, and the addition of a chicken stock cube can often give a vegetable soup the extra taste it lacks. Seasoning too is of importance and often a pinch of paprika or cayenne added with the salt and pepper can make all the difference.

Care should be taken with garnishing – a sprinkling of finely chopped parsley or a little shredded lettuce will give a 'finished' appearance to a bowl of clear or vegetable soup; some finely grated lemon rind or even raw carrot might provide an appetizing colour contrast.

Often the most delicious soup of all can be made from the strangest combination of ingredients. I have blended together some leftover spinach, brussels sprouts, stock made from a game carcase, and stuffing from a roast chicken with delicious results.

Stocks made with raw or cooked leftovers

Rich and nourishing stocks can be made from both raw and cooked poultry carcases, meat bones or fish bones and trimmings. Make your stock in a large saucepan and check, during the cooking time, that the bones are well covered with water. For a brown stock, brown bones and vegetables in a little fat before adding the water. A white stock is made without browning bones or vegetables.

Add vegetable trimmings and peelings to meat stocks to give them extra flavour, and for a well coloured stock, add 1 or 2 roughly chopped tomatoes and the brown skin of an onion.

Always use cold water to make stocks and bring them slowly to the boil to bring out all the flavour of the meat and vegetables.

Strain stock whilst it is still hot, and leave to cool in a really cold place or a refrigerator. All fat will rise to the surface to form a solid layer. The fat should be left on the stock until it is about to be used as this helps to preserve the liquid. To remove the fat, loosen it round the edges of the bowl with a knife and lift it out in one piece.

Meat stock can be kept for up to 4 days in a refrigerator but any stock made with green vegetables should be boiled up daily to prevent sourness.

If you find that stock made from cooked bones is not strong enough, give it more flavour by adding a stock cube or some tomato purée. These will also improve the colour.

Trimmings of bacon, meat gravy, and the remains of stews can all be added to stock to give more taste.

Game Stock from a Raw Carcase*

1 *pheasant carcase (or 2 pigeon, grouse or partridge carcases)*	2 carrots
2 *bacon rinds*	2 sticks celery
½ oz. butter	bouquet garni
2 onions	3–4 pints water
	salt and 6 peppercorns

Chop carcase into four pieces. Remove the outer tough skin of the onions and cut all the vegetables into thick slices.

Heat the butter in a large pan, add carcase, bacon rinds, and vegetables, and cook over a high heat until the bones are well browned on all sides. Pour over enough water to cover, add bouquet garni, a little salt, and the peppercorns.

Bring stock to the boil, skim off any scum from the surface, reduce the heat and simmer for 2–2½ hours. Strain through a fine sieve, leave to cool and remove any fat.

Game Stock from a Cooked Carcase*

Combine cooked carcase with the ingredients listed above but use stock, or water and two stock cubes, instead of water. *Do not brown bacon rinds and bones.* Simmer for 1½ to 2 hours.

Chicken Stock from a Raw Carcase*

1 *chicken carcase and giblets*	water
2 rashers fat bacon	salt
2 onions	8 peppercorns
2 carrots	bouquet garni

Break the carcase into four or five pieces.

Fry the rashers in a large saucepan, without any fat, for 3

minutes. Add the chicken carcase and giblets, and brown quickly in the bacon fat. Pour over enough water to cover.

Wash the onions but leave on the skin, cut into quarters; clean the carrots and cut into half. Add the carrots and onions to the chicken with a little salt, the peppercorns, and a bouquet garni.

Bring the stock to the boil, skim off any scum from the surface, cover and simmer for 2½–3 hours.

Strain the stock through a fine sieve; leave in a cool place until the fat has formed a hard layer on the top. Before using carefully remove the fat, re-skimming the stock if necessary.

Note: The fat off the stock can be used for dripping.

Chicken Stock from a Cooked Carcase*

Follow the instructions for making stock from a raw carcase, add 1 chicken stock cube and simmer gently for 3 hours before straining.

Fish Stock*

2 *lb. fish bones, heads and trimmings*	pinch of thyme
	bay leaf
1 onion	1 teaspoon lemon juice
2 oz. mushrooms or *stalks and peels*	1 pint water
	½ pint white wine
sprig of parsley	salt and pepper

Place all the ingredients in a large pan and season well with salt and pepper.

Bring the stock to the boil, skim off any scum from the surface, cover and simmer for 30–45 minutes. Strain the stock through muslin, and keep in a refrigerator for not longer than 48 hours.

Meat Stock from Cooked Bones★

Beef, mutton, lamb, or veal bones   2 tomatoes
1 onion   salt and pepper
2 carrots   bouquet garni
2 sticks celery   water

Put bones with the vegetables, cleaned and roughly chopped, into a large saucepan. Cover with cold water and bring slowly to the boil. Skim off any scum from the surface, season with salt and pepper, and add the bouquet garni. Cover and simmer for 2–3 hours over a very low heat.

Strain the stock through a hair sieve, leave to cool and skim off all fat from the surface.

For a Dark Stock

Brown the bones and vegetables quickly in a little fat or oil before adding the water.

Vegetable Stock★

Use vegetable trimmings (tough outer leaves, skins and stalks, etc.) to make the stock and use it as a base for soups, sauces, and stews.

1. Light Stock

vegetable peelings and trimmings   4 parsley stalks
1 onion   salt and pepper
1 carrot   3–4 pints water
2 sticks celery

Wash all vegetables, peelings and trimmings carefully and chop roughly. Combine vegetables and water and bring slowly to the boil. Skim off any scum from the surface, season with salt and pepper, add parsley stalks and simmer, with a cover, for about 1½ hours. Strain the stock through a hair sieve.

2. Dark Stock

Brown chopped vegetables in a little butter, oil or bacon fat before adding the water.

Chicken Giblet Stock for Gravy★

chicken giblets (neck, gizzard, and heart)
1 onion
1 carrot
bouquet garni
1 pint water
salt and pepper

Peel and roughly chop onion and carrot. Cover giblets with water, add vegetables, and bouquet garni. Season with salt and pepper, bring to the boil, and simmer for 1½ hours.

Strain the stock, leave to cool. Skim off any fat from the surface and use to make gravy.

Fish Soup★

SERVES 4. Cooking time: about 10 minutes.

1½ pints fish stock
1 onion, finely chopped
1 oz. butter
1 oz. flour
½ pint milk
½ lb. cooked fish (any white fish or salmon will do)
1 tablespoon finely chopped parsley

Melt butter, add onion, and cook over a low heat until onion is soft and transparent, about 3 minutes. Mix in flour and gradually blend in the stock. Bring to the boil, stirring constantly, lower the heat and simmer for a further 3 minutes.

Flake the fish with a fork and add it to the soup with the milk and parsley. Season with salt and pepper and heat through.

Note: For a richer soup, add 2 tablespoons thick cream before serving.

A tablespoon or two of dry Vermouth, white wine, or sherry can be mixed into the soup.

Thick Fish Soup*

SERVES 4. Cooking time: about 30 minutes.

1¼ lb. potatoes	*salmon or tinned tuna or*
1 medium onion	*salmon)*
1½ oz. butter	¼ pint cream
1½ pints milk	salt and pepper
4 oz. cooked fish (*any white fish,*	

Peel and finely chop the onion. Peel and chop potatoes. Heat the butter in a saucepan, add vegetables, and cook gently until the onion is transparent but not brown. Heat the milk to boiling point and pour it over the vegetables. Season with salt and pepper and simmer gently for 20 minutes until potatoes are soft.

Purée the vegetables through a fine sieve, a food mill, or in an electric blender. Return to a clean saucepan.

Flake the fish with a fork, add to the soup, and blend in the cream. Heat gently without boiling and check seasoning before serving.

Cream of Chicken Soup

SERVES 4. Cooking time: about 20 minutes.

1½ oz. butter	2 tablespoons flour
1½ oz. mushrooms	2 pints chicken stock

2 oz. cooked chicken

1 tablespoon finely chopped
parsley

2 egg yolks

¼ pint thin cream

salt and pepper

Wash, dry, and finely chop the mushrooms. Cut chicken meat into very small pieces.

Melt the butter in a saucepan, add mushrooms, and cook over a very low heat until mushrooms are soft, about 4 minutes. Add flour, mix well, and gradually blend in the stock, stirring constantly until the soup is thick and smooth. Add the chicken and parsley, season with salt and pepper, bring to the boil, and simmer for ten minutes.

Beat the egg yolks with the cream, add a little hot soup, mix well, and stir the mixture into the soup. Cook for two minutes without boiling, check seasoning, and serve with a little extra parsley sprinkled over the top.

Curried Chicken or Veal Soup*

SERVES 4.   Cooking time: about 20 minutes.

2½ pints chicken or veal stock

1 oz. butter

1 small onion

1 tablespoon flour

2–4 oz. cooked chicken or veal

1 tablespoon curry powder

Peel and finely chop the onion. Finely chop or mince the meat.

Melt butter, add the onion, and cook gently until onion is soft and transparent. Add the flour and curry powder, mix well, and gradually blend in the stock, stirring constantly until the soup thickens.

Bring to the boil, add meat, and simmer gently for 10 minutes.

Chicken Liver Soup

SERVES 4. Cooking time: about 25 minutes.

1 *chicken liver*	2 oz. rice
2¼ pints chicken stock	salt and pepper
8 oz. frozen peas (or *cooked*	a knob of butter
peas)	3 tablespoons sherry

Finely chop chicken liver. Heat stock until boiling, add rice and cook for 10 minutes. Add peas, and cook until tender, about 8 minutes.

Heat butter, add liver, and brown over a high heat. Drain off fat on crumpled kitchen paper.

Add liver to the soup, stir well, and season with salt and pepper. Mix in the sherry before serving.

Quick Chicken Liver Soup

SERVES 4. Cooking time: about 10 minutes.

1 *chicken liver*	1 tablespoon finely chopped
1 small onion	parsley
butter	salt and pepper
2 tins consommé	

Finely chop the chicken liver; peel and finely chop onion. Heat a little butter, add the onion, and fry over a medium heat until onion is soft. Add the chopped liver and cook for a further 2 minutes. Drain onion and liver on kitchen paper to remove all the fat.

Heat consommé, add onion and liver, season with salt and pepper, and mix in the chopped parsley.

Variations

1. Add two teaspoons of curry powder to the onion and liver.

2. For a more substantial soup, add 1 oz. finely chopped ham or cooked bacon to the soup with the onion and liver.

3. Mix one tablespoon tomato purée and a little cooked rice into the soup.

4. For a sharp flavour, add 2 teaspoons lemon juice and 1 tablespoon sherry.

Chicken Giblet Soup*

SERVES 4.   Cooking time: 1¾ hours.

giblets and neck of 1 chicken	2¼ pints water
2 carrots	½ oz. butter
1 onion	2 tablespoons flour
1 stick celery	salt and pepper
1 stock cube	4 tablespoons sherry or Madeira
bouquet garni	

Clean and roughly chop the vegetables. Cover giblets with cold water and bring slowly to the boil, skim off any scum from the surface, add vegetables, stock cube, and bouquet garni. Season with salt and pepper, and simmer until giblets are tender (about 1½ hours).

Remove giblets and chop the meat finely. Strain soup and remove all fat from the surface.

Heat the butter, add flour, and mix well until browned. Gradually blend in the soup and bring to the boil, stirring constantly. Add chopped meat and sherry. Check seasoning before serving.

Goose or Duck Giblet Soup*

SERVES 4.   Cooking time: 2¼ hours.

giblets and neck of 1 goose or 2 ducks	2½ pints water
2 carrots	½ oz. butter
1 onion	2 tablespoons flour
1 stick celery	salt and pepper
bouquet garni	4 tablespoons sherry or Madeira

Clean and roughly chop the vegetables. Cover giblets with cold water and bring slowly to the boil. Skim off any scum from the surface, add vegetables and bouquet garni. Season with salt and pepper and simmer for about 2 hours until giblets are tender.

Remove giblets and chop the meat finely. Strain soup and remove all fat from the surface.

Heat the butter, add flour, and cook until browned. Gradually blend in soup and bring to the boil, stirring constantly. Add chopped meat and sherry. Check seasoning before stirring.

Turkey Giblet Soup*

Make this in the same way as chicken or goose giblet soup, but increase the proportion of other ingredients in proportion to the size of the turkey giblets.

Note: These three soups can be made richer by the addition of 1 or 2 egg yolks mixed with ¼ pint of cream and whisked into the soup before serving.

Imperial Soup

SERVES 4.   Cooking time: about 10 minutes.

2½ pints well flavoured chicken
   stock
4 *egg yolks*
7 tablespoons cream

4–6 tablespoons sherry
finely chopped parsley
salt and pepper

Heat stock until boiling. Beat egg yolks with the cream and blend in a little of the hot stock. Add egg mixture to the stock and stir vigorously over the heat, without boiling, for 3 minutes. Add sherry, season with salt and pepper, and sprinkle each serving with a little finely chopped parsley.

Game Soup*

SERVES 4.   Cooking time: about 10 minutes.

2 pints game stock
4 *oz. cooked game (pheasant,
   partridge, pigeon, grouse,
   etc.)*
½ oz. butter

1 tablespoon flour
1 tablespoon redcurrant jelly
1 teaspoon lemon juice
3 tablespoons sherry

Cut the meat into very fine shreds.

Melt the butter, add flour, and mix over a moderately hot heat until the flour is lightly browned. Gradually blend in the stock, stirring constantly, and bring to the boil. Reduce the heat, add redcurrant jelly and stir until it has dissolved. Mix in the lemon juice, sherry, and shredded meat. Taste for seasoning.

A Kind of Scotch Broth

SERVES 4. Cooking time: about 20 minutes.

2 pints beef or meat stock	¼ oz. butter
4–6 oz. cooked lamb or mutton	2 teaspoons flour
4 oz. cooked vegetables (a mixture	salt and pepper
of potatoes, carrots, peas,	2 tablespoons cooked rice
cauliflower, etc.)	½ tablespoon finely chopped
1 small onion	parsley

Remove any fat from the meat and cut it into very small strips; dice vegetables; peel and finely chop the onion.

Melt butter, and onion, and cook over a medium heat until onion is golden brown. Sprinkle with flour, mix well, and cook for 1 minute. Gradually blend in the stock, bring to the boil, reduce heat, and add meat and vegetables. Season with salt and pepper, add rice, and simmer for 10 minutes.

Sprinkle the soup with a little finely chopped parsley before serving.

Note: If your stock is not rich or brown enough, add strength to it by blending in a stock cube, a little Bovril, or some tomato purée.

Cabbage Soup

SERVES 4. Cooking time: about 10 minutes.

10 oz. cooked cabbage	salt and pepper
2½ pints stock	2 frankfurter sausages or cooked
1 oz. butter or dripping	pork or beef sausages

Finely shred cabbage; thinly slice sausages. Heat butter or dripping in a saucepan, add the cabbage and cook over a high heat until lightly browned. Pour over the stock and bring to the boil. Add sausages and simmer gently for 5 minutes. Season with salt and pepper.

Variation: Add 1 tablespoon tomato purée and 1 teaspoon caraway seeds to the soup with the cabbage.

Cabbage Soup with Rice and Bacon

SERVES 4.   Cooking time: 25 minutes.

4 oz. cooked cabbage	1 oz. rice
2 oz. bacon	2 pints stock
1 tablespoon olive oil	salt and pepper

Shred cabbage. Remove rinds and finely chop bacon.

Heat oil and cook bacon for 3 minutes without browning. Add rice and cook for a further minute. Pour over stock, mix well, bring to the boil, and simmer for 20 minutes. Stir in cabbage, season with salt and pepper, and serve with grated cheese.

Note: Cooked rice may be used instead of raw, but in that case cook the bacon in just enough oil to prevent it sticking, add stock, and cook for ten minutes. Add the cooked rice with the cabbage.

Thick Vegetable Soup*

SERVES 4.   Cooking time: about 15 minutes.

2½ pints well flavoured stock	beans, cauliflower, cabbage,
1½ tablespoons cornflour	etc., or a mixture of cooked
2 tablespoons water	vegetables
4–6 oz. cooked carrots, peas,	salt and pepper

Mix cornflour with water until smooth.

Heat stock until boiling, add cornflour mixture, and stir constantly over a moderate heat until the soup thickens. Boil for 2 minutes, reduce the heat, add vegetables (chopped if necessary), and season with salt and pepper.

Purée of Vegetable Soup

SERVES 4.   Cooking time: about 10 minutes.

1 *lb. cooked vegetables (celery, cauliflower, brussels sprouts, cabbage, swedes, parsnips, etc.)*	1½ pints meat or vegetable stock
½ oz. butter	salt and pepper
1 tablespoon flour	1 *egg yolk*
	4 tablespoons thin cream

Purée vegetables through a fine sieve or through a food mill. (I find this is easier to do if the vegetables are simmered with a little of the stock for a few minutes to soften them.)

Melt the butter, add flour, and mix well. Gradually blend in the stock stirring continually until the soup comes to the boil and is quite smooth. Add the puréed vegetables, season with salt and pepper and cook gently for 3 minutes.

Beat the egg yolks and cream together, blend in a little of the hot soup and then add the mixture to the soup stirring vigorously. Do not let the soup boil.

Serve the soup with crisply fried croûtons of bread or with a sprinkling of finely chopped, crisply fried bacon.

Carrot Soup

SERVES 4.   Cooking time: 15 minutes.

1 *lb. cooked carrots*	bay leaf
1 *cooked potato*	½ oz. butter
1 small onion	½ pint milk
1 pint white stock (or water and stock cube)	salt and pepper
	finely chopped parsley

Roughly chop carrots. Chop potato. Peel and finely chop onion. Melt butter in a saucepan. Add onion and cook over a moderate heat for 5 minutes without browning. Add carrots, potato, stock, and bay leaf. Bring to the boil, cover, and simmer for 5 minutes. Remove bay leaf and purée the soup through a fine sieve, through a food mill, or in an electric liquidizer. Return to a clean pan, add the milk, season with salt and pepper, and heat through. Garnish with parsley.

Lettuce Soup

SERVES 4.   Cooking time: 10–15 minutes.

1 onion or 2 leeks	salt and pepper
1 oz. butter	2 *egg yolks*
2 pints stock	¼ pint cream
2 tablespoons flour	salt and pepper
outside leaves of 2 large lettuces	

Peel and finely chop onion or thinly slice leeks. Wash, dry, and finely shred lettuce leaves.

Melt half the butter, add onion or leeks and cook over a gentle heat for 3 minutes until soft. Pour over the stock and simmer for 8 minutes.

Mash the remaining butter with the flour and mix until it is smooth, add this to the soup and stir well. Bring to the boil and boil for 3 minutes.

Add shredded lettuce to the soup and season with salt and pepper. Just before serving, beat the egg yolks with the cream, combine this with a little hot soup and stir it vigorously into the soup. Heat through without boiling.

Cauliflower, Broccoli, or Brussels Sprouts Soup

SERVES 4.   Cooking time: about 15 minutes.

8–10 oz. cooked cauliflower, broccoli, or brussels sprouts	½ oz. butter
	2 tablespoons flour
4 oz. lean bacon	2¼ pints stock
1 small onion	salt and pepper

Cut cooked vegetables into small pieces; peel and finely chop onion. Remove rinds from bacon and chop finely.

Brown onion and bacon in the butter, sprinkle over the flour and mix well. Gradually blend in the stock and bring to the boil, stirring constantly. Add the vegetables, season with salt and pepper, and simmer for a few minutes before serving.

Vichyssoise

SERVES 4.   Cooking time: 10 minutes.

2 leeks	½ pint thin cream
1 onion	salt and pepper
1 lb. cooked potatoes	2 tablespoons finely chopped
½ oz. butter	chives
1½ pints stock	

Clean and thinly slice the leeks; peel and finely chop the onion.

Melt the butter in a saucepan, add leeks and onion and cook gently until they are transparent and have absorbed the fat. Add the stock and potatoes and cook for 8–10 minutes until onions and leeks are tender. Pass the soup through a fine sieve, through a food mill, or blend in an electric liquidizer, and return to a clean saucepan. Season with salt and pepper, add cream, and heat through without boiling. Sprinkle with chives and serve.

Potato Soup

Another satisfying soup for winter evenings.
SERVES 4.   Cooking time: about 20 minutes.

1 *lb. cooked potatoes*	1 pint milk
1 onion	1 *egg yolk*
1 oz. butter	¼ pint cream
½ pint white stock (use chicken or water and a chicken stock cube)	salt and pepper
	1 tablespoon finely chopped chives or spring onion tops
pinch chervil	

Peel and finely chop the onion and fry it gently in the butter until soft and transparent, add potatoes, chervil, stock, and milk and simmer gently for 10 minutes. Season generously with salt and pepper.

Pass the liquid and potatoes through a fine food mill or through a fine sieve and pour into a clean saucepan. Whisk the soup over a low heat until it is well blended.

Beat the egg yolk with the cream, blend this with a tablespoon of the hot soup, add to the rest of the soup, and heat through, stirring continually. *Do not boil.*

Mix in the chopped chives before serving.

Leek Soup

SERVES 4.   Cooking time: about 15 minutes.

8–10 *oz. cooked leeks*	1½ pints milk
1 onion	1 chicken stock cube
2 oz. bacon	salt and pepper
1 clove garlic	

Roughly chop leeks. Peel and chop onion. Remove rind and chop bacon. Finely chop garlic. Cook bacon gently for

2 or 3 minutes, add garlic and onion, and cook until onion is soft. Add leeks, milk and stock cube, bring to the boil, and simmer for about 10 minutes. Purée soup through a food mill, a sieve, or in an electric liquidizer. Re-heat and check seasoning before serving.

Minestrone*

If you have some leftover vegetables and some well-flavoured stock in your larder, a hearty minestrone soup will make good use of both ingredients and will provide a warm, filling start to a winter meal.

SERVES 4.   Cooking time: 20 minutes.

2½ pints good stock
1 onion
1 clove garlic
2 tablespoons oil
1 oz. bacon or ham
3 tomatoes

3 oz. *cooked vegetables (carrots, peas, cabbage, leeks, or beans, etc., or a combination)*
¼ teaspoon mixed herbs
1 oz. spaghetti

Peel and finely chop onion; crush garlic; chop bacon or ham; peel and chop tomatoes and cut vegetables into small dice.

Heat oil, add onion, garlic, and ham, and cook for about 3 minutes until onions are transparent but not brown. Add tomatoes and stock, season, and bring to the boil. Toss in the spaghetti, broken into small pieces, and the herbs, and cook for 10 minutes. Add vegetables and continue cooking until spaghetti is tender, about 5 minutes more.

Cream of Pea Soup

SERVES 4.   Cooking time: 20 minutes.

8–10 oz. cooked peas
1 small lettuce
1 small onion
2 pints white stock (use veal
  or chicken stock, or water
  and chicken stock cubes)

1 oz. butter
2 tablespoons flour
4 tablespoons cream
salt and pepper
sprig mint

Clean and shred lettuce; peel and finely chop the onion. Combine lettuce, onion, and stock. Bring to the boil and simmer for 10 minutes, add peas, and cook for a further 5 minutes. Season the soup with salt and pepper, and pass it through a fine food mill or a fine sieve.

Melt the butter in a clean saucepan, add flour, mix well, and gradually blend in the soup stirring constantly until thickened and smooth. Stir in the cream, check seasoning, and sprinkle the soup with finely chopped mint before serving.

3-Minute Soups from Consommé and Leftovers

Tinned consommé is an indispensable part of my store cupboard. In emergencies I use it as a base for a multitude of soups, both hot and cold, depending on the weather. Most of them have no authentic names and for their flavourings rely on the ingredients which are most readily at hand but yet they seem to come up as winners every time.

For a good basic hot consommé to serve 4:

  2 tins beef consommé
  juice of half lemon
  2 tablespoons sherry

Heat consommé, add lemon and sherry, and serve piping hot with croûtons.

For a good basic chilled consommé to serve 4:

Use same ingredients as above; mix, chill until jellied, whip up with a fork, and pile into bowls. Decorate with a blob of sour cream, finely chopped chives, or a thin slice of lemon.

Using leftovers to make a more exciting soup

Hot consommé. Use basic recipe and add:

1. A little ham, cut into very thin shreds.
2. Cooked poultry, cut into thin shreds.
3. Cooked rare roast beef, cut into thin shreds; top with a little whipped cream flavoured with a hint of horseradish.
4. Cooked carrots cut into extra thin *julienne* strips.
5. Cooked peas and a teaspoon of finely chopped mint.
6. Cooked rice, spaghetti or macaroni.
7. A little cooked fresh salmon, white or smoked fish, tinned salmon or tuna fish.
8. Any of the above given an extra little fillip with a teaspoon of curry powder or paste.

Cold consommé. Use basic recipe and add:

1. A little finely chopped pimento or red or green pepper.
2. Finely chopped ham, tongue, corned beef, or tinned spam, etc.
3. Top soup with finely shredded lettuce leaves.
4. Add some finely chopped peeled tomato, grated cucumber or a little crushed garlic to the soup before chilling it.

Consommé with Rice and Tomato

SERVES 4.   Cooking time: about 5 minutes.

2 tins consommé or 2 pints
  clear stock
2 tablespoons tomato purée

3 *oz. cooked rice*
salt and pepper

Heat consommé and blend in tomato purée. Add rice, season with salt and pepper, and heat through.

Note: As with all clear soups, a tablespoon or two of sherry will give this an extra lift.

Consommé Julienne

SERVES 4.   Cooking time: 5 minutes.

  2 tins consommé or 2 pints home-made consommé
  2 oz. *leftover cooked carrots, beans, leeks, cabbage, etc.*
  2 tablespoons sherry
  1 teaspoon lemon juice
  salt and pepper

Cut the vegetables into fine shreds. Heat consommé, add sherry, lemon juice, and vegetables. Season with salt and pepper, and cook gently for 5 minutes.

Fish

I suppose I am particularly fortunate because, living in the country near rivers and the sea, I have a good supply of fresh fish (though I must admit I still have to go to London to find anything exotic). Often I find there is enough cooked fish left over from one meal to stretch happily into a second, and there are a wide variety of recipes calling for cooked fish which I use on these occasions.

If the amount of leftover fish is not adequate for my requirements, then I supplement it with some tinned salmon or tuna – the cost of these is relatively low, especially as I use pink rather than the more expensive red salmon.

Cooked fish adapts well to both cream and sharp spicy sauces, and even the most mundane of fish pies can be made festive by the addition of some prawns or other shellfish.

All fish should be absolutely fresh when it is first cooked, otherwise your made-up dish is not only going to be unappetizing but it could cause tummy trouble. Cooked fish should not be kept for longer than 1–2 days in a refrigerator but, if possible, it should be re-heated and served within 24 hours.

For recipes for cold fish dishes, see pages 35 and 165.

Fish Tart

SERVES 4.   Cooking time: about 50 minutes.

6 oz. plain flour	3 tablespoons sour cream
4 oz. butter	pinch salt

1½ oz. butter
1 large onion
6–8 oz. *cooked fish* (*white fish,
    salmon, etc.*)

3 tomatoes
2 eggs
¼ pint cream
salt, pepper and pinch cayenne
1 oz. grated cheese (optional)

Sift the flour into a bowl with the salt. Rub in 4 oz. butter with fingertips until the mixture resembles coarse breadcrumbs. Add the cream and knead into a smooth dough. Wrap pastry in a cloth and chill for at least an hour.

Roll out pastry and line a 9-inch pie plate. Prick the bottom and bake in a medium hot oven (400°F., Reg. 5) for 10 minutes.

Peel and finely chop onion. Peel and slice tomatoes. Flake the fish with a fork. Beat eggs and cream together. Melt 1½ ozs. butter, add onions, and cook over a low heat until soft but not coloured, about 8 minutes. Arrange fish, tomatoes and onion in the pie shell, season with salt, pepper, and a pinch cayenne, and pour over the beaten egg and cream. Bake in a medium oven (375°F., Reg. 4) for 25–30 minutes until set and golden brown. Grated cheese may be sprinkled over the tart for the last ten minutes of cooking time.

Fish Filling for Savoury Pancakes

SERVES 4. Cooking time: about 25 minutes.

12 savoury pancakes, see page
    110
4 oz. *cooked fish*
2 oz. peeled prawns
6 oz. mushrooms
1 oz. butter
1 tablespoon flour
¼ pint milk
2 tablespoons thick cream

½ tablespoon finely chopped
    parsley
1 tablespoon finely chopped
    chives (optional)
salt and pepper
pinch chili powder
1–2 tablespoons sherry
    (optional)

Flake fish with a fork. Wash and thinly slice mushrooms and cook them gently in ½ oz. butter for 5 minutes until soft. Melt remaining ½ oz. butter, add flour, and mix well. Gradually blend in milk, stirring constantly until sauce is thick and smooth. Bring to the boil and cook for 2 minutes. Add fish, prawns and mushrooms to the sauce. Blend in the cream and chopped parsley and chives. Season with salt, pepper and chili powder. Add sherry.

Spread pancakes with the filling, roll up neatly, arrange in a shallow baking dish, lightly greased, and bake for 15 minutes in a hot oven (425°F., Reg. 6).

Shellfish

Unfortunately it isn't often that one wakes to find some left-over shellfish residing in the larder or refrigerator – lobsters, crawfish, crabs, and fresh prawns are too good and too expensive not to be eaten in one sitting.

But miracles can happen and small amounts of shellfish can be added with great advantage to any freshly made or leftover fish dishes; add them to haddock or salmon in kedgeree or use, with an additional tin of tuna fish, or some frozen prawns, to make a fish cocktail (see page 33).

Note: All fish is susceptible to the action of bacteria (shellfish which has gone 'off' is particularly dangerous) and should not be kept for longer than about 24 hours after being cooked.

Fish Soufflé

2–3 SERVINGS. Cooking time: 20–25 minutes.

1 lb. cooked white fish, salmon, or sea trout (tinned salmon can be used to make up the required weight)

1 oz. butter	salt and pepper
1 oz. flour	2 eggs
¼ pint milk	

Rub the fish through a sieve or through a food mill.

Melt the butter in a saucepan, add the flour, and mix well over a medium heat until the flour and butter form a ball and leave the sides of the pan. Gradually blend in the milk, stirring constantly until the mixture is thick and smooth, add the fish, and leave to cool for 2 minutes.

Beat the egg yolks into the fish mixture one by one until they are well blended, and season the mixture with salt and pepper. Whip the egg whites until stiff, fold them into the fish, and pour into a well-greased soufflé dish. Bake in medium hot oven (400°F., Reg. 5) for 20–25 minutes.

Serve the soufflé at once with a well-seasoned tomato or egg and mustard sauce, see pages 277–8 and 272.

This is not the lightest of soufflés, but it makes a good starter before a small main course. If you want to make it lighter, add an extra egg white.

Savoury Fish Pudding

SERVES 4.   Cooking time: about 35 minutes.

8–12 oz. cooked fish (any white fish, salt fish, smoked fish, salmon or tuna)	½ oz. butter
4 cooked potatoes	2 eggs
1 large onion	1 tablespoon flour
2 tomatoes	¾ pint milk
1 tablespoon chopped parsley	salt and pepper
	pinch celery salt (optional)

Cut fish into ½ inch pieces. Slice potatoes. Peel and thinly slice onion. Peel and chop tomatoes (see page 18).

Heat the butter and cook onions until soft and transparent, about 3 minutes.

Arrange half the potatoes in the bottom of a buttered fire-proof dish. Cover this with the fish, onions, tomatoes and parsley and season with salt, pepper and celery salt. Top with the remaining sliced potatoes.

Beat together with eggs, flour, and milk, and season with salt and pepper. Pour the custard over the potatoes and bake in a hot oven (435°F., Reg. 6) until the custard is set, about 20–25 minutes.

Danish Fish au Gratin

In Denmark they make this fish dish with soused or matjes herring fillets, but I find it adapts well for use with almost any cooked fish.

SERVES 4.   Cooking time: 15–20 minutes.

8–10 oz. cooked fish	2 tablespoons finely chopped
4 cooked potatoes	parsley
2 hardboiled eggs	1 teaspoon finely chopped
1½ oz. butter	capers
1 small onion	salt and pepper
3 tablespoons flour	1–2 oz. grated cheese
½ pint milk	½ oz. butter
3 tablespoons cream	

Cut fish into small pieces. Cut potatoes in thin slices. Chop hardboiled eggs. Peel and finely chop the onion.

Melt the butter, add finely chopped onion and cook until onion is transparent, about 3 minutes. Add flour, mix well, and gradually add milk, stirring constantly until the sauce is thick and comes to the boil. Add parsley and capers, and season with salt and pepper.

Arrange potato slices in the bottom of a baking dish. Place fish pieces and chopped eggs on the potatoes, and pour the sauce over. Sprinkle with grated cheese, dot with ½ oz. butter and bake in a very hot oven (475°F., Reg. 8) for 10–15 minutes until golden brown and hot through.

Fish Croquettes*

SERVES 4.   Cooking time: 2–3 minutes each croquette.

10–14 oz. cooked fish (white fish, mackerel, herring, salmon, etc.)	salt and pepper 2 egg yolks flour
½ oz. butter	1 egg
2 tablespoons flour	brown breadcrumbs
½ pint fish stock or cream or a mixture of both	fat or oil for frying

Flake the fish with a fork (the pieces should not be too small). Heat the butter, add flour, and mix well. Gradually blend in the fish stock or cream and bring to the boil, stirring constantly until thick and smooth. Reduce heat and cook for 2 minutes. Beat in egg yolks, mix in the fish, and season with salt and pepper. Leave the mixture to cool.

Beat the egg. Shape cold fish mixture into 8 croquettes; roll in flour, dip in beaten egg, and then coat all over with brown breadcrumbs.

Fry croquettes in very hot deep fat or oil for about 3 minutes each and drain on kitchen paper. Serve with a sauce tartare or a seafood sauce.

Variations:

1. Add a little finely chopped mushroom cooked in butter.
2. Add some finely chopped parsley and a little chopped onion softened in butter.

Creamed Fish with Prawns and Peas★

SERVES 4. Cooking time: about 20 minutes.

10–14 oz. cooked fish (use any white fish or salmon)	1 oz. butter
	1 oz. flour
4–6 oz. fresh or frozen peeled prawns	¾ pint milk
	salt and pepper
4 oz. cooked peas	

Flake the fish with a fork. Melt the butter in a saucepan, add flour, and mix well. Gradually blend in the milk, stirring constantly until the sauce is thick and smooth.

Fold fish, prawns and peas into the sauce, season with salt and pepper and heat through.

Serve in a ring of creamy mashed potatoes.

Note: 1 tablespoon dry white wine, dry vermouth, or sherry and a tablespoon or two of cream can be added to the fish. For a more piquant dish add 1 tablespoon tomato purée or ketchup and a dash of Worcester sauce.

Fish Cakes★

If one has hearty breakfast-eaters in the family these make a perfect meal for them. You can prepare the fish cakes in advance and leave them in a cool place or in a refrigerator over-night.

Like all of the best things in life, the perfect fish cakes are made from the most expensive commodity. In this case, salmon, freshly cooked, makes the perfect cake but even the more mundane products made from cod or haddock can taste delicious if they are well seasoned and served straight from the pan.

SERVES 4.   Cooking time: about 20 minutes.

1¼ lb. cooked potatoes
½ oz. butter
2 tablespoons cream or milk
8 oz. cooked fish (salmon, cod, haddock, etc.)
1 tablespoon finely chopped parsley

salt and pepper
1 beaten egg
brown breadcrumbs
fat for frying

Flake the fish with a fork. Mash potatoes until smooth with ½ oz. butter and 2 tablespoons cream or milk. Add fish and parsley to potatoes, season with plenty of salt and pepper, and mix well.

Using floured hands, shape the mixture into 8 flat round cakes, dip each cake in beaten egg, coat in breadcrumbs, and fry in shallow fat for about 6 minutes until golden brown on both sides. Drain the fried cakes on crumpled kitchen paper.

Variations:

1. Add 1 teaspoon mixed dried herbs to the mixture.
2. Instead of coating the fish cakes in brown breadcrumbs, dip them in packaged parsley and thyme, or sage and onion stuffing.

Fish with Beetroot

SERVES 4.   Cooking time: about 20 minutes.

½ lb. cooked white fish (haddock, cod, plaice, etc.)
1 oz. butter
1 oz. flour
¾ pint milk
1 egg yolk
1-2 teaspoons English or Dijon mustard (optional)

1 large cooked beetroot (or small tin beetroot)
salt and pepper
1 oz. cheese, grated
paprika

Flake the fish with a fork; cut beetroot into small dice.

Melt butter, add flour, and mix well. Gradually blend in milk stirring constantly over a medium heat until the sauce is thick and smooth. Bring to the boil, remove from the heat and beat in 1 egg yolk. Blend in mustard. Mix in the flaked fish and beetroot, season, and pour into a shallow baking dish.

Sprinkle over the grated cheese and brown under a hot grill or in a hot oven.

Note: For an Eastern touch use half milk and half yoghurt.

Fisherman's Pie

This is one of my household standbys. It's easy to make, delicious to eat, and with some jazzy additions and decorations this everyday dish can become a dinner party starter or lunch party main course. For convenience I have given both the everyday and the smart recipe, although they are basically the same.

SERVES 4.   Cooking time: About 35–40 minutes.

1½ *lb. cooked potatoes*	*haddock, tinned salmon, or*
½ oz. butter	*tuna, etc.*)
1 tablespoon top of the milk	2 hardboiled eggs
¼ *lb. cooked peas (or frozen)*	1½ oz. butter
3 tomatoes	3 tablespoons flour
¼ teaspoon dried sage or	¾ pint milk
thyme	salt and pepper
8 *oz. cooked fish (cod, plaice,*	

Mash potatoes with ½ oz. butter and 1 tablespoon top of the milk until smooth and creamy, season with salt and pepper.

Flake fish with a fork; skin and chop tomatoes (see page 18), cut hardboiled eggs into quarters.

Heat 1½ oz. butter in a large saucepan, add flour, and mix

well. Gradually blend in milk and cook over a medium heat, stirring constantly, until the sauce is thick and smooth. Add peas, tomatoes, herbs, fish, and hardboiled eggs. Mix together lightly and season well with salt and pepper. Turn into a shallow fireproof dish, top with the mashed potatoes, and bake in a medium hot oven (400°F., Reg. 5) for 20–25 minutes until golden brown.

Note: 2 oz. grated cheese can be added to the sauce, or 1 tablespoon finely chopped parsley, or 2 tablespoons tomato purée.

Instead of using mashed potatoes as a topping try using potato crisps or cornflakes, crushed with a rolling pin, instead.

Captain's Pie

This is merely a more sophisticated version of the preceding Fisherman's Pie. The variety of ingredients which you can add to this kind of dish are numerous; all I can do is to offer you the basic recipe and then leave the rest to your imagination.

SERVES 4.   Cooking time: about 35–40 minutes.

1½ lb. cooked potatoes	2 scallops (fresh or frozen)
½ oz. butter	1½ oz. butter
1 tablespoon cream	3 tablespoons flour
1 oz. grated cheese	½ pint milk
pinch paprika	¼ pint cream
6 oz. cooked fish (white fish, tinned or fresh salmon, tuna, etc.)	2 tablespoons dry vermouth or white wine
2 oz. mushrooms	1 tablespoon finely chopped parsley
4 oz. peeled prawns	salt and pepper

Mash potatoes until smooth and creamy with ½ oz butter,

1 tablespoon cream, 1 oz. grated cheese, and a pinch of paprika, season with salt and pepper.

Flake fish with a fork. Wash and thinly slice mushrooms. Chop scallops into small pieces.

Melt butter, add mushrooms and scallops, and cook gently for 3 minutes. Sprinkle over flour and mix well. Gradually blend in milk stirring constantly until the sauce is thick and smooth, taking care not to damage the mushrooms. Bring the sauce to the boil; add fish, prawns, parsley, season with salt and pepper, remove from the heat, and stir in dry vermouth or white wine and ¼ pint cream. Turn into a shallow, fireproof, serving dish, and top with the mashed potato smoothed out evenly and decorated with lines made by running the prongs of a fork over the top.

Cook in a medium hot oven (400°F., Reg. 5) for 20–25 minutes until golden brown.

Cheesy Fish Puff

Not so long ago I would have treated any recipe incorporating puff pastry with extreme caution, because making the puff pastry is inevitably a long and time-consuming job.

Now deep freeze firms have come to our aid and it should be possible to buy first-class frozen puff pastry at any shop which has a deep freeze cabinet. All you have to do is thaw it, roll it, and use it.

SERVES 4. Cooking time: about 30 minutes.

small packet frozen puff pastry, thawed	2 oz. cheddar cheese
	2 large eggs, beaten
6–8 oz. cooked fish (cod, haddock, plaice, smoked fish, tinned tuna, or salmon, etc.)	salt and pepper
	pinch marjoram

Roll pastry into an oblong strip measuring about 12 × 8 inches. Cut in half and place one half on a wetted baking sheet. Roll remaining pastry a little thinner until it is about a quarter of an inch larger all round.

Flake fish with a fork and coarsely grate the cheese. Combine fish, cheese and all but 1 tablespoon of the beaten egg. Season with salt, pepper, and a pinch of marjoram, and spread the mixture on the first piece of pastry. Dampen the edges, cover with the remaining pastry and pinch the edges firmly together. Brush pastry with the remaining beaten egg, and leave to stand in a cool place for at least 15 minutes.

Bake in a hot oven (425°F., Reg. 6) for 20–25 minutes until well risen and golden brown.

Creamed Fish with Potatoes*

SERVES 4.   Cooking time: about 20 minutes.

1 *lb. cooked potatoes*	8–10 *oz. cooked fish (white fish,*
½ oz. butter	*smoked fish, tinned tuna, or*
1 tablespoon cream	*salmon, etc.)*
4 oz. button mushrooms	1 tablespoon finely chopped
1 oz. butter	parsley
1 tablespoon flour	1 oz. grated cheese
½ pint milk	

Mash potatoes with ½ oz. butter and 1 tablespoon cream until smooth, season with salt and pepper, and arrange in a border around a serving dish.

Wash and thinly slice mushrooms. Flake fish with a fork.

Melt 1 oz. butter in a saucepan, add mushrooms, and cook gently for about 5 minutes. Sprinkle over flour and mix well. Gradually blend in milk stirring constantly, but gently, until the sauce is thick and smooth. Add fish and parsley, season with salt and pepper, and cook for a further 3–4 minutes to allow the fish to heat through.

Turn the fish mixture into the centre of the potatoes, sprinkle over the cheese, and brown under a hot grill.

Variations:

1. A border of boiled rice can replace the potatoes.
2. Leftover vegetables (cut into small dice if necessary) can be added to the sauce.
3. Add 1 tablespoon of sherry or dry vermouth to the sauce.
4. $\frac{1}{4}$–$\frac{1}{2}$ teaspoon tarragon and 1 teaspoon lemon juice can be added to the sauce.

Fish à la King

This can be served as a first course or as a lunch or supper dish. Virtually any cooked or tinned fish can be used, and I find this an easy dish to knock up in a hurry using a tin of tuna or salmon.

SERVES 4.   Cooking time: 10–15 minutes.

7–8 oz. flaked cooked or tinned fish	$\frac{1}{2}$ pint water
4 oz. button mushrooms (or use a small tin)	1 chicken stock cube
	$\frac{1}{4}$ pint single cream
$\frac{1}{2}$ green pepper	salt and pepper
2 oz. butter	pinch cayenne
3 tablespoons flour	1 tablespoon sherry or vermouth (optional)

Thinly slice button mushrooms. Finely chop pepper. Heat butter in a saucepan, add mushrooms and pepper, and cook gently for 3 minutes. Remove mushrooms and pepper with a slotted spoon, add flour to the butter, mix well, and gradually blend in water, stirring constantly until the sauce is thick and smooth. Mix in stock cube and stir until it has melted. Add the fish, mushrooms, and pepper to the sauce, blend in the cream, seasoning, and sherry, and heat through without boiling.

Serve the dish with boiled rice.

Finely chopped celery or tinned pimento can be used in place of the green pepper and the dish can be stretched by the addition of small shapes cut from short or puff pastry and baked until golden brown.

Goujons of Cooked Fish

Goujons are small fish found in the Mediterranean and cooked in very light crisp batter. Pieces of cooked fish can be cooked in the same way, and because the batter puffs out in a most amazing way a little goes a long way.

SERVES 4. Cooking time: 5 minutes.

8–10 oz. *firm cooked white fish*	1 teaspoon lemon juice
2 tablespoons olive oil	salt and pepper

Batter

4 oz. plain flour	salt and pepper
3 tablespoons olive oil	1 *egg white*
2 tablespoons water	oil or fat for frying
2 tablespoons milk	

Cut fish into squares the size of a postage stamp. Marinade for 15 minutes in the olive oil and lemon juice seasoned with salt and pepper. Drain well on kitchen paper.

Sieve flour, beat in olive oil, water and milk. Mix until smooth, season with salt and pepper. Beat the egg white until stiff and fold into the batter just before using.

Dip fish pieces in the batter and fry in hot deep fat or oil until they are golden brown and puffed up, about 2 minutes. Drain on kitchen paper to remove excess fat and serve at once with a tartare or seafood sauce.

Note: For a Latin American version of this dish add 1 crushed clove garlic, a pinch chili powder, and a few drops of Tabasco sauce to the marinade.

Scrambled Egg with Haddock

SERVES 4.   Cooking time: about 10 minutes.

8 eggs	2 oz. butter
8 *oz. cooked smoked haddock*	2 tablespoons cream
2 tomatoes	salt and pepper

Buttered toast

Flake the fish, peel and chop the tomatoes, and lightly beat the eggs.

Combine fish, chopped tomatoes, and beaten eggs. Mix in cream and season with salt and pepper.

Melt the butter in a saucepan, add the egg mixture, and cook over a low heat, stirring occasionally, until the eggs are just set.

Serve at once on slices of buttered toast.

Meat

Most cooked meat adapts well, in one form or another, to being re-introduced as a made-up dish. Your choice is limitless and bound by only one thing – the amount of cooked meat you have left.

Beef, since it is usually served underdone, is the most moist and juicy of the cooked meats and it therefore responds well to recipes which require cooking rather than just heating through. To prevent all cooked meats drying out when cold, wrap them lightly in aluminium foil, greaseproof paper or Saranwrap (leaving enough air inside the wrapping to allow the meat to breathe) and never cut, slice or mince meat until you require it.

Meat which has been overcooked in the first place will never improve on the second cooking or heating, so time your roasting or boiling with care and baste the meat frequently during the cooking time to ensure that as much juice as possible is retained.

In most cases meat in made-up dishes should be heated through, not cooked again. It should be minced, very finely chopped, or very thinly sliced so that it heats through quickly. Coarsely chopped or thickly sliced meat tends to be tough and indigestible.

Since meat, like most other cooked foods, tends to lose some of its flavour during the first cooking, extra tastes, spices, and seasonings must be added to the made-up dish.

Use small amounts of cooked meat for making meat sauces to go with spaghetti and other pasta dishes. Use larger amounts of tender cooked meat in recipes which call for thinly cut slices of cooked meat.

For notes on serving cold sliced meat, see page 165.

Drippings and pan juices from roast meat

The fat and juices which come from a joint, combined with any fat which has been added to the meat while it roasts, produce a great deal of goodness which should not be discarded. Use some of the pan juices to make gravy for the roast, tip the rest into a clean bowl, and leave to cool. Store the dripping in a cool place or a refrigerator but do not keep for longer than one week. The meat juices will sink to the bottom of the bowl and make a thick dark jelly which can be used for further gravies or to give flavour to soups, sauces, and stews. The top fat, or dripping, can be used for frying, for basting roast meat or as a delicious and nutritious spread for bread or toast.

To clarify the fat, or dripping, separate it from the meat jelly, bring to boiling point in a clean pan, and strain into a clean bowl. Leave to cool and set hard before keeping in a refrigerator. The fat can be kept for up to fourteen days when it has been clarified in this way.

If the meat glaze, or jelly, at the bottom of the bowl is clear and of a good colour, it can be cut into squares or strips and used instead of aspic jelly as a garnish for cold meat dishes.

Gravy

The best gravies are made from an amalgamation of rich pan drippings from roast meat, flour, and liquid in the form of stock or vegetable water. The gravy should be the consistency of Jersey milk and have a good rich colour. All fat that rises to the surface should be carefully removed.

To make gravy

Drain off nearly all fat from the pan juices leaving the dark meat glaze. Heat the juices, add 1 tablespoon flour and cook over a fast heat until flour is browned. Gradually blend in ½ pint stock or vegetable water and bring to the boil, stirring constantly until the gravy has thickened and is smooth. Season with salt and pepper if necessary.

To give gravy more flavour

Few things help more to give a somewhat uninteresting joint a lift than a gravy which is full of taste and flavour. Sometimes the basic essentials of the pan juices and stock or vegetable water are not enough to provide this so here are a choice of extra ingredients which should make all the difference.

    1-2 tablespoons tomato purée
    a few drops Worcester sauce
    a few drops mushroom ketchup
    ½ a beef or chicken stock cube

Removing fat or grease from the surface of gravy

Sometimes even the best gravy develops a film of fat over the surface just as you are about to serve it. This can be quickly removed by carefully spooning off the fat, by soaking it up with a piece of paper kitchen towelling, or by absorbing it with the corner of a clean tea cloth.

Leftover gravy

Strong rich gravy gives extra taste to brown soups, sauces, and many made up dishes such as shepherd's or cottage pies.

Savoury Meat Pie

Equally good hot or cold, this pie makes a useful dish for lunch, supper, cold buffets, or picnics.

SERVES 4–6.   Cooking time: about 45 minutes.

10 oz. cooked meat	small bunch parsley
2 onions	¼ pint meat glaze, clear gravy,
2 oz. fat bacon	or rich jellied stock
½ oz. lard or dripping	salt and pepper

For the pastry

8 oz. flour	pinch salt
4 oz. butter	milk
2–3 tablespoons iced water	

First make the pastry. Sift flour and salt into a bowl, rub in butter with the fingertips until the mixture resembles coarse breadcrumbs. Mix in enough water to form a stiff dough. Wrap in a cloth and leave to stand in a cold place for 30 minutes. Roll out ⅔ of the pastry and line a shallow pie dish.

Mince the meat. Peel and mince the onion. Remove rinds and mince bacon. Mince or very finely chop the parsley.

Heat lard or dripping. Add onion and bacon and cook over a medium heat for 5 minutes. Add meat, parsley, and meat glaze. Season with salt and pepper, mix well, and cook for a further 5 minutes. Leave meat mixture to cool.

Fill pastry case with cooled meat and juices. Roll out remaining pastry to make the pie lid. Brush edges with a little milk and pinch together to make a good seal. Cut a vent in the centre of the pie and brush all over with milk.

Bake the pie in a hot oven (450°F., Reg. 7) for 10 minutes, then reduce heat to medium hot (400°F., Reg. 5) and cook for a further 20 minutes or until pastry is golden brown.

Cold Meat Diable

Cold dishes served with the sharp pepperiness of a devil sauce were popular throughout the grander English houses in the eighteenth and nineteenth centuries. Then they went out of fashion and nowadays they are all too seldom featured in our cooking. To my mind, a devil sauce does much for any once-enjoyed meat, and it can turn almost any leftover, be it meat, fowl or fish, into a delectable meal.

SERVES 4. Cooking time: about 35 minutes.

8 *thin slices cooked beef, lamb, pork or mutton*
2 medium onions
1 clove garlic
1 tablespoon olive oil
1 tablespoon flour
4 tablespoons strong stock
1 tablespoon vinegar
1 teaspoon sugar
1 tablespoon Dijon mustard
1 teaspoon capers
1 bay leaf
salt and freshly ground black pepper
2 tablespoons browned breadcrumbs
1 tablespoon melted butter

Arrange the slices of beef or cold meat in a fireproof serving dish.

Finely chop onions, garlic, and capers. Heat olive oil in a saucepan, add onions and garlic and cook for 3–5 minutes over a medium heat until onions are soft and golden brown. Sprinkle over the flour, add mustard and vinegar, mix well, and gradually blend in the stock, stirring constantly until the sauce is thick and smooth. Add bay leaf, capers, and sugar. Season with salt and freshly ground black pepper, bring to the boil, and cook gently for 10 minutes. If the sauce becomes too thick, thin it with a little extra stock or water.

Pour the sauce over the meat, sprinkle with breadcrumbs, pour over the melted butter, and cook in a moderately hot oven (380°F., Reg. 4) for 20 minutes until hot through and golden brown.

Risotto Milanese

SERVES 4. Cooking time: 40 minutes.

2 onions	8–12 oz. cooked meat (beef,
1 clove garlic	lamb, or poultry)
3 tablespoons olive oil	salt and pepper
8 oz. rice	grated parmesan cheese
4 oz. mushrooms	1 oz. butter
1–1½ pints stock	

Peel and chop onions. Wash and thinly slice mushrooms. Crush garlic. Cut meat into small dice.

Heat olive oil and cook onions and garlic until golden brown. Add rice and cook for 2 minutes until transparent. Add mushrooms, mix well, and pour over 1 pint stock. Season with salt and pepper. Cover and cook on top of the stove for 20 minutes.

Mix in the meat, add extra stock if necessary (risottos should be moist but not liquid), and continue cooking until the rice is tender. Mix in the grated parmesan and butter before serving.

Serve Risotto with a green or mixed salad.

Meat or Chicken Pilaff

SERVES 4. Cooking time: about 45 minutes.

2 onions	8–12 oz. cooked meat (beef,
6 oz. long grained rice	lamb, mutton, pork, veal
2 oz. bacon	or chicken)
2 oz. mushrooms	salt and pepper
2 oz. butter	pinch cayenne

Peel and chop onions. Wash and slice mushrooms. Chop bacon and cooked meat.

Cook rice in boiling salted water until just tender. Drain, rinse, and dry in a low oven.

Melt the butter, add onions and bacon, and cook over a moderate heat until onions are soft and golden brown. Add mushrooms and cook for a further 3 minutes. Mix in the meat, season with salt, pepper, and cayenne, and cook gently for 5 minutes before adding the rice. Mix lightly with a fork so that all the ingredients are thoroughly combined and pile on a warm serving dish.

Serve the pilaff with a green or mixed salad, and with a bowl of grated cheese.

Meat Provençale

Aubergines, with their distinctive taste and smooth almost slippery texture, combine deliciously with meat. As aubergines produce a lot of juice themselves, the addition of extra gravy or stock in these meat/aubergine combinations is usually unnecessary.

SERVES 4.   Cooking time: about 35 – 40 minutes.

8–12 oz. cooked meat (beef, lamb, mutton, or pork)
2 medium aubergines
3 tablespoons olive oil
2 oz. bacon
1 large onion
3 ripe tomatoes
2 cloves garlic
1 tablespoon parsley, finely chopped
2 tablespoons browned breadcrumbs
1 oz. butter, melted
salt and pepper

Cut aubergines into thin slices lengthwise without removing the skin. Sprinkle slices with salt and leave them to 'sweat' for 10–15 minutes. Dry slices on kitchen paper.

Cut meat into thin strips, dice bacon, peel and chop onion, peel and slice tomatoes (see page 18), crush garlic.

Heat oil and fry dried aubergine slices until lightly browned on both sides, drain well, and arrange on the bottom of a lightly greased baking dish. Cover aubergines with the meat strips.

Add bacon and onion to the oil and cook over a medium heat until golden brown. Add tomatoes, garlic, and parsley, and cook for 3 minutes. Season with salt and pepper, and spread the mixture over the meat and aubergine. Sprinkle over the breadcrumbs, pour over the melted butter, and cook for 20 minutes in a medium hot oven (400°F., Reg. 5) until bubbling and golden brown.

Petty i Panna   Swedish meat and potato hash

This is one of the oldest dishes I remember. It's a classic Swedish recipe, and one which my mother used to make frequently during the war. Probably I used to get bored with it then, but now I regard Petty i Panna as one of the best and most delicious ways there is of using up leftovers of roast beef. In fact the recipe is so simple and so enjoyable that I sometimes think it's almost more delicious than the original roast beef itself.

Lamb can be used in the place of beef, and if you don't fancy mixing a raw egg into your portion the eggs can be fried and arranged on top of the dish before it comes to the table.

The secret of Petty i Panna lies in cutting up all the ingredients really fine and serving it immediately.

SERVES 4.   Cooking time: 30–40 minutes.

5 potatoes	1½ oz. butter
1 lb. cooked beef or lamb	1 tablespoon olive oil
½ lb. bacon	2 onions

1 tablespoon finely chopped parsley

4 fresh eggs

salt and freshly ground black pepper

Peel the potatoes and cut them into really small dice. Cut the meat and bacon into small dice and finely chop the onions.

Heat the butter and oil in a large frying pan, add the potatoes, and cook for about 15 minutes until crisp and golden brown. Remove the potatoes, drain them on crumpled kitchen paper, and keep warm.

Add the onions, meat, and bacon to the fat in the pan, and cook over a moderate heat for about ten minutes, stirring frequently, until the onions and bacon are cooked through. Add the potatoes and cook for a further 5–10 minutes. Season with salt and freshly ground black pepper and mix in the finely chopped parsley.

Arrange the Petty i Panna in four piles on a warm serving dish. Make a hole in the centre of each pile and place in it a raw egg.

Serve at once.

Each person should mix the raw egg into their Petty i Panna as they receive it and season it to their liking with a few drops of Worcester and Tabasco sauce.

Scalloped Meat with Potatoes*

SERVES 4.   Cooking time: about 40 minutes.

1½ lb. cooked potatoes

8–10 oz. cooked meat, poultry, or ham

1 onion

1½ oz. butter

½ pint milk or thin cream

½ teaspoon dry mustard

½ tablespoon parsley, finely chopped

salt and pepper

¼ teaspoon paprika

Thinly slice potatoes. Mince meat through coarse blades of

the mincer. Peel and finely chop the onion. Heat half the butter, add onion and cook for 3–5 minutes until soft and transparent but not brown.

Arrange a layer of potatoes in a buttered baking dish, cover with a little onion and a layer of meat, season, and repeat the layers, finishing with one of potatoes.

Mix milk or cream with the mustard and parsley, season lightly, and pour over the potatoes, dot with remaining butter, and bake in a medium hot oven (400°F., Reg. 5) for 20–25 minutes. Sprinkle over the paprika before serving.

Note: Raw potatoes can be used in this dish, in which case the oven temperature should be lower and the cooking time about 1 hour.

The meat may be cut into small cubes instead of being minced.

Shepherd's Pie*

Surely the most classic of all British leftover dishes!

SERVES 4.   Cooking time: 25–30 minutes.

1 *lb. mashed potatoes*	1 *lb. minced cooked beef or lamb*
1 tablespoon milk or cream	¼ pint strong stock or gravy
2 oz. butter	½ teaspoon Worcester sauce
2 onions	salt and pepper

Melt 1 oz. butter, add it to the mashed potatoes with the milk, season with salt and pepper, and mix well.

Peel and finely chop the onions. Melt the remaining butter in a frying pan, add the onions, and cook until soft. Mix in the meat, moisten with stock and Worcester sauce, and season well.

Place the meat in a lightly greased baking dish, cover with the mashed potatoes, and bake in a hot oven (450°F., Reg. 7) for 30 minutes. The top should be golden brown.

Continental Shepherd's Pie

Shepherd's Pie is not sacred to the British. In France too they have their own version for using up the remains of the joint.

SERVES 4.   Cooking time: 30 minutes.

1 lb. mashed potatoes	1 lb. minced cooked beef or lamb
2 oz. butter	1 tablespoon finely chopped
1 tablespoon cream	parsley
2 onions	2 tablespoons red wine
1 clove garlic	salt and pepper
3 tomatoes	2 oz. grated cheese

Melt 1 oz. butter, add it to the potatoes with the cream, season with salt and pepper, and mix well.

Peel and finely chop the onions, crush the garlic or put through a garlic press, peel and chop the tomatoes. Melt the remaining butter in a frying pan, add the onions and garlic, and cook until soft and transparent. Add the tomatoes and meat, and cook over a medium heat for five minutes. Add the parsley, pour over the wine, season, and mix well.

Place half the potatoes in a greased baking dish, cover with the meat mixture, and top with the rest of the potatoes. Sprinkle over the grated cheese and bake in a hot oven (425°F., Reg. 6) for 30 minutes.

Cottage Pie*

Made on the same principle as a Shepherd's Pie but with less meat and the addition of vegetables in the filling.

SERVES 4.   Cooking time: 40 minutes.

1 lb. mashed potatoes	¾ lb. minced cooked beef or lamb
1 tablespoon milk or cream	¼ lb. frozen peas
1 large onion	¼ pint strong stock or gravy
2 oz. butter	salt and pepper
2 carrots	

Melt 1 oz. butter, add it to the potatoes with the milk or cream, season with salt and pepper, and mix well.

Mince the onion and the carrots through the coarse blades of the mincing machine.

Melt the remaining butter in a frying pan, add the minced onion and carrot, and cook for five minutes over a low heat. Add the meat, peas and gravy, season with salt and pepper, and cook for a further five minutes.

Place the meat in a lightly greased baking dish, cover with the mashed potatoes and bake in a medium hot oven (400°F., Reg. 5) for 40 minutes.

Stuffed Baked Marrow

Marrows are not my favourite vegetable. I find them watery and tasteless, but they *are* cheap when in season and make a useful base for a strongly flavoured meat filling. Cooked minced beef, mutton, or lamb can be used for this dish but not veal, pork, or chicken as the white meats are too bland.

SERVES 4–6.   Cooking time: 1½ hours.

1 medium marrow	1 small tin tomatoes
12 oz. cooked minced beef, mutton, or lamb	3 oz. breadcrumbs
	1 tablespoon tomato purée
1 medium onion	2 teaspoons dried mixed herbs
2 tablespoons olive oil	salt and pepper
2 oz. mushrooms	2 oz. dripping

Wash the marrow, cut a thick slice off the top and scoop out the seeds.

Peel and chop the onion, chop the mushrooms. Heat the olive oil, add the onion and cook for 3–5 minutes until soft. Mix in the mushrooms and meat, and cook for a further five minutes. Break up the tomatoes with a fork, add them to the meat with the breadcrumbs, tomato purée, and herbs. Mix well and season generously with salt and pepper. Fill the marrow with the stuffing, and cover with the top slice.

Melt the dripping in a baking dish, put in the marrow, and bake for 1½ hours in a medium hot oven (400°F., Reg. 5), basting occasionally with the juices in the dish.

Stuffed Marrow Rings

SERVES 4.   Cooking time: 20 minutes.

1 small marrow	pinch savory ⎫ (optional)
6 oz. cooked lamb, mutton, or beef	pinch marjoram ⎭
1 medium onion, peeled and chopped	2 teaspoons flour
	3 tablespoons water
1 oz. butter or dripping	Worcester sauce
2 tomatoes, peeled and chopped	1 tablespoon tomato ketchup
4 tablespoons cooked rice	1 oz. grated cheese
	paprika pepper (optional)

Cut a slice off the top and bottom of the marrow, and cut the rest into four thick slices. Drop the slices into boiling salted water and cook until just soft, about 10 minutes. Cool, and remove the seeds from the centre of the rings.

Heat the fat in a large frying pan, add the onion, and fry until soft. Mix the meat with the onion and cook for a further 3 minutes, add the tomatoes, rice, and herbs, sprinkle over the flour, and mix well. Blend in the water with a few drops of Worcester sauce and the tomato ketchup, cook over a medium heat for 5 minutes stirring well.

Place the marrow rings in a lightly greased baking dish,

fill the centres with the meat mixture, top with the grated cheese and a little paprika pepper. Bake in a hot oven (425°F., Reg. 6) for 20 minutes.

Stuffed Green or Red Peppers

Cooking time: about 20 minutes.
For each serving:

1 red or green pepper	2 oz. *cooked meat, ham, or*
1 tablespoon olive oil	*poultry*
1 small onion	4 tablespoons cooked rice
½ clove garlic	salt and pepper
1 oz. mushrooms	grated cheese

Peel and finely chop onion and garlic. Wash and finely chop mushrooms. Mince meat.

Cut each pepper in half lengthwise and remove the core and all the seeds. Cook pepper halves in boiling water until just tender (8–10 minutes). Drain well and keep warm.

Heat oil, add onion and garlic, and fry until golden. Add mushrooms and cook for 2 minutes. Add rice, and meat, and season well with salt and pepper. Cook for a further 5 minutes. Pack into pepper shells, sprinkle with grated cheese, and brown under a hot grill.

Stuffed Peppers II

SERVES 4.   Cooking time: 50 minutes.

4 green or red peppers	8 oz. *cooked rice*
1 onion	1 oz. butter
4–6 oz. *cooked meat, chicken*	3 teaspoons curry powder
or ham	4 tablespoons cream
2 crisp eating apples	salt and pepper
2 tablespoons mango chutney	

Cut a slice from the stalk end of the peppers and scoop out the core and seeds. Blanch peppers in boiling salted water for 4 minutes.

Mince meat. Peel and finely chop apples. Peel and finely chop onion.

Heat butter in a saucepan and fry the onion until soft. Add meat and cook for 2 minutes. Mix in rice, apples, and chutney, add curry powder and cream, season, and simmer gently for 5 minutes. Pack mixture in pepper cases, and bake in a buttered baking dish for 20–30 minutes in a moderately hot oven (375°F., Reg. 4).

Stuffed Aubergines

SERVES 4.   Cooking time: 40 minutes.

4 aubergines	4 oz. cooked meat, minced (beef, lamb, chicken or ham)
4 tablespoons olive oil	
1 large onion	4 oz. grated cheese
1 clove garlic	salt and pepper
1 medium tin tomatoes	8 anchovy fillets

Cut aubergines in half lengthwise and score the surfaces half the way through in a grid pattern. Sprinkle with salt and fry (flat side down) for 10 minutes in the olive oil. Leave to cool, scoop out the pulp, and chop finely.

Finely chop or mince the onion, crush the garlic, and fry together in the oil until onion is soft and transparent. Add tomatoes, aubergine pulp, minced meat, and 3 oz. cheese. Season well, cook for 2 minutes, and pack mixture in aubergine shells. Place 1 anchovy on each aubergine half, sprinkle with remaining cheese, and cook in a moderately hot oven (375°F., Reg. 4) for 20–30 minutes until skins are soft and the top golden brown.

Stuffed Onions

SERVES 4.   Cooking time: about 1 hour.

4 very large onions	1 oz. meat dripping or bacon
4–8 oz. *cooked meat*	fat
1 oz. fresh breadcrumbs	salt and pepper
1 oz. butter	

Peel and trim onions until uniform. Mince meat. Cook onions in boiling salted water until just soft on the outside, about 10 minutes. Drain well and scoop out a good spoonful from the centre of each one. Chop scooped out onion finely.

Melt butter, add minced meat, breadcrumbs, and chopped onion. Season with salt and pepper, and cook over a moderate heat for 5 minutes.

Stuff onion centres with the mixture. Heat dripping in a casserole dish, add onions, and bake in a medium oven (375°F., Reg. 4) until onions are cooked and golden, about 40 minutes. Baste frequently during cooking time.

Variations:
   1. Add some finely chopped herbs to the stuffing.
   2. Use *ham, boiled bacon or poultry* in place of meat.

Stuffed Bacon Rolls

SERVES 4.   Cooking time: 20 minutes.

6 oz. cooked meat (*ham, or*	1 tablespoon flour
boiled bacon or a combination)	1 tablespoon rich stock or
4 oz. mushrooms	gravy
1 onion	1 *egg yolk*
½ oz. butter	salt and pepper

1 teaspoon finely chopped   8 slices streaky bacon
parsley

Finely chop or mince the meat, finely chop the mushrooms.
Peel and finely chop the onion.

Melt the butter, add the onion and fry for about 3–5 minutes
until soft and transparent, add the mushrooms and meat,
and cook for a further 3 minutes. Sprinkle over the flour, mix
well, and add the gravy. Remove from the heat.

Beat in the egg yolk, season with salt and pepper, and mix
in the finely chopped parsley.

Remove the bacon rinds, spread the stuffing over the rashers,
roll each one up neatly, and place on a greased baking dish.
Cook the bacon rolls in a medium hot oven (400°F., Reg. 5) for
20 minutes.

Serve the bacon rolls with a tomato sauce (see pages 277–8).

Leftover No. 162

This is a very special recipe which until now has only been
made in my own kitchen – at least, as far as I know. A surprisingly large amount of anchovies give the meat a most
subtle flavour. This flavour is impossible to describe and I can
only say that it is *not* fishy but it *is* delicious.

SERVES 4.   Cooking time 30–45 minutes.

1 lb. cooked meat (lamb or beef)   pepper
1 medium onion   1 tin anchovies
2 cloves garlic   1 medium tin tomatoes (14 oz.)
2 sticks celery   1½ lb. potatoes
1½ tablespoons dripping   ½ oz. butter

Mince the meat, peel and chop the onion, finely chop garlic
and celery, peel and slice the potatoes.

Heat the dripping, add onion, garlic, and celery, and cook

over a medium heat for 3 minutes. Add meat, season with pepper, and cook for a further 5 minutes.

Drain the anchovies and reserve the oil; chop the fillets into very small pieces. Mix anchovies and tomatoes with the meat, put into a fireproof dish, cover with sliced potatoes, dot with butter, and pour over the anchovy oil. Bake in a moderately hot oven for 30–45 minutes until the potatoes are soft and golden brown.

Basic Curry (a little on the hot side)

Although this does not strike one as being a hot curry at first, be prepared for a satisfactory burning sensation to hit the mouth and throat a few seconds after each mouthful has gone down. It is as well to have a few cooling accompaniments available, like sliced bananas with lemon juice and grated cucumber in sour cream.

SERVES 4.   Cooking time: about 1 hour.

8–12 oz. cooked meat (beef, lamb, mutton, chicken, or turkey)	$\frac{1}{4}$ pint milk
4 tablespoons curry powder	$\frac{1}{2}$ oz. butter
$\frac{1}{4}$ teaspoon ginger	1 tablespoon oil
$\frac{1}{4}$ teaspoon turmeric	1 onion
$\frac{1}{4}$ teaspoon paprika and cayenne	2 carrots
pinch of chili pepper	1 stick celery
pinch coriander seeds	$\frac{1}{4}$–$\frac{1}{2}$ pint stock
1 tablespoon lime juice	2 tablespoons raisins
4 tables desiccated coconut	3 tablespoons yoghurt

Combine curry powder, ginger, turmeric, paprika, cayenne, chili and coriander seeds in a pestle and mortar and grind well until the coriander seeds are powdered and the ingredients are well mixed. Add the lime juice.

Combine milk, coconut, and butter in a saucepan, bring to the boil and simmer for 5 minutes. Strain the milk and press all the juice from the coconut; add this to the spices and mix well.

Peel and chop the onion, carrots, and celery.

Heat the oil in a large heavy bottomed pan, add vegetables, and cook over a medium heat until onions are golden brown. Add the curry mixture and stock, cover, and simmer gently until the vegetables are soft, about 20–30 minutes. Add meat cut into cubes and the raisins, and continue to simmer very slowly for a further 20 minutes.

Blend in the yoghurt, heat through, and serve the curry on a bed of boiled rice.

Serve the curry with a selection of side dishes (see page 284).

Curried Meat*

SERVES 4.   Cooking time: 1¼ hours.

1½ lb. cooked meat (beef, lamb, veal, pork, mutton, or poultry)	½ pint stock
	¼ pint water
1 onion	1 oz. desiccated coconut
1 oz. butter	2 teaspoons lemon juice
1 small cooking apple	1 tablespoon chutney
½ oz. curry powder	salt and pepper
1 tablespoon flour	

Cut meat into cubes. Peel and chop onion. Peel and chop apple. Combine water and coconut, bring to the boil, simmer for 5 minutes, then strain through a sieve to obtain all the juice from the coconut.

Melt the butter, add onion, and cook over a medium heat for 3 minutes until onion is soft. Add apple and cook for a further 5 minutes. Blend in curry powder and flour, cook for 2 minutes, then gradually add stock and coconut water, stirring constantly until the sauce comes to the boil. Add lemon juice, chutney and seasoning, cover and simmer very gently for 45–60 minutes.

Add the meat to the sauce and cook for 5–10 minutes or until the meat is hot through and tender.

Serve the curry with a collection of accompaniments, see page 284.

Note: Leftover cooked carrots or other vegetables can be substituted for a portion of the meat.

Moussaka★

Anyone who has travelled or holidayed in Greece will recognize this popular Middle Eastern dish. The aubergine/meat combination is always a successful one and I find this one of the very best ways of using up the remains of a joint of beef or lamb. You can make moussaka with veal but the flavour is not quite as strong and you have to be careful to season the dish well.

SERVES 4.   Cooking time: 60–75 minutes.

2 large aubergines	2 tablespoons red wine
4 tablespoons olive oil	2 tablespoons tomato purée
3 large onions	2 eggs
1 *lb. cooked meat (lamb, mutton, beef, or veal)*	¼ pint thin cream
	salt and pepper
4 ripe tomatoes	2 oz. grated cheese
¼ pint stock	

Cut aubergines into thin slices. Peel and finely chop onions, peel and slice tomatoes, and mince the meat.

Heat half the oil in a frying pan, add aubergine slices, sprinkle with salt, and fry over a medium heat for 5 minutes until soft. Remove aubergines with a slotted spoon, add remaining oil, and cook onions until soft and golden brown. Remove onions, add meat to the juices in the pan, and mix well. Pour over stock and red wine and blend in tomato purée. Season well with salt and pepper and arrange layers of aubergine slices, onions, meat and sliced tomatoes in a lightly greased baking dish.

Bake in a medium oven (375°F., Reg. 4) for 30 minutes.

Combine and beat together the eggs and cream, season with salt and pepper, and pour the custard over the meat. Sprinkle with grated cheese and return to the oven for a further 20 minutes until a golden brown crust has formed.

Note: A small pinch of sage, thyme or rosemary can be added to the meat.

Mary's Minced Meat Casserole

SERVES 4. Cooking time: about 60 minutes.

This dish is a kind of a moussaka without the aubergines. I make it when those vegetables are not available, and find it a pretty good alternative to the real thing.

1 lb. cooked beef, lamb, or mutton	1 tablespoon finely chopped parsley
1 lb. ripe tomatoes	½ teaspoon mixed herbs
1 medium onion	½ pint white sauce (see page 270)
1 small tin tomatoes	2 egg yolks
1 tablespoon olive oil	salt and pepper
¼ pint red wine	

Mince the meat. Peel and slice tomatoes and onion.

Heat the oil, add onions, and cook over a medium heat for 3 minutes; add meat, raise the heat and brown for a few minutes. Stir in the tinned tomatoes, red wine and parsley; season with salt and pepper, add the mixed herbs, and simmer gently for 10 minutes.

Fill a buttered fireproof dish with alternative layers of the meat mixture and the sliced tomatoes. Beat 2 egg yolks into the white sauce, season it well with salt and pepper, and pour over the meat. Bake in a medium hot oven (400°F., Reg. 5) for 30 minutes.

Note: 1–2 oz. grated cheese can be sprinkled over the sauce before baking.

Meat and Cabbage Casserole

SERVES 4.   Cooking time: about 20 minutes.

1 cabbage	½ tablespoon flour
1 clove garlic	¼ pint stock
1 tablespoon dripping	3 tablespoons fresh white
8–10 oz. *cold meat (beef, lamb,*	breadcrumbs
mutton, or pork)	½ oz. melted butter
3 tablespoons tomato purée	salt and pepper

Clean and shred the cabbage and cook it in boiling salted water for 10–15 minutes until tender.

Crush garlic and brown lightly in the dripping. Add meat, sprinkle over the flour, and cook for 2 minutes. Mix in tomato purée and stock, season with salt and pepper, add cabbage, and cook over a low heat for 10 minutes. Put the mixture into a lightly buttered fireproof dish, sprinkle over the breadcrumbs, pour over the melted butter, and brown under a hot grill.

Savoury Minced Meat★

Mince always seems to be a most popular dish with children, probably because it is easy to eat. This version is cooked with children in mind so the seasoning should be kept on the light side. If it is to be an 'adults only' dish I would suggest increasing the quantity of Worcester sauce, adding a little tomato purée and also a few drops of Tabasco sauce.

SERVES 4.   Cooking time: about 40 minutes.

1 *lb. cooked meat, beef, lamb,*	½ pint well flavoured stock
pork, or mutton	1 teaspoon Worcester sauce
4 oz. mushrooms	1½ lb. potatoes
1 onion	1 egg, beaten
½ oz. butter	1 oz. butter
small tin tomatoes	salt and pepper

Peel the potatoes and boil them until soft in salted water. Mince the meat. Peel and chop onion. Clean and chop mushrooms.

Melt ½ oz. butter, add onion and cook until golden brown. Add mushrooms and cook for 2 minutes. Add meat, tomatoes, and Worcester sauce. Season with salt and pepper, cook for 5 minutes then stir in enough stock to make the mixture moist but not too mushy. Cover and simmer for 10 minutes.

Mash the potatoes with 1 oz. butter, season with salt and pepper, and mix in the beaten egg. Surround a serving dish with potato, fill the centre with the mince, and bake in a hot oven for 5 minutes to brown the top of the potatoes.

Minced Meat and Tomato Patties*

SERVES 4.   Cooking time: about 20 minutes.

8 *oz. cooked meat (beef, lamb,*	½ tablespoon tomato ketchup
mutton, or pork)	½–1 teaspoon Worcester sauce
8 oz. tomatoes	salt and pepper
1 medium onion	flour
½ oz. butter	butter or dripping for frying

Mince the meat. Peel tomatoes and chop flesh finely. Peel and finely chop onion. Heat the butter, add onion, and cook over a moderate heat until it is soft, about 3 minutes. Combine meat, tomatoes, and onion. Add tomato and Worcester sauce, season with salt and pepper and mix well.

Form the mixture into flat cakes using floured hands. Fry cakes in butter or dripping until well browned on both sides.

Mushroom and Minced Meat Patties*

SERVES 4.   Cooking time: about 20 minutes.

8 oz. cooked meat (beef, lamb,   Worcester sauce
   mutton, or pork)   salt and pepper
1 medium onion   2 egg yolks
8 oz. mushrooms   flour
½ oz. butter   butter or dripping for frying
mushroom ketchup

Mince meat. Peel and finely chop onion. Wash and finely chop mushrooms. Melt the butter, add onions, and cook over a moderate heat until soft, about 3 minutes. Add mushrooms, and cook for a further 2 minutes.

Mix the onions and mushrooms with the meat, add a little mushroom ketchup and Worcester sauce, season with salt and pepper, and bind the mixture with the egg yolks. Use floured hands to form the mixture into eight flat cakes.

Fry the cakes in butter or dripping until well browned on both sides.

Meat and Potato Croquettes*

SERVES 4.   Cooking time: about 20 minutes.

10–12 oz. cooked meat (beef,   10–12 oz. cold, leftover, mashed
   lamb, or mutton)   potatoes
1 large onion   ½ oz. butter

4–8 tablespoons gravy
flour
1 beaten egg
1 tablespoon finely chopped
parsley

breadcrumbs
salt and pepper
fat or oil for frying

Mince the meat. Peel and finely chop the onion. Melt the butter and fry onion until soft. Combine meat, potatoes, onion and parsley, add enough gravy to make into a thick paste, and season with salt and pepper. Form into croquette shapes (thick sausage shapes), roll in flour, then in beaten egg and breadcrumbs. Fry the croquettes until golden brown in deep fat or oil.

Shepherd's Omelette

SERVES 4. Cooking time: about 10 minutes.

6 eggs
4 tablespoons cream or milk
salt and pepper
1 onion, finely chopped

6 oz. minced cooked beef, lamb,
  or veal
few drops Worcester sauce
1½ oz. butter

Beat eggs lightly with the cream or milk, season with salt and pepper.

Heat the butter in an omelette pan large enough to take all the ingredients; add onion and cook for 1 minute. Add the meat to the onion and cook until lightly browned. Mix in a few drops of Worcester sauce and pour over the egg mixture. Cook the omelette over a medium heat until it is lightly set, lifting it every now and then with a fork to allow raw liquid from the top to cook through.

Turn on to a warm serving dish and serve at once.

Caribbean Meat Patties

SERVES 4.   Cooking time: about 8 minutes each patty.

4 bananas	1 teaspoon Worcester sauce
4 rashers bacon	salt and pepper
1 *lb. cooked lamb, mutton, or beef*	butter for frying

Peel and mash the bananas. Coarsely mince the bacon and meat. Combine all the ingredients and season with salt and pepper. Form into patties and fry them in butter or fat until golden brown on each side.

Sliced Meat in Bagatelle Sauce*

A strong, piquant sauce, which gives zest to any cold sliced meat.

SERVES 4.   Cooking time: 25 minutes.

8 *slices cooked meat (beef, lamb,*	1 teaspoon Dijon mustard
mutton, or pork)	1½ tablespoons redcurrant
1½ oz. dripping or pan juices	jelly
1 small onion	2 tablespoons red wine
2 tablespoons flour	salt and pepper
2 teaspoons capers	
½ pint stock (or water and	
stock cube)	

Peel and very finely chop onion. Finely chop capers. Melt dripping, add onion, and cook over a medium heat until golden brown. Mix in flour and cook over a high heat until it is browned. Add capers and gradually blend in the stock, stirring constantly until the sauce comes to the boil. Lower the heat, add mustard, redcurrant jelly, and wine, and cook gently until jelly is melted.

Arrange the slices of meat in a fireproof dish, pour over the sauce, and heat through in a medium hot oven (400°F., Reg. 5) for 15 minutes.

Lasagne with Meat and Tomato Sauce

SERVES 4.   Cooking time: about 45 minutes.

6 oz. lasagne	1 small tin tomatoes
10 oz. *cooked beef, lamb, or mutton*	pinch sage
	pinch oregano
2–3 tablespoons olive oil	4 oz. grated cheese
1 onion	salt and pepper
2 oz. mushrooms	

Mince the meat. Peel and finely chop the onion, and wash and chop the mushrooms.

Cook the lasagne in boiling salted water for 15–20 minutes until tender. Drain well, and pat dry on kitchen paper.

Heat the oil and cook the onion for about 3 minutes until soft. Add mushrooms and cook for a further 2 minutes. Mix in meat, tomatoes, and herbs, and season with salt and pepper. Simmer gently for 10 minutes.

Lay a sheet of lasagne on a greased baking dish, cover with a layer of sauce, sprinkle with grated cheese, and cover with a second layer of lasagne. Repeat the layers finishing with one of the meat sauce sprinkled with cheese. Bake in a medium hot oven (400°F., Reg. 5) for 20–30 minutes.

Noodles with Meat Sauce

An Italian sauce with strong garlic flavouring.

SERVES 4. Cooking time: about 20 minutes.

1 medium onion	pinch sage
2 cloves garlic	pinch oregano
3 oz. bacon	4 tablespoons stock
1 tablespoon olive oil	salt and freshly ground black
6 oz. *cooked meat (lamb,*	pepper
mutton, or beef)	8 oz. noodles
1 tablespoon tomato purée	grated cheese

Cook the noodles in boiling water, according to the directions on the packet, while the sauce is being made. Cooking time for noodles varies considerably with different types and brands.

Peel and finely chop the onion. Crush garlic or squeeze through a garlic press. Chop bacon and mince the meat.

Heat the oil, add bacon, onion, and garlic, and cook over a medium heat until onion is golden brown. Add meat, mix well, and blend in tomato purée and stock. Add herbs, season with salt and pepper, and simmer for 10–15 minutes.

Pour the sauce over the noodles and serve with grated cheese.

Meat Sauce for Spaghetti*

Needless to say this sauce can also be served with noodles, lasagne, or any of the other forms of pasta which need a sauce.

SERVES 4, or can be stretched to 6. Cooking time: 10 minutes.

10 oz. cooked meat (beef, lamb, mutton, or veal)
1 large onion
2 tablespoons olive oil
3 tablespoons tomato purée
¼ pint water ⎫
1 chicken stock cube ⎬ or ¼ pint strong stock
1 tablespoon tomato ketchup
¼ teaspoon Worcester sauce
1 tablespoon red wine
salt and pepper

Mince the meat. Peel and finely chop onion. Heat oil, add onion, and cook over a fast heat until golden brown. Add meat, mix well, and brown all over. Stir in tomato purée, water and stock cube (or stock). Add tomato ketchup, Worcester sauce, and wine, season with salt and pepper, and simmer for 5 minutes.

Pour the sauce over cooked spaghetti or pasta, and serve with grated cheese.

Meat, Mushroom and Herb Sauce for Spaghetti or Pasta

This is a much stronger-tasting sauce than the plain *meat sauce for spaghetti*.

SERVES 4. Cooking time: 20 minutes.

½ lb. cooked meat (beef, lamb, mutton, or veal)
1 large onion
2 cloves garlic
4–6 oz. mushrooms
1 stick celery
3 ripe tomatoes
1 tablespoon tomato purée
½ oz. butter
2 tablespoons olive oil
¼ pint stock (or water and stock cube)
1 tablespoon finely chopped parsley
pinch dried thyme
pinch dried sage
salt, pepper
grated cheese

Mince meat. Peel and finely chop onion and garlic. Wash and finely chop mushrooms. Finely chop celery. Peel and chop tomatoes.

Heat butter and olive oil. Add onion, garlic and celery, and cook over a moderate heat until onion is golden brown. Add mushrooms and cook for 3 minutes. Add meat and brown over a high heat. Add tomatoes, tomato purée, stock and herbs. Season with salt and pepper, and simmer for 15 minutes.

Serve with spaghetti or macaroni, etc., and with a bowl of grated cheese.

Savoury Pancakes*

Pancakes, stuffed with a savoury filling and served piping hot, either as a first or main course, are one of my favourite ways of using up leftovers. Once made, the pancakes can be kept, covered with a polythene bag, in a refrigerator for up to five days, and used as they are required. (If you find they stick together, warm them gently for a few minutes in a low oven.)

Use a non-stick pan, or an omelette pan, for cooking the pancakes, and fry them in olive oil rather than butter to prevent sticking.

Cooking time: about 3 minutes for each pancake.

Makes 12–14 pancakes.

6 oz. plain flour	2 tablespoons soda water
2 eggs	salt and pepper
¾ pint milk	olive oil
1 oz. melted butter	

Sift flour into a bowl, add eggs, and beat them well into the flour. Gradually beat in milk, melted butter, and soda water, and finish with a wire whisk or rotary beater until the batter is smooth. Season with salt and pepper, and, whenever possible, leave for an hour before using to improve the batter.

Heat about 2 teaspoons of olive oil in an omelette pan until smoking, add about 1½ tablespoons batter and tilt the pan so that it spreads out evenly. Cook the pancake over a medium heat until golden brown, flip over, and cook for a further minute on the other side. Stack pancakes until they are required.

Savoury Pancakes Stuffed with Cooked Meat or Poultry

SERVES 4.   Cooking time: about 60 minutes.

10–12 oz. minced cooked lamb,
  beef, ham, or chicken
1 oz. butter
1 onion, chopped
1 oz. flour

½ pint milk
salt and freshly ground black
  pepper
12 pancakes

Follow recipe for pancakes given above and keep them warm.

Melt the butter in a saucepan, add onion, and cook over a medium heat until onion is transparent but not brown. Add flour and mix well. Gradually add the milk, stirring constantly until the sauce is thick and smooth. Season with plenty of salt and freshly ground pepper, and mix in the minced meat. Fill the pancakes with the meat mixture, roll up neatly, arrange in a lightly buttered baking dish, and heat through in a medium hot oven (400°F., Reg. 5) for 15 minutes.

Variations:

1. Add a tablespoon tomato purée, a dash of Worcester sauce, and some finely chopped parsley to the filling.

2. Use less minced meat and add to the filling some thinly sliced mushrooms cooked in a little butter.

Beef Marikoff

Despite its grand name, this is really a kind of Beef Stroganoff made with cooked meat, instead of the raw meat which must be used in the classic dish.

I would stipulate that the beef you use should be from the centre of a cold roast joint and definitely on the pink side.

SERVES 4.   Cooking time: 10–15 minutes.

14–16 oz. *cooked tender beef*
1 oz. butter
1 large onion
2 tablespoons tomato purée
salt and pepper
pinch paprika
¼ pint cream
1 teaspoon lemon juice } or ¼ pint sour cream

Cut the meat into thin strips about 1 inch long. Peel and thinly slice the onion and separate into rings.

Melt the butter, add onion rings, and cook for 3 minutes until they are soft and transparent. Add beef, tomato purée, lemon juice and cream (or sour cream), and simmer gently for 5 minutes. Season with salt, pepper, and a pinch of paprika.

Serve with boiled rice and garnish with a little finely chopped parsley.

Beef Olives*

SERVES 4.   Cooking time: about 30–35 minutes.

8 *thin slices undercooked roast beef*
8 *thin slices ham*
2 oz. mushrooms
1 tablespoon flour
½ pint richly flavoured stock
salt and pepper
finely chopped parsley

Finely chop mushrooms and fry them gently in $\frac{1}{2}$ oz. butter for 3 minutes.

Place a slice of ham on each slice of beef and spread with a little of the mushroom. Season with salt and pepper and roll up neatly. Secure the rolls with string or with cocktail sticks.

Heat $1\frac{1}{2}$ oz. butter in a frying pan, add rolls, and brown on all sides. Arrange the rolls in a baking dish. Add flour to the juices in the pan and mix well. Gradually blend in the stock and stir over a medium heat until the sauce is thick and smooth. Season the sauce and pour it over the meat.

Bake rolls in a medium hot oven (400°F., Reg. 5) for 20–30 minutes, and sprinkle with finely chopped parsley before serving.

Note: Red wine may be added to the sauce in place of some of the stock.

If your stock is not rich enough, add a tablespoon tomato purée or half a stock cube.

Beef and Horseradish Rolls

This is one of my favourite ways of serving cold roast beef, and I have a selfish habit of saving the undercut or fillet of a sirloin joint for this purpose. The meat must be cut in really thin slices. One of the best investments I have ever made was to buy a slicing machine, for, besides making the meat look more attractive, the slicer can produce at least three slices to my one.

For each serving:

2 *thin slices undercooked roast beef*	salt and pepper
	lettuce leaves
1 tablespoon horseradish sauce	1 tomato
2 tablespoons cream	

Lightly whip the cream, mix it with the horseradish sauce,

and season with salt and pepper. Spread beef slices with the sauce and roll up neatly. Arrange rolls on a bed of fresh, crisp, lettuce, and garnish with slices of peeled tomato.

Miroton of Beef

Another classic leftover dish. It can be made with cooked, boiled or roast beef, and should be served with boiled new potatoes or mashed potatoes. I find this a good dinner-party dish, as it can be made well in advance.

SERVES 4.   Cooking time: 40 minutes.

1 *lb. cooked beef*	1 teaspoon French mustard
4 onions	1 tablespoon tomato purée
1 clove garlic	salt and freshly ground black
1½ oz. butter	pepper
1 oz. flour	1 tablespoon finely chopped
2 teaspoons vinegar	parsley
¾ pint stock	

Peel and finely chop the onions. Crush the garlic or put through a garlic press.

Melt the butter, add the onions and garlic, and cook until soft and transparent. Mix in the flour, stirring constantly until the mixture becomes golden and leaves the side of the pan. Gradually blend in the vinegar and stock until the sauce is thick and smooth. Mix in the mustard and tomato purée, season, bring to the boil, and simmer gently for 20 minutes.

Cut the beef into wafer-thin slices, arrange them in a shallow fireproof dish, and pour over the sauce. Sprinkle over the chopped parsley, and heat through in a medium hot oven (400°F., Reg. 5) for 15–20 minutes.

Note: The top of the dish can be sprinkled with breadcrumbs and a little melted butter, and browned in a hot oven.

Macaroni and Beef Pie

SERVES 4. Cooking time: about 30 minutes.

8–10 oz. cooked beef	2 tablespoons flour
1½ oz. butter	½ pint stock
1 large onion	salt and pepper
1 clove garlic	8 oz. macaroni
1 large green pepper	2 oz. grated cheese
3 tomatoes	

Finely chop meat. Remove core and seeds from the pepper and finely chop the flesh. Peel and chop the onion. Finely chop or crush garlic. Peel and chop tomatoes. Cook macaroni in boiling salted water for 12 minutes, drain well.

Melt butter, add onion, garlic, and pepper, and cook for 5 minutes. Add tomato, and cook for a further 3 minutes. Mix in the flour and blend in the stock until the mixture comes to the boil. Add meat and macaroni, and season with salt and pepper. Turn into a baking dish, sprinkle with cheese, and bake in a medium oven (375°F., Reg. 4) for 20–25 minutes.

Cheesy Beef Pie

SERVES 4. Cooking time: about 30 minutes.

10–12 oz. cooked beef	1 tablespoon anchovy paste
8 oz. cooked potatoes	4 oz. grated cheese
2 eggs	freshly ground black pepper

Mince beef and potatoes together. Blend in egg yolks, anchovy paste, and 2 oz. grated cheese. Season with plenty of freshly ground black pepper.

Whip egg whites until they are stiff but not dry, and fold them into the meat mixture. Turn into a lightly greased baking dish, sprinkle with remaining cheese, and bake in a medium oven (375°F., Reg. 4) for 30–35 minutes.

Red-Flannel Hash

SERVES 4.   Cooking time: about 30 minutes.

2 oz. bacon
1 oz. dripping
1 large onion
½ lb. cooked salt beef, brisket, or corned beef
4–6 oz. cooked beetroot
¾ lb. cooked potatoes

2 tablespoons finely chopped parsley
2 tablespoons double cream
salt and freshly ground black pepper
4 eggs

Remove rinds from bacon and cut into small pieces. Peel and finely chop the onion. Flake or finely chop the meat. Cut beetroot and potatoes into small dice. Heat the dripping in a large frying pan (preferably a non-stick pan), add bacon, and cook for 2 minutes. Remove bacon, add onions, and cook until onions are soft but not brown. Lift out onions with a slotted spoon and combine them with the bacon, meat, beetroot, potatoes, parsley, and cream. Mix together gently, and season with salt and pepper.

Reheat the fat in the pan, add the hash, and press it down flat and smooth with the back of a spoon. Cook over fairly high heat until the hash is well browned on the bottom, about 20 minutes. Invert the hash on to a warm serving dish and serve with fried or poached eggs.

Piquant Salt Beef

The remains of a joint of salt beef, brisket, or silverside are delicious served cold with a salad. However, on a chilly day, and as a change from cold meat, this dish has an unusual flavour, and is quick to make.

SERVES 4.   Cooking time: about 30 minutes.

8 *slices cooked salt beef, brisket,*
   or silverside
4 tablespoons Piccalilli (juice
   only)
½ tablespoon flour
¼ pint water
1½ lb. potatoes
½ oz. butter
1 tablespoon cream
salt and pepper

Peel the potatoes, and cook them in salted water until soft. Mash them with ½ oz. butter and 1 tablespoon cream, and season with salt and pepper. Keep potatoes warm whilst preparing the meat.

Dip the slices of meat into the Piccalilli juice, flour the slices lightly, and arrange them in a shallow baking dish. Pour over the water and cook the meat in a medium hot oven (400°F., Reg. 5) for 15–20 minutes.

Serve the meat on a bed of creamy mashed potatoes. Garnish with chopped parsley.

Réchauffé of Lamb or Mutton*

SERVES 4.   Cooking time: 30 minutes.

1–1½ *lb. cooked lamb or mutton*
1 onion
¾ oz. butter
1 tablespoon flour
¾ pint stock or gravy
1 tablespoon mushroom ketchup
salt and pepper
finely chopped parsley

Cut meat into small cubes. Peel and chop onion. Heat butter, add onion, and cook over a moderately high heat until onion is golden brown. Add flour, mix well, and cook for a few minutes until flour is lightly browned. Gradually blend in stock, stirring constantly, until the sauce comes to the boil and is thick and smooth.

Add mushroom ketchup and meat to the sauce, season with salt and pepper, and cook gently for 20 minutes.

Serve with mashed potatoes or rice, and garnish with a generous sprinkling of finely chopped parsley.

Note: Some mushrooms, thinly sliced and cooked in a little butter, can be substituted for some of the meat.

Lamb with Mushrooms★ '

SERVES 4.   Cooking time: 15 minutes.

1 oz. butter	1½ gills gravy, stock, or tinned
2 onions	consommé
8 oz. mushrooms	2 tablespoons sherry
12 oz. (or 8 slices) cooked lamb	salt and pepper

Peel and thinly slice onions. Wash and thinly slice mushrooms. Shred lamb or leave in slices. Heat butter, add onions, and cook for 3 minutes over a moderately high heat until golden but not brown. Add mushrooms and cook for a further 2 minutes. Add meat and gravy, stock or consommé, season with salt and pepper, and cook for 10 minutes. Stir in sherry and check seasoning before serving.

Serve the lamb with boiled rice or mashed potatoes.

Lamb in Rich Orange Sauce★

SERVES 4.   Cooking time: 35–40 minutes.

10–12 oz. cooked lamb	2 tablespoons flour
6 oz. mushrooms	½ pint stock
1 large onion	4 anchovies
1 oz. butter	2 tablespoons sweet pickle
	(I use Branston Pickle)

1 tablespoon redcurrant jelly
grated rind and juice of 1
  orange

2 tablespoons red wine
  (optional)
salt and pepper

Cut lamb into neat cubes. Wash, dry and thinly slice mushrooms. Peel and chop onion. Chop anchovies. Melt butter, add mushrooms and onion, and cook over a moderate heat for 5 minutes until onion is golden brown, add meat and cook for a further 3 minutes. Sprinkle over the flour, mix well, and blend in the stock. Bring to the boil and cook for 2 minutes. Lower the heat and mix in the anchovies, pickle, redcurrant jelly, orange rind and juice, and wine if you are using it. Season with salt and pepper, and cook over a low heat for 20 minutes.

Serve in a ring of boiled rice or mashed potatoes, and garnish with finely chopped parsley or segments of orange.

Lamb Pilaff

SERVES 4–6.   Cooking time: 30–35 minutes.

8–12 oz. cooked lamb
8 oz. long grain or Patna rice
3 tablespoons olive oil
1 large onion
2 oz. blanched split almonds
2 tomatoes
1 oz. seedless raisins

pinch allspice
pinch cinnamon
pinch thyme
1–1½ pint stock
salt and freshly ground black
  pepper

Cut lamb into small cubes. Peel and chop onion. Peel and chop tomatoes. Heat oil in a heavy pan. Add onions and cook over a medium heat for 3 minutes. Add rice and almonds and cook for a further 3 minutes until rice is transparent. Add chopped tomatoes, raisins, spices, thyme, and 1 pint stock. Stir well, cover, and cook over a low heat for 20 minutes, adding more stock if the rice dries out too much. Add meat, mix well, season with salt and pepper, cover, and cook for 5–10 minutes until rice is soft and all the liquid has been absorbed.

Cardinham Special (Spiced Lamb Loaf)*

SERVES 4–6. Cooking time: 30–40 minutes.

8–10 oz. cooked lamb
1 large onion
3 oz. bacon
2 oz. cheddar cheese
1 tablespoon parsley, finely
  chopped

pinch sage
salt and pepper
2 eggs
3 tablespoons tomato juice

Mince the lamb with the onion, bacon and cheese. Combine these with 1 tablespoon finely chopped parsley and a pinch of sage, season with salt and pepper.

Beat the eggs, add the tomato juice, and mix the liquid with the dry ingredients. Place the mixture in a well-greased loaf tin, and bake in a moderately hot oven (400°F., Reg. 5) for 30–40 minutes until the loaf is set and a knife put through the middle comes out clean.

Turn out the loaf and serve with a tomato sauce (p. 277).

Pork Chin Chow*

This is a dish I invented on the spur of the moment with ingredients readily available in my kitchen. I must admit to being quite proud of it, and it's certainly a recipe which I shall use frequently in future.

SERVES 4. Cooking time: about 20 minutes.

1 lb. cooked pork
1 medium onion
2 large carrots
4 sticks celery
2 oz. butter
1 tablespoon apricot jam

2 tablespoons chutney
½ teaspoon Worcester sauce
¼ pint water
1 stock cube
salt and pepper

Thinly slice the pork, then cut slices into narrow shreds. Peel and thinly slice onion. Clean carrots and cut into matchstick strips. Thinly slice celery.

Heat butter in a large frying pan. Add onion, carrots, and celery, and cook over a medium heat until vegetables are soft but not browned, about 8 minutes. Add meat, mix well, and cook for a further 5 minutes. Blend in jam, chutney (finely chopped if necessary), and Worcester sauce. Dissolve stock cube in the water, add to the meat, and simmer gently for 5 minutes – the vegetables should still be on the crisp side. Season with salt and pepper.

Serve with rice or noodles.

Pork, Apple and Vegetable Bake*

SERVES 4.　Cooking time: 45 minutes.

8 *thin slices pork*	1 tablespoon dripping
2 cooking apples	1 tablespoon brown sugar
1 large onion	$\frac{1}{4}$ pint cider
2 carrots	salt and pepper

Peel, core and slice the apples. Peel and finely chop the onions and cut carrots into thin matchstick strips.

Heat dripping, add onions and carrots, and cook until onions are soft, about 3 minutes. Remove the vegetables and place them in the bottom of a greased baking dish.

Fry pork slices in the dripping until lightly browned on both sides. Arrange meat on the vegetables, cover with apple slices, season with salt and pepper, and sprinkle the brown sugar over. Pour the cider over and bake in a medium oven (375°F., Reg. 4) for 35–40 minutes.

This dish goes well with mashed potatoes and cabbage.

Savoury Pork Shepherd's Pie★

SERVES 4.   Cooking time: about 45–50 minutes.

10 *oz. cooked pork*	¼ teaspoon dried sage
1 large onion	¼ teaspoon rosemary
1 tablespoon dripping	1 tablespoon tomato ketchup
1 8 oz. tin tomatoes	salt and pepper
1 tablespoon flour	¾–1 *lb. cooked mashed potatoes*

Mince meat and onion through the coarse blades of a mincer.

Heat dripping, add onion, and cook until golden brown. Add meat and brown over a high heat. Mix in flour, cook for 2 minutes and then add tinned tomatoes, sage, rosemary, and tomato ketchup. Season with salt and pepper, put in a baking dish, and top with mashed potatoes.

Bake the pie in a medium hot oven (400°F., Reg. 5) for 35–40 minutes.

Pork with Sweet and Sour Sauce★

SERVES 4.   Cooking time: about 20 minutes.

10–12 *oz. cooked pork*	4 tablespoons sugar
1 medium onion	4 tablespoons vinegar
3 carrots	3 tablespoons soy sauce
3 tablespoons oil	1 tablespoon cornflour
4 oz. bean sprouts or finely chopped celery	½ pint water
	salt and pepper

Cut meat into thin strips, peel and coarsely chop the onion, and cut carrots into small dice.

Heat the oil in a saucepan. Add onions and carrots, and cook for 3–4 minutes until onions are soft and transparent but not brown. Add meat with the bean sprouts or celery, and cook for a further 10 minutes over a medium heat.

Combine the sugar, vinegar, soy sauce, cornflour, and water, and mix until smooth.

Pour the sauce over the meat, bring to the boil, and stir gently until the sauce is thick and translucent – this should take about 5–8 minutes.

Serve the meat on a bed of noodles or fluffy boiled rice.

Pork Chow Mein

'Chow Mein' is an Americanized term for any Chinese dish which includes meat and vegetables. If you like Chinese food, this is an easy example of it to make in your own home, and one which makes good use of leftover cooked pork. Tins of bean sprouts can be bought from most good delicatessen shops.

SERVES 4.   Cooking time: about 15 minutes.

10–12 oz. cooked pork	1 tin bean sprouts
2 tablespoons olive oil	3 tablespoons soy sauce
2 onions	3 tablespoons cornflour
4 sticks celery	¾ pint stock

Cut meat into thin shreds. Peel and thinly slice onions. Thinly slice celery and drain bean sprouts. Heat the oil in a deep frying pan, add onions and celery, and cook without browning for 5 minutes. Add meat, bean sprouts, and soy sauce, and cook for a further 2 minutes. Blend cornflour with the stock, pour over the meat and vegetables, bring to the boil, stirring constantly. Lower the heat and cook for 3 minutes.

Serve Chow Mein with fried rice and crispy noodles (these can also be bought in tins).

Veal with Tuna Fish Sauce

In Italy they cook a joint of veal, usually the fillet, and leave it to get cold in order to make this classic dish. If you have some cooked veal in the larder, the sauce will make it into something to be proud of.

SERVES 4.   No cooking.

8 *thin slices tender cooked veal*
½ pint mayonnaise
1 teaspoon lemon juice
1 small tin tuna fish
6 anchovies

Arrange veal slices in a shallow dish. Drain tuna fish and pound with 2 anchovy fillets in a pestle and mortar (or press through a sieve) until smooth. Add tuna to the mayonnaise with the lemon juice and check seasoning.

Pour the sauce over the veal, decorate with remaining anchovies, and chill well before serving.

Veal Paprika

SERVES 4.   Cooking time: about 45 minutes.

8–10 *thin slices cooked veal*
1 oz. butter
1 large onion
1 tablespoon flour
¼ pint stock
1 tablespoon tomato purée
¼ pint sour cream (or cream and 1 teaspoon lemon juice)
salt and pepper
1 teaspoon paprika

Melt butter and quickly fry veal slices until golden brown. Arrange slices in a lightly greased baking dish. Peel and thinly slice onion, and separate slices into rings. Add onion to the pan juices and cook over a moderately high heat until onion is golden brown. Sprinkle over the flour, mix well, and cook for 1 minute. Gradually blend in the stock and tomato purée. Cook for 3 minutes. Lower heat, add sour cream, season with salt and pepper, and stir in the paprika.

Pour the sauce over the meat and bake in a medium hot oven (375°F., Reg. 4) for 20–30 minutes.

Note: The veal and sauce can be served in the centre of a bed of rice or mashed potatoes.

Creamed Veal*

SERVES 4. Cooking time: about 15–20 minutes.

1 *lb. cooked veal (or lamb or chicken)*	¼ pint chicken or white stock
4 oz. mushrooms	2 tablespoons finely chopped parsley
1 oz. butter	1 teaspoon lemon juice
2 tablespoons flour	2 oz. grated cheese
¼ pint milk	salt and pepper

Mince meat. Wash and chop mushrooms. Melt butter, add mushrooms, and cook gently for 3 minutes. Sprinkle over the flour and mix gently. Gradually add milk and stock, stirring constantly until the sauce comes to the boil and is thick and smooth. Add meat and chopped parsley, and season with salt and pepper. Add lemon juice, and cook gently for 10 minutes.

Pour the mixture into a lightly greased baking dish, sprinkle the surface with grated cheese, and brown in a hot oven or under a hot grill.

Note: Chopped cooked vegetables can replace some of the meat.

Cannelloni Toscana

The true Italian cannelloni are made from squares of freshly made pasta, filled and rolled into neat pancakes. In this country one can buy a packet of Italian dried cannelloni, already made into hollow giant-macaroni shapes.

I first had this particular cannelloni dish (there are hundreds of variations) in a beach-side restaurant in Tuscany, and I can truthfully say that my own version, made from leftover cooked veal and spinach and using the dried commercial pasta, is not so very different.

SERVES 4.   Cooking time: 40–50 minutes.

8 cannelloni	2 oz. butter
½ lb. cooked veal	3 tablespoons stock or gravy
¼ lb. cooked spinach (use leftover, fresh, tinned, or frozen)	2 eggs
	salt and pepper
1 slice bread	½ pint béchamel sauce, see
milk	page 279
1 small onion	1½ oz. grated cheese

Remove crusts from bread and soak it in a little milk until soft. Lightly squeeze bread to remove excess milk. Mince together the meat, spinach, and bread. Peel and grate onion. Heat butter, add onion, and cook over a fast heat until golden brown. Add meat mixture and cook until brown. Mix in stock and cook for 10 minutes.

Beat eggs, add them to the meat mixture, and mix well. Season with salt and pepper.

Cook cannelloni until tender in boiling, salted water. Drain well and pat dry on kitchen paper. Fill with the meat mixture and arrange in a lightly-buttered serving dish. Pour over the béchamel sauce, sprinkle with grated cheese, and bake in a hot oven (425°F., Reg. 6) for 20 minutes.

Serve the cannelloni with a green or mixed salad.

Leftover Dishes made with Ham and Tongue

Home-cooked ham or tongue inevitably provide a good few servings of cold meat to help with the budget. The sliced, chopped or minced meat can be served in any number of ways, and can be easily stretched by the addition of a sauce or of other ingredients. Don't merely stick to the more conventional 'ham or tongue sandwiches' or the 'cold platter' of sliced cold meat. There are a lot of exciting dishes to be made from these remains and, unlike so many cooked meats, their flavour is just as good the second time around.

Go easy on the salt when producing made-up dishes from both ham and tongue as both these can be a little on the salty side.

If the meat is to be served cold, in slices, serve a sauce on the side to add interest, and take care to cut the slices as thinly as possible.

Ham Mimosa

A useful dish which can also be made with cooked chicken.

SERVES 4.   Cooking time: about 10 minutes.

6 hardboiled eggs	2 tablespoons Dijon or English
4 *oz. cooked ham or chicken*	mustard
1½ oz. butter	1 tablespoon cream
3 tablespoons flour	1 *egg yolk*
¾ pint milk	salt and pepper

Cut meat into small dice. Chop hardboiled eggs but reserve 2 of the yolks. Heat butter, add flour, and mix well. Gradually blend in the milk, stirring constantly until the mixture comes to the boil and is thick and smooth. Add mustard to the

sauce and cook for 3 minutes. Beat cream with the egg yolk
and blend it into the sauce – *do not boil*. Season with salt and
pepper, lightly mix in chopped eggs and ham, and arrange in a
shallow serving dish. Garnish with 2 hardboiled egg yolks,
rubbed through a coarse sieve, and serve with triangles of toast
or fried bread.

Macaroni con Pomidori

SERVES 4.   Cooking time: about 35 minutes.

6 oz. macaroni	pinch basil
1 large tin tomatoes	salt and pepper
½ oz. butter	2–4 oz. ham, chopped
1 onion, chopped	2 oz. grated cheese
2 cloves garlic, crushed	

Melt butter, add chopped onion and crushed garlic, and
cook for about 4 minutes over a low heat until onion is transparent. Add tomatoes and basil, and season with salt and pepper.
Bring the sauce to the boil, cover, and simmer for 15 minutes.

Meanwhile cook the macaroni in boiling salted water until
just tender, about 15 minutes. Drain it well.

Add the chopped ham to the tomato sauce, and place
alternate layers of macaroni and sauce in a greased baking dish.
Sprinkle over the grated cheese, and bake in a medium hot
oven (400°F., Reg. 5) for 15 minutes.

Spaghetti can replace the macaroni in this dish, and minced
cooked meat can be used in the place of ham.

Mini Meat Patties

These small meat pies are equally good eaten either hot or cold,
and make a useful picnic dish.

Makes about 12 patties.   Cooking time: about 40 minutes.

Pastry
8 oz. flour
4 oz. salted butter
2–3 tablespoons iced water

Filling

8 oz. pork sausage meat	pinch sage
4 oz. *ham or cooked meat*	pinch thyme
1 small onion	salt and pepper
4 sprigs parsley	2 tablespoons gravy or stock
2 oz. mushrooms	beaten eggs

To make the pastry, rub the fat into the flour, using fingertips, until the mixture resembles coarse breadcrumbs. Add
enough water to make a soft dough, knead lightly, wrap in a
cloth and chill for half an hour.

Mince the ham, onion, parsley, and mushrooms. Mix well
with the sausage meat and season with salt and pepper; add
the herbs and gravy or stock.

Roll pastry out thinly and cut into rounds to line 12 patty
tins. Place a spoonful of filling in each case pressing it down
tightly with the back of a spoon. Cover with a second slightly
smaller round of pastry, moisten the edges with a little water
and pinch them tightly together so that the patty is well-sealed
and the juices cannot escape. Cut a vent in the surface and brush
with beaten egg. Bake the patties for 10 minutes in a moderately
hot oven (400°F., Reg. 5), then lower the heat to 350°F., Reg. 4
and cook for a further 20–30 minutes until golden brown. Turn
out, and leave to cool on a wire rack or eat at once.

Rich Ham Quiche

SERVES 6.   Cooking time: about 35 minutes.

Pastry

8 oz. plain flour	pinch salt
4 oz. butter	3–4 tablespoons iced water

Filling

4 oz. grated cheese (preferably Gruyère)	$\frac{1}{4}$ pint cream
	salt and pepper
2 eggs	12 oz. ham

Make pastry by rubbing the butter into the flour and salt with the fingertips. Mix to a smooth dough with the water. Chill for 30 minutes in a refrigerator. Roll out thinly, line a flan case, prick the bottom with a fork and bake 'blind' in a hot oven (425°F., Reg. 6) for 10 minutes.

Beat eggs with the cream, mix in cheese, and ham, and season with salt and pepper. Pour filling into flan case, and bake in a hot oven (425°F., Reg. 6) for 15–20 minutes until set.

Ham and Cheese Soufflé

A good first course to start off a dinner party, or a light luncheon or supper dish to serve with a green or mixed salad. Like all soufflés it waits for no man and must be served immediately it is cooked.

SERVES 4.   Cooking time: 30–40 minutes.

1 oz. butter	salt
$\frac{1}{2}$ oz. flour	cayenne pepper
$\frac{1}{4}$ pint milk	4 oz. cheddar cheese, grated
3 egg yolks	4 oz. ham
3 egg whites	

Melt the butter in a medium large saucepan, add the flour, mix well, and cook for 1 minute. Gradually add the milk, stirring constantly over a medium heat until the mixture just comes to the boil. Remove from the heat and leave to cool for 2 minutes.

Beat the egg yolks into the mixture one at a time, and season with salt and cayenne. Mix in the grated cheese and ham.

Whisk the egg whites until stiff, blend a spoonful into the soufflé and then lightly fold in the remainder. Pour the mixture into a buttered 6-inch soufflé dish and bake in a medium oven (375°F., Reg. 4) for 25–30 minutes until well risen.

Serve at once.

Ham Omelette

SERVES 4.   Cooking time: about 15 minutes including filling.

6 eggs	½ pint milk
4 tablespoons cream or milk	1 tablespoon cream
salt and pepper	salt and pepper
2 oz. butter	6 oz. ham
2 tablespoons flour	

Lightly beat eggs with cream or milk, and season with salt and pepper. Chop ham into small dice.

Heat 1 oz. butter in a saucepan, add flour, mix well, and gradually blend in the milk, stirring constantly over a medium heat until thick and smooth. Season with salt and pepper, fold in the diced ham, and keep the filling warm until omelettes are cooked.

Heat ½ oz. butter in an omelette pan, add half the egg mixture, and cook over a fast heat until just set. Lift omelette with a fork as it cooks to allow raw liquid on top to cook through.

Pour half the ham filling on to the omelette, fold in half and slide on to a warm dish. Repeat the process with the remaining butter, eggs, and filling. Serve at once.

Note: The mixture can be made into individual omelettes and can be sprinkled with cheese and browned quickly under a grill before being served.

Omelette à la Paysanne

SERVES 4. Cooking time: about 10 minutes.

6 eggs	1 medium onion
4 tablespoons milk	1½ oz. butter
¼ lb. *ham or sausage*	salt and pepper
2 *boiled potatoes*	

Beat the eggs lightly with the milk, and season with salt and pepper. Chop ham or sausage and potatoes into small dice. Finely chop the onion.

Heat the butter in an omelette pan large enough to hold all the ingredients; add onion, cook for 2 minutes, then add diced ham or sausage and potatoes and cook until the mixture is lightly browned. Pour over the eggs and cook over a medium heat until the omelette is just set. Lift the omelette with a fork as it cooks to allow raw egg liquid on the top to cook through.

Turn out on to a warm serving dish and serve at once.

Ham and Mushroom Rolls (hot)*

This is a sophisticated version of the recipe for Creamed Ham and Mushrooms, see page 135. It is simple but delicious!

SERVES 4. Cooking time: for the filling, 10–15 minutes; for browning, 5 minutes.

8 *thin slices ham*
¾ lb. button mushrooms
2 oz. butter
1 tablespoon flour
¼ pint milk

1 tablespoon chopped chives
(parsley will do instead)
salt and pepper
¼ pint double cream

Thinly slice the mushrooms and cook them in boiling salted water for three minutes, drain well and leave to dry.

Melt the butter in a saucepan, add the flour, and cook over a medium heat stirring well until the butter and flour are well mixed. Gradually blend in the milk, still stirring, until the sauce is thick and smooth. Bring to the boil and cook for 2 minutes.

Add three quarters of the sliced mushrooms to the sauce with the chopped chives. Season with salt and pepper.

Spread each slice of ham with mushroom sauce, roll them neatly and arrange them in a lightly buttered fireproof dish. Cover the slices with the remaining sliced mushroom, pour over the cream, and brown under a grill or in a hot oven for 5 minutes.

Ham Rolls Stuffed with Rice (cold)

thin slices ham, allow 2–3 slices
per serving
For each slice:
2 *oz. cooked rice*
1 tablespoon mayonnaise

2 teaspoons chopped mustard
pickle
6 sultanas
salt and pepper

Combine the cooked rice with mayonnaise and mustard pickle, add the sultanas, and season with salt and pepper.

Spread the rice mixture on slices of ham, roll up neatly, and arrange on a bed of lettuce leaves with a garnish of sliced tomatoes.

Ham and Chicken Savouries*

Makes 8 savouries (3–4 servings). Cooking time: 10–15 minutes.

4 oz. cooked chicken $\Big\}$ or any combination of the two
4 oz. cooked ham
1 large onion
2 tablespoons packet parsley and thyme stuffing
2 eggs, lightly beaten
salt and pepper
flour

Mince the ham and chicken together and coarsely grate the onion. Mix together the meat and onion, add the parsley and thyme stuffing, season with salt and pepper. Bind mixture with beaten eggs, and leave to stand in a refrigerator for 15 minutes.

Using well-floured hands, shape the mixture into 8 flat cakes about 2½–3 inches in diameter, fry them in hot fat for at least five minutes on each side until golden brown.

Serve the savouries with mashed potatoes and a tomato sauce (see page 277).

Ham Filling for Savoury Pancakes*

SERVES 4. Cooking time: about 30 minutes excluding pancakes.

12 pancakes (see page 110)	¾ pint milk
6 oz. ham	1 tablespoon sherry
1½ oz. butter	salt and pepper
4 oz. mushrooms	2 oz. grated cheese
2 tablespoons flour	paprika

Finely chop the ham. Thinly slice the mushrooms.

Melt butter over a medium heat, add mushrooms, and cook for three minutes without browning. Stir in the flour and gradually add milk. Bring to the boil, stirring constantly until sauce is thick and smooth. Add ham and sherry, and season with salt and pepper.

Spread some filling over the centre of each pancake, roll up loosely, and arrange in a baking dish. Sprinkle with grated cheese and a very little paprika. Bake in a hot oven (425°F., Reg. 6) for 15–20 minutes until cheese is golden brown and pancakes are piping hot through.

Creamed Ham and Mushrooms on Toast

SERVES 4.   Cooking time: about 15 minutes.

8 oz. cooked ham	½ pint milk
½ lb. mushrooms	salt and pepper
3 oz. butter	4 slices toast
2 tablespoons flour	

Finely slice or chop the mushrooms, and cook them gently in 1 oz. butter until soft, about 3 minutes. Chop the ham.

Melt the remaining 2 oz. butter in a saucepan, add the flour and cook over medium heat, stirring constantly, until butter and flour are well mixed. Gradually blend in the milk, still stirring, and cook until the sauce is thick and smooth.

Add the cooked mushrooms and chopped ham to the sauce, season with salt and pepper, heat through, and pour over 4 slices of freshly made toast.

Devilled Tongue

Not a very attractive name for a dish, but nevertheless a most delicious way of serving slices of tongue. Serve the slices with a tomato sauce (see page 277), with mashed potatoes and a green salad.

For each serving:

2 *slices tongue*	½ teaspoon lemon juice
1 dessertspoonful Dijon mustard	breadcrumbs
pinch cayenne pepper	butter for frying

Mix together the mustard, cayenne, and lemon juice. Spread both sides of the tongue slices with the mixture, and spread them with breadcrumbs, pressing the crumbs into the meat with the back of a spoon to make sure they stick well.

Fry the slices in hot butter until lightly golden brown.

Tongue Véronique*

SERVES 4. Cooking time: 45 minutes including making the sauce.

8 *slices cooked tongue*	1 oz. raisins
1½ oz. butter	2 oz. almonds
1 medium onion	2 tablespoons sherry
2 oz. mushrooms	1 tablespoon finely chopped
1 large carrot	parsley
½ oz. flour	salt and pepper
½ pint stock	

Peel and finely chop the onion, thinly slice the mushrooms, and cut the carrot into small dice.

Melt the butter, add the onion, and cook over a high heat until they are golden brown. Add the mushrooms and diced carrot, and cook for a further five minutes, stirring constantly. Blend in the flour, and gradually mix in the stock stirring all the time until the sauce is smooth, then mix in the raisins and almonds. Cover and simmer for fifteen minutes; add the sherry and chopped parsley, and season well. Arrange the slices of tongue in a greased baking dish, pour over the sauce, and

bake in a medium hot oven (400°F., Reg. 5) for 15 minutes.
Serve the tongue with creamy mashed potatoes.

Bacon

Rashers of cooked bacon left over from breakfast can be kept
in a refrigerator for up to forty-eight hours. Use chopped
cooked bacon as a garnish for soups or salads, add it to fillings
for omelettes or stuffed vegetables, mix it into rice or pasta
dishes, or combine it with cold scrambled egg, chopped
watercress, sliced tomatoes or lightly fried chopped mushrooms as a filling for sandwiches.

Bacon Rinds

Recently I bought one of those flat parcels of vacuum-packed
streaky bacon and found to my horror when I opened it that
all the rinds had been cut from the bacon. When I asked the
grocer about this, he told me that many housewives preferred
their bacon without rinds as it saved time and trouble. Now
that really seemed extraordinary to me, for it doesn't after all
take more than a few seconds to cut off bacon rinds with a pair
of kitchen scissors. The rinds contain the flavour of the bacon
itself, and the fat produced by rendering down the rinds is
invaluable for cooking with, or for sealing pastes, pâtés and
potted meats.

Add bacon rinds to vegetable, meat, and poultry stocks for
flavouring.

Cook the rinds over a gentle heat or in a slow oven to produce bacon fat for cooking or sealing. Strain the fat through a
hair sieve or a piece of muslin and keep it for up to two weeks
in a refrigerator.

Crisply-fried bacon rinds can be crumbled to sprinkle over
soups and salads or left whole to serve with drinks. Fry the

rinds, without extra fat, over a high heat until they curl up and become golden brown. Drain well on crumpled kitchen paper.

Buying Bacon

However convenient the pre-packed varieties of bacon may be, nothing beats the flavour or the taste of rashers cut from a piece as you buy it. I ask my grocer to cut it extra-thin as I find the thinner the bacon, the quicker to cook and more economical it is. If you prefer to buy your bacon in packs, remember to check from the outside of the packet the date by which it should be eaten.

Bacon trimmings can often be bought for next to nothing from your local grocer and are invaluable as a flavouring ingredient for all stocks.

Sausages

How often I seem to misjudge the amount of sausages to cook for breakfast or lunch! Here are a few ideas for using up cooked beef or pork sausages for those who may find themselves in this predicament.

1. Thinly slice cold cooked sausages and add to meat or vegetable soups for the last five minutes before serving.
2. Cut cooked sausages into thick slices to add to stews or casseroles for the last 10–15 minutes of cooking time.
3. Use in sandwiches.
4. Thinly slice cooked sausages lengthwise, arrange them on a slice of toast, spread with a little mustard, cover with some grated cheese, and toast under a hot grill to serve as a snack or supper dish.
5. Mince cooked sausages and add to minced meat or chicken for made-up dishes.
6. Cut cooked sausages into 1 inch chunks, wrap in thinly rolled out puff pastry, brush with milk or beaten egg, and bake in a hot oven until pastry is golden brown. These make good accompaniments for soups, casseroles, or drinks.

Poultry and Game

Chicken

Christmas is not the only time to expend your energy on left-over poultry, with that everlasting cold turkey. Chicken, for instance, is probably the best basis for any leftover cookery.

Raw or cooked chicken carcases can be used as a base for countless soups. The meat itself forms the background of a hundred varieties of different flavourings. Six ounces of cooked chicken or turkey can be stretched to produce an adequate supper dish for four people; twelve ounces can provide an elegant salad for the most sophisticated gourmet.

When buying a chicken, try to make sure that you get a fresh, not a frozen one. You may have to pay a little extra, but the cost will be repaid in the flavour and the moist texture of the flesh. Insist that you always have the giblets of the bird, as these are invaluable for making stocks and gravies.

A good way to save on the housekeeping bills is to buy two chickens at once. Cook them together (saving heating costs), serve one hot, and use the remains and the carcases to make a number of different dishes.

One useful tip that I resort to quite often when trying to stretch small amounts of chicken to their utmost, is that the texture of tuna fish is surprisingly like that of the barnyard fowl. In emergencies, a tin of tuna can be mixed with the chicken and increase the portions to almost miraculous lengths.

Cooked chicken tends to be rather tasteless, and care should be taken to add enough flavouring to make it interesting. A wing or leg of cold roast chicken served with a limp salad is dreary – the same meat, chopped, mixed with a few compatible ingredients, and folded into a spiced mayonnaise, will not only stretch further but taste far better.

It would be impossible to cover the multitude of dishes which can be produced from cooked chicken; I can only offer you a number of my own favourites and leave you to ring the changes as your imagination, and the choice of ingredients which you have to hand, allows. All I suggest is that you make use of even the smallest part of the bird, and never insult a carcase by throwing it unused into the dustbin.

Turkey

In America small turkeys make popular family food at all times of the year, but in this country we still seem to keep them for a Christmas treat. However, smaller birds are now being bred here and I have no doubt that before long they will become as popular as they are in the States; certainly, with their left-over potential, they make a most economical buy.

All dishes made with cooked chicken can be used for turkey. The only thing to remember is that in dishes served in a white or cream sauce, the white and not the dark meat of the bird should be used.

Duck

I have put in a few recipes for using up the remains of a cooked duck but have kept them to a minimum since, if your family is anything like mine, I have yet to see much remaining of a roast duck at the end of a meal. However, nobody can eat the bones, and a really strong, richly-tasting stock can be made from the carcase and giblets.

Game

Small amounts of cooked game can be potted, or used to make a rich and nourishing soup. Here again the carcase of raw or cooked birds makes a really good strong stock and should not be discarded. See game stock on page 46.

Paella

The classic paella has its origins in Spain, and is curious because it is made with a combination of meat and fish. The ingredients can be varied depending on what you have handy. Authentic paella should be cooked on top of the stove but for this version oven cooking is more suitable.

SERVES 4.   Cooking time: 40 minutes.

12 oz. cooked chicken
2 oz. ham or bacon
1 large onion
3 tablespoons oil
8 oz. long grained rice
good pinch saffron
2 tablespoons hot water
4 oz. prawns, cooked and peeled

4 oz. cod or firm white fish, cooked and cut in 2" lengths
4 oz. peas, fresh or frozen
1 small tin red pimento
1½ pints stock
salt, pepper, pinch cayenne
finely chopped parsley

Cut chicken into cubes. Finely chop bacon or ham. Peel and chop onion. Cut fish into 2-inch pieces. Chop red pimento. Soak saffron in the hot water for 20 minutes.

Heat oil in a large fireproof dish (an enamelled serving dish with a lid is ideal). Add onion and cook without browning for 3 minutes. Add bacon or ham and the rice, and stir over a moderate heat until rice is transparent. Pour over the stock and saffron, mix well, cover, and cook in a moderate oven (350°F., Reg. 3) for 20 minutes.

Cook peas in boiling salted water for 8 minutes.

Mix peas and chopped pimento into the rice, and season with salt, pepper, and a pinch cayenne. Arrange chicken, fish, and prawns on the surface, return to the oven and cook for a further 20 minutes.

Serve the paella straight from the dish with a generous sprinkling of finely chopped parsley over the top.

Chicken or Turkey à l'Estragon

The subtle flavouring of tarragon and lemon juice is delicious with chicken or turkey. The slight sharpness is especially good on Boxing Day when the dish can be made from leftover slices of turkey.

SERVES 4.   Cooking time: 30 minutes.

8–12 *slices chicken or turkey*	2 teaspoons lemon juice
1 oz. butter	salt and pepper
2 tablespoons flour	8 oz. rice
½ pint milk	1 oz. butter
½ tablespoon chopped dried tarragon	

Soak the tarragon in the lemon juice for ten minutes. Melt the butter, add flour, and mix well. Gradually blend in the milk, stirring constantly until the sauce is thick and smooth. Bring to the boil, add tarragon and lemon juice, and cook gently for 5 minutes. Season the sauce with salt and pepper.

Cook rice in boiling salted water for 20 minutes or until tender. Rinse with warm water and dry in a warm oven. Mix in 1 oz. butter and arrange the dried rice in a circle around the outside of a serving dish. Fill the centre with chicken or turkey slices and pour over the sauce. Cover with foil to prevent rice becoming too dry and heat in a moderately hot oven (400°F., Reg. 5) for about 15 minutes until hot through.

Note: A little fresh, finely chopped tarragon can be sprinkled over the dish before serving.

Chicken Soufflé

A good way of making a small amount of cooked chicken stretch to four generous servings.

SERVES 4.   Cooking time: about 60 minutes.

4–6 oz. *cooked chicken*	2 oz. plain flour
grated rind of ½ lemon	½ pint warm milk
2 teaspoonfuls finely chopped parsley	3 large eggs
3 oz. butter	salt and pepper

Mince cooked chicken. Heat butter until melted, add flour, and mix well. Gradually blend in the warm (not boiling) milk, stirring constantly until the mixture is thick and smooth. Remove from the stove and mix in the minced chicken, lemon rind, and chopped parsley. Season with salt and pepper.

Separate eggs and beat whites until stiff. Beat yolks, one by one, into the soufflé base and then lightly fold in the beaten whites. Pour into a well greased 2-pint soufflé dish and bake for about 45 minutes in a medium hot oven (400°F., Reg. 5).

Serve at once.

Chicken Pilaff with Salted Almonds

SERVES 4.   Cooking time: 25 minutes.

2 oz. butter
1 large onion
1 green pepper
8 oz. long grained or Patna rice
1 pint chicken stock (or water
  and stock cube)

8 oz. *cooked chicken*
salt and pepper
1 oz. salted almonds
8 rashers bacon

Peel and finely chop onion. Remove core and seeds from the pepper and chop finely. Cut chicken into small dice.

Heat 1 oz. butter in a heavy-bottomed pan. Add onion and pepper, and cover over a gentle heat until onion is soft and transparent. Add the rice, stir well, and cook until rice becomes transparent. Add stock, bring to the boil, mix well, cover and simmer for about 20 minutes until the rice is cooked and the liquid absorbed. Add chicken and remaining butter, and season with salt and pepper.

Cut each bacon rasher into two and roll each bit up neatly. Bake rolls in a hot oven for 5 minutes.

Serve the pilaff surrounded with bacon rolls and scatter the salted almonds over the top.

Creamy Chicken Pie

SERVES 4.   Cooking time: 20–30 minutes.

Pastry
8 oz. flour
salt and pepper

4 oz. butter
1½–2 tablespoons water

Filling
1 oz. butter
2 tablespoons flour
½ pint milk
8 oz. *cooked chicken*
2 hardboiled eggs

1 tablespoon chopped chives
  or onion tops
1 tablespoon chopped parsley
½ gill cream
salt and pepper

For the Pastry

Rub the butter into the flour with fingertips until the mixture resembles coarse breadcrumbs. Season with a little salt and pepper and add enough water to form the mixture into a firm dough. Chill for 15–30 minutes.

For the Filling

Melt the butter in a pan, add flour, and mix well. Gradually blend in the milk, stirring constantly until thick and smooth. Cut the chicken into cubes, add it to the sauce with the hard-boiled eggs (chopped), chives, and parsley. Blend in the cream, season with salt and pepper, and pour into a pie dish.

Roll out the pastry, cover the pie, brush with milk, and make a small hole to allow any air to escape. Cook the pie in a hot oven (425°F., Reg. 6) for 20–30 minutes until pastry is golden brown.

The pie can be served hot or cold, but is better hot.

Devilled Chicken Bones

I once actually met a man who every morning used to make his choice for breakfast from a selection composed of pickled salmon, grilled kidneys, devilled chicken bones, kedgeree, and a few rather mundane dishes like bacon and fried eggs. The thought impressed me so much that I once tried serving devilled chicken's legs for breakfast at my own home – without success. The sight of those sharp-smelling, highly seasoned joints, oozing with flavour, was too much for my guests first thing in the morning.

Now I serve devilled bones as strictly lunch or supper dishes. They are equally delicious hot or cold. Serve them hot with boiled rice and a green vegetable or salad, or serve them cold for a summer lunch or a picnic.

For each chicken joint (wing or leg):

1 dessertspoonful Dijon mustard
salt
pinch cayenne pepper
few drops Worcester sauce
melted butter

Combine the mustard with a little salt, cayenne, and Worcester sauce. Cut incisions in the meat with a sharp knife, rub the mustard mixture into these, brush with melted butter, and grill until golden brown.

Chicken in Barbecue Sauce

SERVES 4.   Cooking time: 20 minutes.

10–12 oz. cooked chicken, diced
1 large onion
2 cloves garlic
1 tablespoon olive oil
1 medium tin tomatoes (14 oz.)
2 teaspoons Worcester sauce
2 teaspoons lemon juice
2 teaspoons soft brown sugar
1 teaspoon made mustard
Tabasco sauce
$\frac{1}{4}$ lb. frozen peas
salt and pepper

Peel and finely chop the onion, crush the garlic or put through a garlic press.

Heat the oil in a saucepan, add the onion and garlic, and cook over a medium heat for 3–5 minutes until soft. Add the tomatoes, Worcester sauce, lemon juice, sugar, mustard, and a few drops of Tabasco sauce. Mix well, bring to the boil, cover, and simmer for 10 minutes. Add the frozen peas and the chicken, season, and cook over a medium heat for a further 10 minutes.

Serve the chicken in the centre of a ring of fluffy boiled rice.

Chicken Robbelin*

This is another dish in which tuna fish and chicken combine successfully.

SERVES 4.   Cooking time: sauce, about 15 minutes; browning time, 5–10 minutes.

6 oz. *cooked chicken*
7 oz. tuna fish (a medium tin)
1 medium onion
2 oz. butter
2 tablespoons flour
½ pint milk

4 oz. frozen peas or *cooked*
  vegetables
1 tablespoon sherry
2 oz. grated cheese
salt and pepper

Chop the chicken into small dice. Drain and flake the tuna. Peel and finely chop the onion.

Melt the butter, add onion, and cook over a medium heat until transparent but not brown. Add the flour, mix well, and gradually blend in the milk stirring constantly until the sauce is thick. Bring to the boil and cook gently for 2 minutes.

Add the chopped chicken, tuna fish, and vegetables to the sauce, and continue to cook until the vegetables are tender (if cooked vegetables are used, merely heat through). Add the sherry with half the grated cheese, and season with salt and pepper. Pour into a fireproof dish, sprinkle with the remaining cheese, and brown under a grill or in a hot oven for about 5 minutes.

Madders' Chicken Morocco

Ideas for many of the dishes in this book have been begged, borrowed or stolen from friends all over the world. This way of serving chicken is the invention of a portrait painter called

Madelaine Rampling (known to her friends as Madders). Although she professes not to be any good in the kitchen, this dish, at least, is delicious; it can be used to transform a shop-bought, pre-cooked chicken or to jazz up the remains of a home-cooked bird.

SERVES 4. Cooking time: 20 minutes.

4 cooked chicken joints or 12 oz. diced cooked chicken
1½ tablespoons olive oil
salt and pepper
juice and coarsely grated rind of two oranges
2 tablespoons honey
2 oz. split almonds
2 tablespoons whisky

Season the chicken with salt and pepper. Heat the oil, add the chicken and brown on all sides. Transfer the chicken to a hot serving dish, add the orange rind, orange juice, honey and almonds to the juices in the pan, and cook for five minutes over a medium heat, stirring well. Pour the sauce over the chicken and bake in a medium hot oven (400°F., Reg. 5) for fifteen minutes.

Heat the whisky until just bubbling, pour it over the chicken and set it alight immediately. Bring the dish to the table while it is still flaming, and serve with rice and a green salad.

Chicken à la King

SERVES 4–6. Cooking time: about 15 minutes.

10–12 oz. cooked chicken
8 oz. mushrooms
1 green pepper
1 stick celery
1 oz. butter
2 tablespoons flour
½ pint chicken stock
2 tablespoons cream
salt and pepper
2 egg yolks
4 tablespoons double cream
1 tablespoon finely chopped parsley

Dice the chicken. Wash and thinly slice mushrooms. Core, seed and chop pepper. Chop celery.

Heat the butter in a heavy saucepan, add pepper and celery, and cook for 3 minutes. Add mushrooms and cook for a further 2 minutes until celery is soft. Sprinkle over the flour, mix well, and gradually blend in the stock. Add chicken pieces and bring to the boil, reduce the heat, stir in 2 tablespoons cream, season with salt and pepper, and simmer for a few minutes.

Beat egg yolks with double cream, add to the chicken mixture and cook, stirring constantly, over a low heat for a few minutes until the sauce thickens.

Garnish Chicken à la King with finely chopped parsley.

Note: 1 tablespoon sherry may be added to the sauce.

The dish can be served with mashed potatoes, boiled rice, or triangles of crisply fried bread.

Chicken Fritters Maryland

It is amazing quite how far one can stretch a small quantity of cooked meat if one tries. I worked out these quantities on the basis of four servings, but the finished dish could happily have fed five or six hungry people.

SERVES 4–6. Cooking time: about 20 minutes.

6 oz. cooked chicken	¼ pint milk
1 oz. butter	salt and pepper
1 onion	4 rashers bacon
½ green pepper	2 bananas
4 oz. flour	deep fat or oil for frying
2 eggs	

Finely chop chicken. Peel and chop onion. Finely chop

pepper. Combine flour, egg yolks and milk, and beat with a wire whisk until smooth. Heat butter, add onion and pepper, and cook for 3 minutes until soft. Mix chicken, onion and pepper into the batter mixture, and season with salt and pepper.

Fry bacon, without fat, until crisp. Lightly fry bananas, cut into thick slices, in bacon fat. Keep bacon and bananas hot whilst cooking the fritters.

Whip egg whites until stiff, fold lightly into the batter, and drop from a tablespoon into very hot deep fat or oil. Cook fritters for about 3 minutes until puffed and golden brown. Drain on kitchen paper, and serve at once with the bacon and bananas.

Maidenwell Special★

SERVES 4. Cooking time: about 45 minutes.

1 onion	1 tablespoon flour
1 stick celery	1 teaspoon lemon juice
3 oz. dripping	¼ pint stock
12 oz. *cooked chicken*	salt, pepper and pinch paprika
4 oz. *leftover vegetables (peas, beans, cauliflower or carrots, etc.)*	10–12 oz. *mashed potatoes*

Peel and chop onion, chop celery, mince chicken, and chop leftover vegetables if necessary.

Heat dripping, add onion and celery, and cook over a medium heat for about 4 minutes until the onion is soft and transparent. Add chicken and vegetables and cook for a further 5 minutes. Blend in flour, mix well, and cook for 2 minutes before adding lemon juice and stock. Season with salt, pepper, and a pinch of paprika, and put into a fireproof serving dish. Cover with mashed potatoes and bake in a medium hot oven (400°F., Reg. 5) for about 30 minutes until golden brown.

Curried Chicken Filling for Vol-au-Vents and Croustades

SERVES 4.   Cooking time: 35–40 minutes.

8 vol-au-vent cases, see page 231	2 tablespoons flour
½ pint milk	10–12 oz. *cooked chicken*
bayleaf	1 oz. butter
small onion	1 small onion
pinch mace	2 teaspoons curry powder
1 oz. butter	salt and pepper

Heat the milk with the bayleaf, small onion and a pinch mace, over a low heat for 5 minutes. Strain to remove onion and bayleaf. Melt 1 oz. butter, add flour, and mix well. Gradually blend in the milk and bring to the boil, stirring constantly until the sauce is thick and smooth. Season and cook for 2 minutes.

Finely chop 1 small onion. Dice chicken. Melt 1 oz. butter, add onion and curry powder, and cook over a low heat until onion is soft, about 5 minutes. Add the sauce and mix in the chicken. Fill the vol-au-vent cases with the curried chicken and heat through in a medium oven (375°F., Reg. 4) for 15–20 minutes.

Cooked Meat Pasties

The true Cornish Pasty is, of course, made with raw meat and raw vegetables but the same principle can be applied to pastry cases filled with cooked meat and vegetables. The only thing to bear in mind is that since the ingredients have already been cooked they will not produce the juices which make a good pasty so delicious; to make up for this I add a knob of butter or a spoonful of leftover gravy or pan drippings to the filling.

Makes 4 pasties.   Cooking time: 25–30 minutes.

Pastry
12 oz. flour
3 oz. butter
3 oz. lard

2–3 tablespoons water
salt and pepper

Filling
10 oz. *cooked chicken, ham, or luncheon meat (or a mixture)*
6 oz. *cooked vegetables (peas, beans, carrots or potatoes)*
1 small onion
salt and pepper
butter, gravy or pan drippings

Rub the fat into the flour with fingertips until the mixture resembles coarse breadcrumbs. Season with a little salt and pepper, and add enough water to form the mixture into a stiff dough. Chill for 15–30 minutes, then roll out thinly and cut into four 7-inch circles.

Cut the meat and vegetables into small dice and finely chop the onion. Place a quarter of meat and vegetables in the centre of each pastry circle, season with salt and pepper and dot with a little butter, gravy, or pan drippings. Damp the edges of the pastry and pinch them tightly together, folding the edge over to seal the pastry and give a crinkled effect. Brush with a little milk and bake the pasties in a hot oven (425°F., Reg. 6) for 25–30 minutes.

Gelda's Fancy

A quick supper dish with an unusual flavour and a golden cheese crust.

SERVES 4.   Cooking time: about 20 minutes.

4 hardboiled eggs	½ pint milk
6 oz. *chicken or ham*	1 teaspoon mustard
6 anchovy fillets	salt and pepper
1½ oz. butter	2 tablespoons cream
2 tablespoons flour	2 oz. grated cheese

Roughly chop hardboiled eggs. Finely chop chicken or ham and anchovies. Melt butter, add flour, and mix well. Gradually blend in milk, stirring constantly over a medium heat until sauce comes to the boil and is thick and smooth. Mix in mustard, add eggs, chicken or ham, and anchovies. Season with salt and pepper, blend in the cream, and pour into a fireproof serving dish. Sprinkle over the grated cheese and brown under a grill or in a hot oven until golden brown.

Mr T's Chicken or Turkey Toasts

This is a sort of supper dish that goes down well with husbands and children.

SERVES 4.   Cooking time: about 20 minutes.

8 *thin slices chicken or turkey*	2 oz. cheese
½ *lb. cooked cauliflower, carrots, or broccoli spears*	4 slices bread
	butter
¼ pint mornay sauce, see page 186	

Grate cheese. Toast bread and spread with butter. Arrange slices of meat on the toast, cover with the vegetables, sliced if necessary. Pour over the sauce and top with a generous sprinkling of grated cheese.

Heat in a medium hot oven (400°F., Reg. 5) for 15 minutes until golden brown and bubbling.

Chicken Livers

The liver of the chicken has a taste peculiar to itself, rich and
full of flavour. It always seems a shame not to put it to some
good use rather than cooking it with the rest of the giblets
to make gravy – the trouble is that the liver, though so rich,
is not very large. Here are some suggestions for ways of using
one chicken liver.

1. Finely chop or mince the liver and add it to poultry stuffing.
2. Finely chop chicken liver, fry lightly in a little butter, and
   add to meat, poultry, or vegetable soups.
3. Add finely chopped, lightly fried chicken liver to sauces or
   gravy.
4. Add chopped, lightly fried chicken liver to risottos or pilaffs.

For other recipes using chicken liver, see pages 52–3 and
276.

Spaghetti with Chicken Liver Sauce

SERVES 4.   Cooking time: about 30 minutes.

1 *chicken liver*	2 oz. butter
1 oz. mushrooms	2 eggs
4 rashers bacon	salt and pepper
1 clove garlic	8 oz. spaghetti

Cook spaghetti in boiling salted water until tender. Drain
and keep warm.

Meanwhile make the sauce. Wash, dry and finely chop
chicken liver and mushrooms. Remove bacon rinds and finely
chop bacon. Crush garlic. Beat eggs with a wire whisk until
smooth.

Heat butter, add bacon and garlic, and cook for 4 minutes.

Add chicken liver and mushrooms, and cook for a further 4–5 minutes until liver is tender.

Place spaghetti in a saucepan. Mix in beaten egg and chicken liver mixture, season with salt and pepper, and cook over a low heat until egg is just beginning to set, about 5 minutes.

Serve at once.

Leftover Stuffing from a Chicken or Turkey

It is not very often that one has enough stuffing left over from a bird to bother using it again. But there are exceptions, such as the everlasting leftovers that spring from a large Christmas turkey. This recipe makes good use of the cooked stuffing left over on any occasion.

cooked sausage, chestnut, or   beaten egg
any other kind of stuffing or   breadcrumbs
forcemeat   fat for frying

Using floured hands shape the stuffing or forcemeat into small balls about the size of a walnut. Dip them in beaten egg, coat them in seasoned breadcrumbs and fry until golden brown in hot fat.

Serve the stuffing balls with any poultry or meat dish, with stews or casseroles.

Stuffed Goose Neck

You may not often eat goose, but when you do make sure you are given the whole of the neck with the bird. The skin of the neck can make a wonderful meal. Stuff it with chopped goose liver, minced pork or veal, onion and herbs and serve it hot with red cabbage or cold with salad.

SERVES 4. Cooking time: 45 minutes. (It doesn't look all that much but this is a *really* rich dish.)

1 *goose neck*	salt and pepper
1 *goose liver*	3 tablespoons fresh white
1 medium onion	breadcrumbs
1 tablespoon parsley	2 eggs, beaten
pinch sage	

Peel off the skin from the goose neck (use the bones for stock). Finely chop the liver and mince the onion. Combine liver, onion, parsley, sage, seasoning and breadcrumbs. Bind with the beaten eggs and pack the stuffing in the neck skin.

Sew up each end of the neck and roast in goose fat for 40 minutes in a medium oven (375°F., Reg. 4). Leave to cool.

Remove stitches and cut into slices before serving.

Note: Thin slices of stuffed goose neck are delicious to serve as part of a mixed hors d'oeuvres.

Turkey Porjarski

The authentic version of these mock cutlets is made with raw chicken breasts, but I find the basic recipe adapts well to both cooked turkey and cooked chicken.

SERVES 4. Cooking time: 10–15 minutes, plus about 10 minutes for the sauce.

12–16 oz. *cooked turkey or chicken*	butter for frying
	2 oz. mushrooms
4–6 oz. white bread	½ oz. butter
milk	1 tablespoon flour
salt and pepper	½ pint milk
beaten egg	1–2 teaspoons mushroom
flour	ketchup (optional)
dry breadcrumbs	

Mince cooked turkey or chicken through the coarse blades of a mincer. Soak bread until soft in enough milk to cover. Squeeze out excess milk.

Mix together the minced meat and bread, and season with salt and pepper. Using floured hands shape the meat mixture into 8 cutlet shapes, dip in beaten egg and coat in breadcrumbs. Fry the cutlets in butter until crisp and golden on both sides, about 10–15 minutes.

Thinly slice the mushrooms and cook them gently for 5 minutes in ½ oz. butter, sprinkle with 1 tablespoon flour, mix lightly and gradually blend in the milk, stirring until the sauce comes to the boil and is smooth. Add mushroom ketchup, season with salt and pepper, and cook for 3 minutes.

Pour the sauce over the cutlets before serving.

Devilled Turkey

SERVES 4. Cooking time: 20 minutes.

8 slices cooked turkey	1 teaspoon Worcester sauce
2 oz. softened butter	grated rind and juice of
2 teaspoons dry mustard	½ lemon
1 tablespoon sherry	salt, pepper, and pinch cayenne

Combine and mix the mustard, sherry, Worcester sauce, grated lemon rind, lemon juice and seasoning. Rub the mixture into the turkey slices and leave to marinade for at least 30 minutes. Spread with the softened butter and grill under a hot flame or bake in a moderately hot oven (400°F., Reg. 5) for 15 minutes.

Turkey or Chicken Rasputin

SERVES 4.   Cooking time: 20–25 minutes.

1 lb. cooked turkey or chicken	2 egg yolks
2 sticks celery	salt, pepper and pinch paprika
1 large onion	2 tablespoons dry sherry or
1 green pepper	white wine
2 oz. butter	breadcrumbs
3 tablespoons flour	1 oz. butter
¾ pint chicken or turkey stock	

Clean and chop celery. Peel and chop onion. Remove core and seeds of pepper and finely chop flesh. Heat 2 oz. butter, add vegetables, and cook over a medium heat for 5 minutes until golden brown. Mix in the flour and gradually add the stock, stirring constantly until the sauce comes to the boil and is thick and smooth. Remove from the heat and beat in egg yolks one by one. Add sherry and seasoning.

Mix in the turkey and cook over a low heat for a further 5 minutes. Turn into a lightly buttered baking dish, top with breadcrumbs, dot with butter, and brown under a high grill or in a hot oven for a few minutes.

Turkey Slices in Wine Sauce

SERVES 4.   Cooking time: 30 minutes.

8 thin slices turkey	¼ pint red wine
2 oz. butter	pinch cinnamon
½ lb. redcurrant jelly	salt and pepper

Use some of the butter to grease a shallow baking dish.

Combine the remaining butter, redcurrant jelly, wine and

seasonings in a saucepan, and heat until the jelly is melted and the mixture just comes to the boil.

Arrange turkey slices in the baking dish, pour over the sauce, cover with foil, and heat in a medium oven (350°F., Reg. 4) for 20–25 minutes.

Serve the turkey with baked potatoes and a green vegetable.

Turkey Tetrazzini

SERVES 6.   Cooking time: 45 minutes.

8 oz. spaghetti	½ pint cream
2 oz. butter	2 oz. grated Parmesan cheese
2 oz. flour	¾–1 lb. cooked turkey
1 pint white stock	1 6 oz. tin mushrooms
2 tablespoons sherry	salt and pepper

Cook the spaghetti until only just tender in boiling water. Drain well.

Dice cooked turkey, thinly slice mushrooms.

Melt the butter, add flour, mix well, and gradually add the stock, stirring constantly over a medium heat until the sauce is thick and smooth. Stir in sherry and cream, and remove from the heat. Mix the turkey, cheese and mushrooms with the sauce, season with salt and pepper, and place in a lightly buttered fireproof dish. Bake in a moderate oven (350°F., Reg. 3) for about 25 minutes until hot through and golden brown.

Duck Pilaff

Ducks are an expensive commodity and every scrap of meat from the carcases should be used and stretched to the utmost.

A pilaff or risotto is a useful way to make the best of these small amounts of meat.

SERVES 4.   Cooking time: about 40 minutes.

8 oz. rice	2 rashers bacon
stock (preferably made from the duck carcase)	1½ oz. butter
8–12 oz. *cooked duck*	¼ pint gravy
1 large onion	salt and pepper

Peel and chop the onion. Cut meat into thin strips. Remove rind and chop the bacon.

Cook the rice in the stock until tender, strain off the excess liquid (this can be used again). Heat the butter, add onion and bacon, and cook over a medium heat until the onion is golden brown and soft, about 5 minutes. Mix in the meat and gravy, stir lightly, season with salt and pepper. Add the rice and heat through before serving.

Duck with Tuna Fish Sauce

SERVES 4.   No cooking.

8 *thin slices cooked duck*	1 tablespoon tomato ketchup
3 tablespoons mayonnaise	2 tablespoons cream
1 small tin tuna fish	salt and pepper

Drain oil from tuna fish and pound to a smooth paste in a pestle and mortar (or pass through a fine food mill or fine sieve). Blend fish with the mayonnaise, ketchup, and cream, and season with salt and pepper.

Mask slices of duck with the sauce and decorate with chopped aspic (see page 282) and watercress.

Duck with Ginger and Pineapple Sauce

Serving quantities depend on the amount of cooked duck you
have available. Allow about 3–4 oz. per serving.
Cooking time: 10–15 minutes.

cooked duck
1 small tin pineapple titbits
6 pieces preserved ginger
¼ pint ginger syrup

2 teaspoons cornflour
salt and pepper
2 teaspoons soy sauce
rice

Cut the duck into neat cubes the same size as the pineapple.
Thinly slice preserved ginger.

Heat pineapple juice with ginger syrup in a small pan. Mix
cornflour to a smooth paste with a little water, add to the fruit
juice and bring to the boil, stirring all the time. Cook until
the sauce thickens and becomes shiny and mix in the duck,
pineapple, and ginger. Simmer for 5 minutes, season with salt
and pepper and 2 teaspoons soy sauce, and serve with boiled
rice.

Cold Dishes and Salads

The great advantage of using leftover meat, fish, and vegetables to make cold dishes or salads is that the main ingredient does not need to be re-cooked and therefore loses none of its flavour. Since cooked meat, fish, and vegetables tend to dry out after cooling it is important to provide a sauce or dressing which will help to combat this drying or to marinade the meat before it is used. Aspic or tomato jelly also serves the same purpose if the leftover is made into a mould.

Salads and cold dishes should be served well chilled, and like all other leftover dishes they should be attractively garnished with, perhaps, a few slices of tomato or cucumber, a sprig of watercress, or some thin strips of pimento.

Make sure that all salad ingredients are fresh, well-coloured, and crisp, as nothing looks less appetizing than wilted lettuce leaves, discoloured tomatoes, or yellowing watercress.

To stretch meat or other leftovers for a cold dish, add cooked or tinned vegetables, a little tinned meat, salmon or tuna, or a rich well-flavoured sauce.

After turning out jellied moulds or mousses, return them to a refrigerator until the last minute as, especially in hot weather, they have a tendency to flop and go soggy.

Salmon and Prawn Mousse

SERVES 4 as a main course.   SERVES 6 as a first course.   No cooking.

8–10 oz. *cooked salmon* (tinned salmon or tuna may be used)

4–6 oz. peeled prawns (fresh or frozen)

3 oz. butter
¼ pint double cream
salt and pepper
1 tablespoon gelatine

3 tablespoons cold water
1 teaspoon lemon juice
¼ pint boiling water
½ teaspoon dried tarragon

Flake fish with a fork and cream the flesh with the butter until smooth. Season with salt and pepper, and rub through a sieve or through a food mill (this can be done in an electric liquidizer). Whip the cream until stiff but not dry, and fold with the prawns into the salmon mixture.

Dissolve the gelatine in cold water, add lemon juice, dried tarragon and boiling water, mix well, and strain through a fine sieve. Leave jelly in a cool place until it begins to set.

Line a mould with the setting jelly (see page 282), leave to set hard, and then fill the centre with the salmon mixture and chill for at least 2 hours. Turn the mousse out and serve it with wedges of lemon.

Salmon Mould

SERVES 4.   No cooking.

1 *lb. cooked or tinned salmon*
4 oz. soft butter
¼ pint double cream
4 anchovy fillets
1 teaspoon lemon juice
pepper

pinch paprika
½ pint aspic jelly (see page 281)
¼ cucumber
1 tablespoon white wine
   vinegar

Pass the salmon through the fine blades of a mincer and mix with 4 oz. butter.

Drain and finely chop the anchovy fillets.

Blend the fish mixture with cream, anchovies, and lemon juice. Season with pepper and a little paprika.

Pour liquid aspic jelly into a round mould. Swirl it round

the mould until set and coating the sides and bottom. Fill with salmon mixture and chill for at least an hour.

Turn out the mould and decorate with thin slices of peeled cucumber dipped in vinegar.

Salad Niçoise

This dish makes a good starter or an attractive light summer main course. It is a winner for slimmers, and I eat it frequently after a period of over-indulgence. It should, to be genuine, be made from tuna fish but I find that cooked flaked white fish, salmon, or even the remains of a kipper from breakfast, do equally well.

SERVES 4. No cooking.

8 oz. cooked fish (*cod, plaice, sole, haddock, kippers, tinned tuna, or salmon*)
1 green pepper
1 small onion
8 anchovy fillets
milk
10 black olives
2 hardboiled eggs
1 tomato

1 lettuce heart
2 tablespoons olive oil
1 tablespoon white wine vinegar
½ teaspoon Dijon mustard (optional)
1 clove garlic, finely crushed
salt and freshly ground black pepper

Flake fish with a fork. Remove core and all seeds from the pepper and cut flesh into thin strips. Peel, thinly slice, and separate onion into thin rings. Soak anchovies in milk to remove excess salt and squeeze dry. Cut eggs into quarters and peel and slice tomato. Cut lettuce into quarters.

Arrange lettuce quarters around a serving bowl, place flaked fish in the centre, and garnish with green pepper, anchovies, olives, hardboiled eggs, and sliced tomatoes.

Combine olive oil, garlic, mustard and vinegar, season with salt and freshly ground black pepper, mix well, and pour the dressing over the salad.

Chill salad before serving.

Note: If you use a salty fish like smoked haddock or kippers go easy on the seasoning in the dressing.

Fish and Pimento Salad

SERVES 4. Cooking time: 5 minutes.

8–12 oz. cooked white fish
1 small tin pimentos
¼ lb. fresh or frozen peas

½ pint mayonnaise (see page 265)
1 lettuce
½ cucumber (optional)

Flake fish with a fork. Drain and finely chop the pimentos. Cook and drain the peas. Clean and finely shred the lettuce.

Combine fish, pimentos, peas, and mayonnaise, and mix lightly, season if necessary.

Arrange the fish mixture on a bed of finely shredded lettuce, and decorate with thin slices of peeled cucumber. Chill before serving.

Serving cold sliced meat

One of the most obvious ways of serving cold roast meat (boiled brisket, silverside, or salt beef) is to produce it cold, cut into slices, with salad. This is, of course, one of the quickest ways to prepare the remains of yesterday's joint and it can be delicious – but only if a few major rules are followed.

Cold meat *must* be cut in very thin slices. Thick slices tend to be tough and indigestible.

The meat should be cut at the very last minute or it loses colour and becomes dry. If it has to be cut some time before the meal, cover the sliced meat with a slightly damp cloth, foil, Saranwrap, or dampened greaseproof paper.

Meat that has been over- or under-cooked should be used for made-up dishes and not served as cold sliced meat. Correctly cooked, beef should be under-cooked and definitely on the pink side. Lamb should also be just a little pinkish. Pork, and mutton, on the other hand, should be well cooked and have no sign of bloodiness.

Except for beef, which when cut from the best joints in wafer-thin slices is juicy and rose red, most cold meat does not look very appetizing. To make up for the lack of colour special attention should be paid to the presentation and garnishing of the dish. Parsley sprigs, aspic jelly, watercress, tomatoes, cucumber, and shredded lettuce, can all help to make cold meat look more attractive.

Because cold meat tends to be rather a dreary meal, try to serve a variety of it, such as a couple of ounces of thinly-sliced ham and tongue mixed with the meat.

Serve the meat with a good choice of pickles, chutneys, mustard, and sauces.

Serve cold roast beef with mustard and horseradish sauce; lamb and mutton with mint jelly, or mint sauce, and red-currant jelly; pork with apple sauce and horseradish.

Most salads go well with cold meat and the best ever vegetable accompaniment is a baked potato in its jacket. For ways to serve baked potatoes, see page 203.

Cold Meat in Fresh Tomato Sauce

This is a good way to use up the remains of a cold joint when tomatoes are at their best, and cheapest, but it can be made just as well with a sauce made from tinned tomatoes (see page 277).

SERVES 4.   No cooking.

1 *lb. thinly sliced cold cooked
    beef, lamb, or mutton*
4 ripe tomatoes
1 large clove garlic, finely
    chopped
1 tablespoon finely chopped
    parsley
grated rind of half lemon

½ tablespoon fresh finely
    chopped chervil and basil
    (or ¼ tablespoon dried)
4 tablespoons olive oil
1 tablespoon white wine
    vinegar
salt and freshly ground black
    pepper

Arrange the thin slices of meat in a shallow serving dish.

Skin tomatoes (see page 18), remove pips and finely chop the flesh. Combine and mix well the tomato, garlic, herbs, olive oil, vinegar, lemon peel, and enough salt and freshly ground pepper to season. Pour the sauce over the meat and leave to stand in a refrigerator or cold place for at least two hours before serving.

Mixed Meat Salad with Mayonnaise

SERVES 4.   Cooking time: 2 minutes.

4 *oz. cooked beef or lamb*
4 *oz. ham*
4 *oz. tongue*
2 *oz. mushrooms*
juice ½ lemon

4 *oz. cooked vegetables (peas,
    beans, or carrots)*
¼ pint mayonnaise
salt and pepper
lettuce

Cut the meat into fine shreds. Chop beans or dice the carrots. Thinly slice the mushrooms. Blanch mushrooms in lemon juice and boiling salted water for 2 minutes. Drain well.

Combine all the ingredients, mix with the mayonnaise, season with salt and pepper, and arrange on a bed of lettuce leaves. Chill before serving. Serve with rice and green or mixed salad.

Variations:

1. Use curried instead of plain mayonnaise.

2. Add a little horseradish sauce to the mayonnaise.
3. Toss the salad in a Cumberland sauce (see page 273) instead of mayonnaise.

Note: Make half a quantity of the recipe and serve as part of an hors d'oeuvre.

Beef Salad

Use any cold beef for this dish, which is ideal for lunch on a hot summer's day as it is sharp and refreshing.

SERVES 4. No cooking.

10–12 oz. *cooked beef*
4 tablespoons olive oil
1½ tablespoons white wine vinegar
1 teaspoon Dijon mustard (or ½ teaspoon dry mustard)
2 teaspoons finely chopped capers

2 teaspoons finely chopped parsley
¼ teaspoon chopped tarragon
salt and pepper
4 *cooked potatoes* (8 *if they are new*)
2 hardboiled eggs

Cut beef into matchstick strips. Combine olive oil, vinegar, mustard, capers, parsley and tarragon, and season with salt and pepper. Marinade beef in the dressing for at least 4 hours.

Thinly slice potatoes and chop hardboiled eggs. Arrange potatoes around the edge of a serving dish, pile beef in the centre, and garnish with chopped egg.

Cold Beef at its Best

I had this dish in the internationally famous Harry's Bar in Venice and couldn't wait to get home to try it. My version wasn't on a par with Harry's but was delicious nevertheless.

Later I discovered that the correct way to make the dish is from wafer-thin slices of *raw* beef – not an idea which appeals to many people.

Thin slicing is all important for this dish, so make sure your carving knife is razor sharp.

SERVES 4. No cooking.

12–16 oz. underdone good quality roast beef (sirloin or fillet)
¼ pint mayonnaise
2 teaspoons Dijon mustard (or 1 teaspoon made English mustard)
1–3 tablespoons thin cream

Cut the meat into even, wafer-thin slices, and trim off any fat or gristle. Arrange slices on a serving dish.

Beat mustard into mayonnaise and blend in enough cream to make a thick pouring consistency. Check seasoning and pour the mayonnaise in a wavy pattern over the meat. Garnish with watercress or chopped lettuce.

Beef and Vegetables in Aspic

Read the notes about aspic on page 282.

SERVES 4. No cooking.

8–12 oz. lean undercooked beef
4 oz. cooked peas
8 oz. cooked carrots
½ pint aspic jelly (see page 281)
2 tablespoons red wine
3 tablespoons olive oil
1 tablespoon white wine vinegar

1 tablespoon finely chopped parsley
1 tablespoon finely chopped capers
salt and pepper

Cut meat into thin matchstick strips and marinade for at least an hour in the combined olive oil, vinegar, parsley, capers, and seasoning. Drain, and pat the meat dry with kitchen paper. Cut carrots into thin slices.

Add the red wine to the aspic jelly and line a mould with about a quarter of the jelly. Press the carrots, dipped in a little jelly, into the sides and bottom of the mould, and fill the centre with alternate layers of peas and meat. Pour the aspic over each layer and leave to set before arranging the next layer. Finish with remaining aspic and chill in a refrigerator until set. Turn out and garnish with salad.

Beef Stroganoff Salad

SERVES 4. No cooking.

10–12 oz. *undercooked roast beef*
vinaigrette dressing (see page 274)
2 onions
18 black olives

8 oz. mushrooms
½ pint sour cream
salt and pepper
½ teaspoon paprika

Cut beef into thin shreds. Peel and thinly slice onions and separate into rings. Remove stones and cut olives into thin slices. Wash, dry, and thinly slice mushrooms. Marinade onions, olives, and mushrooms in vinaigrette dressing for 30 minutes. Drain well and combine with meat, sour cream, and paprika. Season with salt and pepper and chill before serving.

A rice salad goes well with this dish.

Cold Pork with Horseradish and Apple Sauce

The attractive, pink coloured sauce is the special feature of this Swedish method of serving cold roast pork. Don't be put off by the fact that the sauce calls for beetroot juice. It is now possible to buy small tins of sliced beetroot with vinegar, and the juice from these tins is ideal for the purpose.

SERVES 4. No cooking.

8 *slices pork*
$\frac{1}{4}-\frac{1}{2}$ pint apple purée
3 tablespoons horseradish sauce

2 tablespoons beetroot juice
salt and pepper

Arrange pork slices in a shallow serving dish. Combine apple purée, horseradish, and beetroot juice. Season with salt and pepper, and spread the sauce over the meat. Chill before serving, and garnish with chopped watercress or lettuce.

Ham Mousse – I*

SERVES 4. No cooking.

8 *oz. ham*
$\frac{1}{2}$ pint mayonnaise
1 tablespoon Dijon mustard
1 tablespoon finely chopped
  pickle

2 tablespoons double cream
salt and pepper
1 tablespoon gelatine
2 *egg whites*

Mince the ham through the fine blades of a mincing machine. Mix ham with the mustard, pickle, mayonnaise, and cream. Season with salt and pepper.

Dissolve the gelatine in a little hot water and mix it into the ham mixture. Whip the egg whites until stiff, fold them into the ham, turn the mousse into a dampened mould, and chill until set.

Turn out the mousse, and garnish it with watercress, sliced tomatoes or sliced cucumber.

Ham Mousse – II*

SERVES 4. No cooking.

8 *oz. ham*
½ pint clear stock
1 tablespoon gelatine

¼ pint double cream
salt, pepper and a pinch
    cayenne

Mince the ham through the fine blades of a mincing machine. Dissolve the gelatine in a little hot stock, and mix it into the ham with the rest of the stock. Season with salt, pepper, and a pinch cayenne.

Whip the cream until thick, fold it into the ham mixture, and turn the mousse into a dampened mould. Chill the mousse until set, unmould to serve, and garnish with watercress, sliced tomatoes, sliced hardboiled eggs, or cucumber.

Ham or Beef and Potato Salad

I made this for a buffet party recently and it had a great success. On that occasion I used ham, but I have also made the same salad with thin strips of cold roast beef and found it equally delicious. Cooked potatoes can be used in the place of raw ones.

SERVES 4. Cooking time: about 30 minutes for the potatoes.

1½ lb. potatoes
2 oz. bacon rashers
6 *oz. ham or cooked beef*
2 hardboiled eggs
¼–½ pint mayonnaise

1 tablespoon finely chopped
    parsley
1 tablespoon finely chopped
    gherkins

Peel potatoes and cook in salted water until soft but not floury. Leave to cool, then cut into small neat cubes. Cut ham or beef into thin matchstick strips and chop hardboiled eggs.

Remove rinds from bacon and fry rashers until crisp. Drain on kitchen paper, and chop or crumble into small pieces.

Mix parsley and gherkins into the mayonnaise, fold in meat and hardboiled eggs, and arrange the salad in a serving dish. Sprinkle over the bacon, and chill before serving.

Cold Chicken with Peas and Tarragon Mayonnaise

SERVES 4.   Cooking time: about 20 minutes.

8 *slices cooked chicken*	2 teaspoons dried tarragon,
8 oz. spaghetti	finely chopped
4 *oz. cooked peas*	1 teaspoon lemon juice
½ pint mayonnaise	salt and pepper

Arrange chicken in a shallow serving dish. Cook spaghetti in boiling salted water for about 15 minutes until tender. Drain and cool.

Soak tarragon in lemon juice and mix with the mayonnaise, season with salt and pepper if necessary.

Combine cooled spaghetti with half mayonnaise and the cooked peas. Arrange spaghetti around the chicken, and spoon remaining mayonnaise over the chicken.

Chill before serving.

Ham or Chicken and Rice Salad

SERVES 4.   Cooking time: about 20 minutes.

½ lb. rice	3 tablespoons oil
4 *oz. cooked ham or chicken*	1 tablespoon white wine
4 *oz. cooked peas (fresh or frozen)*	vinegar
1 green pepper	salt and freshly ground black
1 teaspoon Dijon mustard	pepper

Cut ham or chicken into small dice. Core, remove seeds, and finely chop green pepper.

Combine the oil, mustard and vinegar, and season with salt and freshly ground black pepper.

Cook rice in boiling water (see page 235), rinse in cold water, drain well, and toss in the vinaigrette dressing. Leave to cool.

Add meat, pepper, and peas to the rice, and chill the salad before serving.

Serve with a green or mixed salad.

Curried Ham Rolls

SERVES 4.   No cooking.

8 *thin slices ham*	¼ pint mayonnaise
½ *lb. mixed cooked vegetables*	1½ teaspoons curry powder
(*potatoes, carrots, beans,*	1 teaspoon lemon juice
beetroot, peas, etc.)	

Cut the vegetables into small dice. Dissolve curry powder in the lemon juice, add to the mayonnaise, and mix well. Mix the vegetables into the mayonnaise, spread on the slices of ham, and roll each one up neatly.

Arrange the ham rolls on lettuce leaves, garnish with slices of tomato and cucumber, and serve chilled.

Autumn Ham Salad

Although it can be made at other times of the year, this combination of ham and apples is best when made with the first of the Cox's. It is a satisfying salad and makes a good lunch dish.

SERVES 4.   No cooking.

4–6 oz. *ham*
3 crisp eating apples
2 sticks celery
1 head chicory

1 *lb. cooked potatoes*
4 oz. cheddar cheese
½ pint mayonnaise (see page 265)

Chop the ham, cut peeled apples into small cubes, thinly slice the celery and chicory, and dice the potatoes and cheese.

Combine all the ingredients, mix well, and chill before serving.

Ham Rolls with Asparagus

For each serving:

2 *thin slices ham*
4 *cooked asparagus spears*
(*fresh, frozen, or tinned*)

lettuce leaves
2 tablespoons mayonnaise
1 teaspoon tomato ketchup

Mix tomato ketchup with the mayonnaise. Roll ham neatly around the asparagus, and arrange rolls on a bed of crisp lettuce leaves. Mask the rolls with the mayonnaise, and decorate with an extra piece of asparagus.

Tangy Tongue Salad

Follow the directions for making Beef Salad on page 168, substituting *tongue*, cut into matchstick strips in place of the beef.

Serving Cold Sliced Poultry and Game

Slices and joints of cold roast poultry or game can be delicious if the meat is not dry and the dish looks attractive. All stuffings should be removed from the bird and kept separately in the larder or refrigerator. The cold stuffing can be cut into thin slices and served with the meat.

The breast of the bird should be cut into thin slices and the joints left whole. Allow at least one large joint, one small joint and a slice of breast, or three slices of breast, for each serving. Cold sliced ham or tongue go well with both poultry and game and will help the meat to go further.

Arrange the meat attractively on a serving dish and garnish with watercress, chopped aspic, sliced tomatoes, cucumber and shredded lettuce, etc.

Serve cold chicken, poultry or game with a green or mixed salad and baked potatoes or a rice salad.

Serve chicken with mayonnaise, turkey with cranberry sauce; duck and wild duck with redcurrant jelly and an orange salad; game with redcurrant jelly or Cumberland sauce, see page 273.

Chicken and Ham Velouté

SERVES 4.   Cooking time: about 10 minutes.

8 oz. cooked chicken	salt and pepper
8 oz. cooked ham	pinch cayenne
1 oz. butter	¼ teaspoon mixed herbs
2 tablespoons flour	2 egg yolks
½ pint chicken stock	1 tablespoon powdered gelatine
¼ pint milk	

Finely chop or mince chicken and ham. Heat butter, add flour and mix well. Gradually blend in half the chicken stock and the milk, stirring constantly until the sauce thickens and comes to the boil. Add mixed herbs, season with salt, pepper, and a pinch cayenne. Beat in egg yolks and cook, without boiling, for 3 minutes. Leave to cool.

Dissolve gelatine in the remaining stock and mix into the sauce. Add ham and chicken, mix well, and turn into a mould. Chill in a refrigerator until set. Turn out and serve garnished with sliced tomatoes, cucumber, or chopped lettuce.

Chicken and Tomato Ring

SERVES 4.   Cooking time: 5 minutes.

¼ pint tomato juice
¼ teaspoon chopped tarragon
salt and pepper
½ oz. gelatine

12 oz. cooked chicken
1 bunch watercress
vinaigrette dressing

Heat tomato juice with tarragon and season with salt and pepper. Simmer for 3 minutes and strain. Dissolve gelatine in the hot tomato juice. Leave to cool and thicken.

Cut chicken into small dice. Add to the almost-set tomato juice and pour into a ring mould. Chill in a refrigerator until set. Turn out and fill the centre with watercress dipped in vinaigrette dressing.

Curried Chicken and Rice Salad

SERVES 4.   Cooking time: about 5 minutes (excluding rice).

8 oz. cooked chicken
1 oz. blanched almonds
2 oz. butter
½ lb. mushrooms
1 tablespoon lemon juice
1 teaspoon curry powder
2 tablespoons pineapple
   (2 rings)

1 teaspoon finely chopped
   onion
1 tablespoon mango chutney
8 oz. cooked rice (2½ oz.
   uncooked)
salt and pepper

Chop pineapple and chutney, and thinly slice mushrooms. Melt butter, and cook almonds over a high heat until golden. Add mushrooms and lemon juice, season with salt and pepper, and cook for 2 minutes, mix in curry powder and leave to cool.

Mix all the ingredients together and stir thoroughly. Turn into a serving dish and chill well.

Chicken and Pâté in Aspic

An attractive-looking dish and one which would make a good main course for a summer lunch party. The aspic jelly can be home made, made from packaged aspic jelly crystals, or from bottled jelly. Tinned consommé with a little added gelatine can also be used in the place of aspic.

SERVES 4.   No cooking.

4 slices pâté
8 *thin slices cooked chicken with the skin removed*
1 red pimento (tinned) for garnish
¾ pint aspic jelly (see page 281)
1 tablespoon sherry or Madeira

Mix the sherry with the aspic jelly.

Cover the bottom of a shallow glass serving dish with a thin layer of liquid aspic jelly and leave to set. Place the four slices of pâté on the aspic and arrange the slices of chicken (with all skin removed) in a pattern on top. Garnish the chicken with very thin strips of red pimento and pour over enough aspic to cover.

Leave to set for at least an hour before serving.

Chaudfroid of Chicken or Turkey

SERVES 4.   Cooking time: about 15 minutes.

8–12 *thin slices cooked chicken or turkey*

1 oz. butter
2 tablespoons flour
4 tablespoons chicken stock

Sauce
½ pint milk
1 small onion, peeled and sliced
6 peppercorns
pinch mace
bayleaf
pinch salt

½ tablespoon powdered gelatine
2 tablespoons double cream
salt and pepper

Garnish
½ pint aspic jelly, see page 281
watercress
red pimento

Heat milk, without boiling, with the onion, peppercorns, mace, bayleaf, and a pinch of salt. Cook for 5 minutes and strain through a fine sieve. Melt the butter, add flour, and gradually mix in the milk, stirring constantly until the sauce is thick and smooth.

Dissolve gelatine in the stock and blend into the sauce with 2 tablespoons double cream. Season with salt and pepper and leave to cool.

When the sauce is cold and beginning to set coat each slice of chicken or turkey generously. Arrange the slices on a serving dish and garnish with chopped aspic jelly, watercress and thin strips of red pimento.

Chicken Mousse – I*

SERVES 4.   Cooking time: about 15 minutes.

2 eggs
¼ oz. butter
½ tablespoon flour

¼ pint milk
salt and pepper
½ oz. (1 tablespoon) gelatine

1 gill water
2 tablespoons double cream
1 tablespoon lemon juice

1 tablespoon sherry
10–12 oz. cooked chicken

Melt the butter, add flour, and mix well. Gradually blend in the milk stirring constantly until the sauce comes to the boil and is thick and smooth. Lower heat, beat in the egg yolks, and season with salt and pepper.

Dissolve gelatine in hot water and mix into the sauce. Leave to cool. Beat in cream, lemon juice, and sherry.

Cut chicken into small dice or mince through the coarse blades of a mincing machine. Fold chicken into the sauce and leave in a cool place until the mixture is beginning to set. Whip egg whites until stiff, fold lightly into the chicken mixture, and turn into a dampened mould. Leave to set firm, turn out, and garnish with cucumber, tomato, and lettuce.

Chicken Mousse – II*

SERVES 4. Cooking time: about 15 minutes.

10–12 oz. cooked chicken
¼ pint stock
2 tablespoons clear gravy
2 tablespoons flour
½ teaspoon mixed herbs

1 tablespoon sherry
1 tablespoon powdered gelatine
salt and pepper
¼ pint double cream, whipped
½ pint aspic jelly (see page 281)

Remove all fat and skin from the meat and chop it into small pieces.

Heat stock and gravy together, add a little to the flour to make a smooth paste, add this to the hot liquid, bring to the boil, and cook over a medium heat, stirring constantly, until thick and smooth. Add the herbs and sherry, season with salt and pepper.

Melt the gelatine in a little hot stock, mix it well with the sauce, and leave to cool but not set.

Pour a thin layer of aspic into a large mould or some small individual moulds and leave to set.

Add chicken to the sauce and fold in the whipped cream, fill the mould with mousse and leave to set in a refrigerator or a cold place.

Turn the mousse out on to a bed of lettuce leaves and garnish with thin strips of pimento, thin slices of tomato, slices of hardboiled egg, or cooked vegetables tossed in a vinaigrette dressing.

Chicken and Almond Salad

SERVES 4.   No cooking.

12 oz. cooked chicken
2 sticks celery
2 oranges

$\frac{1}{4}$–$\frac{1}{2}$ pint mayonnaise
2 oz. salted almonds

Cut chicken into small dice. Chop celery. Peel orange, remove all white pith and membrane, and chop flesh. Cut salted almonds into thin slivers.

Reserve a few salted almonds for decoration, combine and mix the other ingredients, and arrange the salad on a bed of lettuce leaves or on a serving dish. Sprinkle over remaining almonds and chill before serving.

Special Chicken and Pineapple Salad

On the whole, I do not advocate combinations of meat and fruit, but I have to admit that this chicken and pineapple partnership is a very successful one. The dish can be made with tinned pineapple but fresh fruit gives a much better flavour, and the salad looks very special served from pineapple shells.

SERVES 4.   Cooking time: 20 minutes.

8 oz. long grained or Patna rice	1 teaspoon dry mustard
1 small green pepper	1 tablespoon white wine
2 tomatoes	vinegar
1 medium pineapple	3 tablespoons olive oil
12 *oz. cooked chicken*	salt and pepper

Cook the rice in boiling salted water until tender, about 20 minutes. Rinse well and drain. Combine the dry mustard, vinegar and oil, mix well, and season with salt and pepper. Toss the warm rice in the dressing and leave to cool.

Remove the core and seeds from the pepper and finely chop the flesh. Peel and finely chop the tomatoes. Cut pineapple in half lengthwise, carefully scoop out the flesh, discard the core, and cut the pineapple into small cubes. Cut up the chicken.

Mix chopped pepper, tomato and pineapple with the cooled rice and the chicken, pile into the pineapple cases and chill before serving.

Turkey Mayonnaise

SERVES 4.   Cooking time: about 20 minutes.

6 oz. long-grained or Patna rice	salt and pepper
½ pint mayonnaise	12 *oz. cooked turkey*
2 tablespoons cream	8 anchovy fillets
1 tablespoon finely chopped parsley	3 tomatoes
1 tablespoon finely chopped chives	

Cook the rice in boiling salted water until tender, about 20 minutes. Rinse in cold water, drain well, and mix in half the mayonnaise and the chopped chives and parsley. Season with salt and pepper.

Cut the turkey in thin slices. Peel and thinly slice the tomatoes.
Arrange the rice on a serving dish. Top with a layer of dark
meat and then a layer of white. Mask the turkey with the remaining mayonnaise thinned with the cream. Decorate with
anchovy fillets and thin slices of tomato.

Macaroni Salad

SERVES 4.   No cooking.

6 oz. *cooked macaroni*
6 oz. cheddar cheese
½ red or green pepper
2 sticks celery

1 tablespoon finely chopped
chives or spring onion tops
¼ pint vinaigrette dressing
(see page 274)

Coarsely chop the macaroni, grate the cheese, finely
chop pepper and celery.

Combine all the ingredients and toss well in a vinaigrette
dressing.

Variation:
Use ¼ pint mayonnaise instead of the vinaigrette dressing.
Add 1 small tin drained tuna, 4 chopped anchovy fillets and
4 chopped black olives, and serve the salad as a main luncheon
or supper dish.

Vegetables

Every part of a vegetable should be put to good use, and it saddens me to see people throwing away things like onion skins and beetroot tops which could help to give flavour to a dish or even make a dish in their own right.

All vegetables contain a good proportion of their value in their skins, and almost all outside leaves and peelings should be cleaned and used by themselves or in conjunction with meat bones to make stock for use in soups, gravy, or sauces. The brown skin of onions, the skin of tomatoes and mushroom peelings are particularly good for giving flavour and colour to stock.

Cooked vegetables can quickly be re-heated to serve as a vegetable for another meal. Like all leftovers they should be used as quickly as possible and should not have been over-cooked in the first instance. Colour, as always, is of great importance, and since most vegetables tend to fade a little when they are cooked it is always worth adding a little extra colour by sprinkling the re-heated dish with chopped parsley, chives, or pimento.

Vegetables can be re-heated in a wide variety of ways; small amounts can be added to meat dishes or omelettes, or can give flavour and body to soups. Obviously the quickest way of re-heating is to toss the cooked vegetables in some melted butter until they are hot through, but they can also be served in a number of interesting and delicious sauces which will not only jazz up the vegetable but also double the quantity of the dish.

Small amounts of cooked vegetables of all varieties can be combined together in one made-up dish and can be used for almost all the recipes in this book which call for a quantity of just *one* vegetable.

Make use of every bit of the vegetables you have – even the smallest amount can be put to some good use and will help to improve your next meal.

Reheating Cooked Vegetables in Butter

This way of re-heating vegetables takes only a couple of minutes and can be delicious if the vegetables were crisp and tasty to start with.

Allow 1 oz. butter for each 8 oz. cooked vegetables, and cut the vegetables into small slices or dice to enable them to heat through as quickly as possible.

Heat the butter, add vegetables, season with salt and pepper, and toss over a moderately high heat until vegetables have absorbed the butter and are hot through.

For root vegetables such as carrots, parsnips or turnips, add a little sugar to the butter.

A sprinkling of finely chopped parsley added to the vegetables will help to give flavour and colour to the dish.

Combinations of two or more cooked vegetables can be cut to the same size and re-heated in this way.

Poor Man's Asparagus

I first read this recipe in an eighteenth-century cookery book. It was described as being exactly the same in taste as asparagus and a suitable dish to serve as a course by itself. Although I cannot honestly say that I rate the vegetable as highly, it does make a good companion to any main course and is different enough to cause comment. The taste is subtle rather than out-standing.

SERVES 4.   Cooking time: 20–30 minutes.

the leaves of 1 large or 2 small cauliflowers
melted butter or sauce Hollandaise

Trim off all the green part of the leaves so that only the centre white stalk remains. Scrape the stalks with a sharp knife to remove any coarse fibrous edges, and prepare in the same way as you would celery stalks. Cut stalks into even lengths of little-finger thickness and drop into boiling salted water.

Cook for 20–30 minutes until tender. Drain and serve with melted butter or an Hollandaise sauce.

French Peas

SERVES 4.   Cooking time: about 8 minutes.

½ oz. butter
1 lettuce (or the outer leaves
  of two lettuces)
2 rashers bacon
1 small onion
½ lb. cooked peas
salt and pepper

Wash and shred lettuce. Chop bacon, and peel and chop onion. Melt butter in a saucepan, add bacon and onion, and cook for 6 minutes over a medium heat without browning. Add peas and lettuce and heat through.

Cooked Vegetables with Ham in a Mornay Sauce

SERVES 4.   Cooking time: 20 minutes.

12–16 oz. cooked vegetables
  (*carrots, cauliflower, cabbage,
  etc.*)
4 oz. cooked bacon or ham
½ pint milk
1 small onion
pinch mace
½ oz. butter
1 tablespoon flour
salt and pepper
2 oz. grated cheese

Slice or chop vegetables. Chop cooked bacon or ham. Peel and roughly chop onion.

Combine milk, onion, and a pinch mace in a saucepan, heat and cook, without boiling, for 5 minutes. Strain the milk.

Heat butter, add flour, and mix well. Gradually blend in the milk, stirring constantly, until the sauce comes to the boil and is thick and smooth. Beat in 1½ oz. grated cheese, season with salt and pepper, and cook for 2 minutes.

Mix vegetables and bacon or ham into the sauce, turn into a lightly buttered serving dish, sprinkle over remaining cheese, and brown in a hot oven or under a hot grill.

Vegetables with a Hollandaise Sauce

Leftover vegetables which have *not* been overcooked can be reheated in a colander or steamer over boiling water for 5–10 minutes until hot through. Serve the vegetables with a Hollandaise sauce, see page 270.

Fried Cooked Vegetables

Cooked vegetables well seasoned with salt and pepper and pepped up with a teaspoon of lemon juice or a few drops of Tabasco sauce, can be lightly fried in butter, dripping or bacon fat.

Cabbage with Egg and Cheese Sauce

Small amounts of leftover vegetables can be stretched to very reasonable proportions by the addition of a rich sauce and hard-boiled eggs.

SERVES 4.   Cooking time: 35 minutes.

8 *oz. cooked cabbage*	3 oz. cheese, grated
2 hardboiled eggs	1 egg yolk
1 oz. butter	2 tablespoons cream
2 tablespoons flour	salt and pepper
½ pint milk	

Finely shred cabbage. Chop eggs. Melt butter, add flour and mix well. Gradually add milk, stirring constantly until the sauce comes to the boil and is thick and smooth. Add 2 oz. cheese, and cook for 3 minutes over a low heat.

Beat the egg yolk with the cream, blend the mixture into the sauce; season with salt and pepper. Mix in the cabbage and hardboiled eggs and turn into a lightly greased baking dish. Sprinkle with the remaining cheese. Bake in a hot oven (450°F., Reg. 7) for 10–15 minutes until golden brown (or brown under a grill).

Note: This recipe can be made into a good supper dish with the addition of some chopped bacon or ham and some peeled and chopped tomatoes.

Cabbage with Sweet and Sour Sauce

SERVES 4.   Cooking time: about 10 minutes.

12–16 *oz. cooked cabbage or* carrots	3 tablespoons sugar
	3 tablespoons vinegar
2 tablespoons olive oil or ½ oz. butter	1 tablespoon cornflour
	salt
½ pint water	

Finely shred cabbage or thinly slice carrots. Combine sugar, vinegar, water and cornflour.

Heat oil (for the cabbage) or butter (for the carrots), add vegetables and cook for 1 minute. Pour over liquid, bring to the boil, and stir gently until the sauce thickens and becomes translucent. Season with a little salt.

Hot Cabbage Salad

SERVES 4.   Cooking time: 10 minutes.

12–16 oz. cooked cabbage
¼ pint white wine vinegar
2 teaspoons sugar

1 small onion
1 teaspoon caraway seeds
4 rashers bacon

Shred cabbage. Peel and finely chop onion. Remove rinds and fry bacon rashers until crisp. Drain rashers on kitchen paper and crumble or chop finely.

Combine vinegar, onion, sugar, and caraway seeds in a saucepan, bring to the boil, and simmer for 5 minutes. Stir in cabbage, heat through, and season with salt and pepper. Sprinkle bacon over before serving.

Spiced Cabbage

SERVES 4.   Cooking time: about 20 minutes.

12–16 oz. cooked cabbage
1 small tin tomatoes
½ teaspoon caraway seeds

salt and pepper
2 oz. grated cheese

Chop the cabbage roughly, combine it with the tomatoes and caraway seeds, season with salt and pepper, and cook for ten minutes over a medium heat, stirring gently. Place cabbage mixture in a lightly buttered baking dish, sprinkle the grated cheese over, and brown under a grill or in a hot oven.

Fried Cabbage and Rice

SERVES 4. Cooking time: 5 minutes.

6 oz. cooked cabbage
4 oz. cooked rice
2 oz. butter

1 oz. almonds, shredded
salt and pepper

Shred the cabbage. Heat butter in a frying pan, add almonds
with a good pinch of salt, and cook until almonds are golden
brown. Add cabbage and rice, mix well, and fry over a medium
heat for about 5 minutes. Season with pepper and more salt
if necessary.

Scalloped Leeks

SERVES 4. Cooking time: 20 minutes.

1 lb. cooked leeks
1 oz. butter
3 tablespoons flour
½ pint vegetable water or milk
4 tablespoons cream

1 egg yolk
salt and pepper
2 oz. grated cheese
paprika (optional)

Cut the leeks into bite-sized pieces.

Heat the butter, add flour, and mix well. Gradually blend
in vegetable water or milk and stir constantly over a medium
heat until thick and smooth. Season with salt and pepper.

Beat cream and egg yolk together, add to the sauce, and cook
without boiling for 2 minutes. Mix in the leeks and pour into
a baking dish. Sprinkle with grated cheese and a little paprika
(optional) and bake in a hot oven (450°F., Reg. 7) for ten
minutes until golden brown.

Vegetable Patties

SERVES 4. Cooking time: 10 minutes for the sauce; 6-8 minutes each for the patties.

½ lb. cooked vegetables (carrots, parsnips, swedes, beans, peas, or any combination)	¼ pint milk
	salt and pepper
	1 beaten egg
1 oz. butter	dried breadcrumbs
1 oz. flour	fat for frying

Cut the vegetables into pea-sized dice.

Melt the butter in a small saucepan, add the flour, mixing well until the butter and flour form a ball and leave the sides of the pan; gradually add the milk, stirring constantly over medium heat until the mixture is thick and smooth.

Add the vegetables to the sauce and season generously with salt and pepper. Leave to cool.

Using hands dusted with flour, shape the mixture into flat cakes about 2 inches in diameter, brush with beaten egg, and coat with dried breadcrumbs. Fry in hot shallow fat until golden brown on both sides.

Variations:

1. Add 2 oz. grated cheese to the sauce.
2. Add a chopped hardboiled egg to the sauce.
3. Add 2 tablespoons finely chopped onions to the sauce.

Vegetable Pie*

SERVES 4. Cooking time: 15-20 minutes.

½ lb. cooked vegetables (carrots, beans, peas, etc.)	½ lb. mashed potatoes
	1 oz. butter

1 oz. flour

½ pint milk

salt and pepper

1 tablespoon finely chopped
parsley

4 oz. grated cheese

Cut the vegetables, except the peas, into small dice.

Melt the butter in a saucepan, add the flour, and mix well until the butter and flour form a ball and leave the sides of the pan. Gradually add the milk, stirring constantly, over a medium heat until the mixture is thick and smooth.

Add the vegetables, parsley and half the cheese to the sauce, mix well, and season generously with salt and pepper. Pour into a baking dish, top with the mashed potatoes, and sprinkle with the remaining cheese. Bake in a medium hot oven (400°F., Reg. 5) for 15 – 20 minutes until golden brown.

Vegetable and Macaroni Cheese

SERVES 4.   Cooking time: about 40 minutes.

¼–½ lb. cooked vegetables (carrots,
peas, beans, marrow)

3 oz. macaroni

1½ oz. butter

1½ oz. flour

¾ pint milk

6 oz. grated cheese

salt and pepper

Cut the vegetables into small dice.

Boil the macaroni until tender, about 10 minutes, in salted water, drain well.

Melt the butter in a saucepan, add the flour, and mix well. Gradually add the milk, stirring constantly over a medium heat until the mixture is thick and smooth. Mix in 4 oz. grated cheese and season with salt and pepper.

Combine the vegetables and macaroni with the cheese sauce, pour into a baking dish, sprinkle over the remaining cheese, and bake in a medium hot oven (400°F., Reg. 5) for 20–25 minutes until golden brown.

Variation:

Add peeled and chopped tomatoes to the vegetables, or 1 medium onion finely chopped and gently fried in a little butter until soft.

Creamed Vegetables with Sausages

Although this recipe is for leftover boiled vegetables, it can also be made with vegetables which have already been served in a cream sauce – you need about a pint of creamed vegetables.

SERVES 4.   Cooking time: 20 minutes.

½ *lb. cooked vegetables (carrots, beans, cauliflower, marrow, or cabbage)*	½ pint milk
	1 tablespoon cream
	salt and pepper
1 oz. butter	1 lb. pork sausages
1 oz. flour	

Cut the vegetables into thin slices.

Melt the butter in a saucepan, add the flour and make a roux; gradually add the milk, stirring constantly over a medium heat, until the mixture is thick and smooth, blend in the cream, season with salt and pepper.

Fry the sausages until well-browned and cut them into thin slices.

Add the vegetables and sausage slices to the sauce, pour into a fireproof dish, and bake in a medium oven (375°F., Reg. 4) for about 20 minutes until hot through.

Serve as a light lunch or supper dish or with roast meat or poultry.

Spanish Vegetable Flan

Can be served as a lunch or supper dish or as a vegetable accompaniment for cold or hot meat.

SERVES 4 as a supper dish; SERVES 6 as a vegetable dish.
Cooking time: about 50 minutes.

Pastry

8 oz. plain flour	pinch salt
4 oz. butter	3–4 tablespoons iced water

Filling

8 oz. cooked leeks	2 oz. grated cheese
3 tomatoes	¼ pint double cream
8 oz. cooked potatoes	salt and pepper

Make pastry by rubbing the butter into the flour and salt with the fingertips. Mix to a smooth dough with the water. Chill for 30 minutes in a refrigerator. Roll out thinly, line a flan case, prick the bottom with a fork and bake 'blind' in a hot oven (425°F., Reg. 6) for 10 minutes.

Chop leeks. Peel and thinly slice tomatoes. Thinly slice potatoes.

Arrange half the leeks, tomatoes and potatoes in the half-baked flan case. Cover with half the cheese and fill the case with the remaining vegetables, arranged in an attractive pattern. Sprinkle with salt and pepper, pour over the cream, and cover the surface with the remaining grated cheese. Bake in a hot oven (425°F., Reg. 6) for a further 25–30 minutes until golden brown.

Serve hot, cut into slices.

Note: The dish can also be served cold and makes a good 'extra' to take on picnics.

Pan Haggerty

This dish, I believe, has its origins in the North of England and was a popular 'stretching' recipe during the slump. The original dish (which I was given by a lady from the North) was made with onions, potatoes and cheese only, but I often add chopped bacon or ham to make a supper dish.

SERVES 4.   Cooking time: 30–40 minutes.

1½ *lb. cooked potatoes*   3 oz. dripping
1 large onion   salt and pepper
4–6 oz. grated cheese

Cut potatoes into thin slices. Peel and finely chop onion. Heat half the dripping in a large frying pan, add onion, and cook until soft, about 3 minutes. Remove and drain onions, add remaining dripping to the pan, and arrange layers of potato, onion, and cheese in the pan, seasoning each layer with plenty of salt and pepper. Cover and cook for 15–20 minutes. Remove lid and brown under a hot grill.

Pan Haggerty can either be turned out or served straight from the pan.

Variations:

1. Cook 2 oz. finely chopped bacon with the onions.
2. Add a layer of chopped chicken, ham or meat when cooking the Pan Haggerty.

Spring Vegetable Loaf

If you have only a few of these cooked vegetables in your refrigerator or larder the rest can easily be cooked up in a few minutes. The proportions of the vegetables can be increased or decreased if necessary; they are only a guide.

SERVES 4.   Cooking time: about 25 minutes.

½ lb. cooked young carrots	1½ tablespoons finely chopped
1 small lettuce	parsley
½ lb. cooked potatoes (preferably new)	½ oz. flour
	2 oz. grated cheese
½ lb. cooked cauliflower	1½ gills milk
small tin petits pois (or ¼ lb. cooked small peas)	1 egg, beaten
	small milk loaf
small packet frozen beans	salt and pepper
1½ oz. butter	

Dice carrots. Shred lettuce. Dice potatoes. Break cauliflower into sprigs. Strain peas and cook beans.

Melt butter, add all the vegetables, and heat over a moderate flame for 5 minutes. Add parsley and mix well. Sprinkle with flour and gradually add the milk, stirring gently but constantly until the sauce is thick and smooth. Stir in 1 oz. grated cheese and the well-beaten egg. Season with salt and pepper.

Cut a neat slice off the top of the loaf. Scoop out all the soft bread from inside and fill with the vegetable mixture. Sprinkle with grated cheese and bake in a hot oven (425°F., Reg. 7) for 15 minutes.

Vichy Carrots

A French way of serving carrots. Traditionally it is made with raw baby carrots, but I find it a good way to use up any leftover carrots. Slice old ones very finely, leave small new carrots whole.

SERVES 4.   Cooking time: about 10 minutes.

1–1½ *lb. cooked carrots*
2 oz. butter
1 clove garlic, crushed or put through a garlic press
1 tablespoon finely chopped parsley
salt and pepper

Melt the butter in a saucepan, add the garlic, and cook for 2 minutes over a low heat. Add the carrots and heat them gently, shaking the pan, until they absorb the butter and take on a glazed appearance. Sprinkle over the parsley and season with a little salt and pepper.

Variation: Vichy Carrots and Potatoes

Use a mixture of cooked carrots and potatoes. Dice the vegetables and cook in the same way as Vichy Carrots.

Bubble and Squeak

A really traditional 'leftover' dish.

During the Depression, bubble and squeak frequently made an appearance as a main dish. Diced or thinly sliced boiled beef was mixed with mashed potatoes and cooked shredded cabbage, the lot was fried together and it was served as a meal on its own with a generous sprinkling of vinegar.

The name of this dish comes from the noise made by cabbage as it is fried.

Cooking time: about 15 minutes.

equal quantities of *cooked cabbage and mashed potatoes*
salt and pepper
butter for frying

Shred the cabbage and mix with the mashed potato, season if necessary.

Heat the butter in a heavy frying pan, add the cabbage

and potato, press down to flatten and cook over a high heat until the bottom is well browned, lower the heat, and continue to cook until hot through.

Invert the bubble and squeak on to a hot serving dish so that the browned side is upwards.

To serve as a main dish

Add chopped leftover meat and some finely chopped onion to the cabbage and potato and cook in the same way.

Colcannon

This is the Irish version of bubble and squeak.

SERVES 4.   Cooking time: 25–30 minutes.

1 *lb. cooked potatoes*	8 *oz. cooked cabbage*
2 *oz.* bacon fat	salt and pepper
1 onion	

Mash potatoes. Peel and finely chop onion. Shred cabbage. Heat bacon fat, add onion, and cook over a moderate heat, without browning, for 3 minutes. Add potatoes and cabbage, mix well, and season with salt and pepper. Turn into a lightly greased pudding basin and cook in a moderately hot oven for 20 minutes. Turn out on to a serving dish.

Cheese and Vegetable Quiche

Leftover cooked peas, carrots, beans, and cauliflower can all be used in this quiche recipe, either by themselves or in a combination. It is a versatile pie that can be served hot or cold, as a starter or as a main dish. It is also good for a picnic.

SERVES 6.   Cooking time: about 35 minutes.

Pastry

8 oz. plain flour	pinch salt
4 oz. butter	3–4 tablespoons iced water

Filling

½ oz. butter	¾ pint milk
2 oz. bacon	3 eggs
1 small onion	2 oz. grated cheese
6 oz. *cooked vegetables*	salt and pepper

Make pastry by rubbing the butter into the flour and salt and mixing to a dough with iced water. Leave pastry in a cold place before rolling it out thinly. Line a flan tin, prick the bottom with a fork and bake 'blind' in a hot oven (425°F., Reg. 6) for 10 minutes.

Remove rinds and chop bacon. Peel and finely chop onion and chop vegetables. Fry bacon and onion in the butter for about 3 minutes until onion is soft and transparent.

Beat eggs with the milk, mix in cheese, and season with salt and pepper. Add bacon, onion, and vegetables to the custard and pour into the half-baked case.

Bake the quiche in a hot oven (425°F., Reg. 6) for about 15–20 minutes until custard is set.

Green Omelette

SERVES 4.　Cooking time: about 20 minutes.

1½ oz. butter	6 eggs, lightly beaten
2 onions, chopped	salt and pepper
1 lb. *cooked spinach, cabbage, broccoli, or spring greens*	

Melt the butter, add chopped onion, and cook over a moderately high heat in a large pan until the onions are golden brown.

Add the green vegetables, lower the heat, and cook for a

further 2 minutes. Pour over the lightly beaten eggs, season with salt and pepper, and cook over a slow heat until the omelette is well browned on the bottom and just set through, about 10 minutes.

Turn on to a hot dish and serve at once.

Russian Salad

A useful way of using up a variety of leftover cooked vegetables. Three varieties at least should be used. Peas are essential, and if you have none of these left over then cook a ¼ lb. bag of frozen ones. Cooked carrots, potatoes, turnips, celery, swede, beans, and beetroot can all be incorporated in the salad.

SERVES 4.   No cooking.

approximately 1 *lb. cooked*   1 tablespoon thin cream
   mixed vegetables   salt and pepper
½ pint mayonnaise (see page 265)

Cut the vegetables into small dice and mix them together.

Add the cream to the mayonnaise, season well, and add to the vegetables. Stir gently with a wooden spoon to make sure the vegetables are all well coated with the mayonnaise. Chill before serving.

Cooked Vegetables in a Vinaigrette Dressing

If you have a large enough quantity use French beans, small broad beans (or larger beans with the skins removed), cauliflower or leeks by themselves for this recipe. Other cooked vegetables should be mixed together with three or more varieties being used: e.g. cooked carrots, peas and runner beans.

SERVES 4.   No cooking.

approximately 1 *lb. cooked*
  vegetables
1 teaspoon mustard
3 tablespoons olive oil
1 tablespoon white wine
  vinegar

salt and pepper
1 tablespoon finely chopped
  parsley

For a plain salad: cut French beans into two-inch lengths;
remove the skins from large broad beans; break cauliflower
into small sprigs; cut leeks into thin slices or leave whole if
they are young.

For a mixed salad: cut the vegetables into small dice. Combine
the mustard, olive oil and vinegar, mix well, season with salt
and pepper, and mix in the finely chopped parsley. Pour the
dressing over the vegetables and mix gently with a wooden
spoon.

Chill before serving.

Vegetables in a Jellied Mould

This is a summer dish, perfect to serve with cold meats or
salads. Use your imagination to make a pretty and colourful
mould by layering different kinds of leftover cooked vegetables.

The aspic can be made from any clarified meat, poultry, or
vegetable stock. A little sherry or white wine added to the
stock makes a world of difference to the taste. For clarifying
stock see page 45.

SERVES 4.   No. cooking.

  1½ pints clarified vegetable, meat or poultry stock
  4 tablespoons sherry or white wine
  2 tablespoons powdered gelatine
  1½ *lb. cooked mixed vegetables (carrots, beans, peas, cauliflower or*
    asparagus, etc.)
  tomatoes for garnishing

Dissolve the gelatine in clarified stock, add wine, and leave until almost set. Cut any large vegetables into thin slices or small dice.

Pour a thin layer of the aspic jelly into a round mould; swirl it round until it coats the sides, and refrigerate until well set. Fill the mould with vegetables and pour over remaining aspic until the vegetables are covered. Leave in a cold place until set. Turn out and garnish with sliced or quartered tomatoes.

Note: The mould can be served with a mayonnaise as a first course.

Spinach Salad

SERVES 4. No cooking.

8–10 *oz. cooked leaf spinach*
3 tablespoons olive oil
1 tablespoon white wine vinegar
salt and freshly ground black pepper
2 tablespoons pine nuts or sesame seeds

Make sure that the spinach is well drained. Roast pine nuts or sesame seeds in a hot oven for a few seconds until golden brown, leave to cool. Combine olive oil and vinegar, season with salt and pepper, and mix well. Toss spinach in the dressing, sprinkle the pine nuts or sesame seeds over and chill before serving.

Potatoes

The potato is the most readily available vegetable eaten by the average British household, the most popular and the most inexpensive. It is also about the most difficult to judge when it comes to quantities. Luckily this is no problem. Potatoes lend themselves well to being recooked and served in a different guise, so it is often worth cooking double quantities in order to keep a store of cold potatoes on hand. Small quantities of cooked potatoes can be stretched to serve again as a vegetable by being combined with other ingredients, or they can be incorporated into soups or laid in a thin layer to finish off a stew or casserole. Many of the most delicious potato recipes demand that the vegetable should be cooked before work on the dish can begin.

Using Leftover Baked Potatoes

Baked potatoes cooked in their skins are so delicious that one tends to overestimate the quantity required. I have had several opportunities to experiment with re-heating them.

For each serving:

1 *potato baked in its jacket*	2 teaspoons grated cheese
3 teaspoons melted butter	salt and pepper
2 teaspoons milk or cream	cayenne pepper

Cut off and discard a slice from the top of the potato. Carefully scoop out the inside taking care not to damage the skin.

Mash the potato with 2 teaspoons melted butter, the milk or cream and the cheese; season with salt and pepper, and beat until smooth. Fill the potato skin with this mixture and top with a fine sprinkling of cayenne.

Brush the skin with 1 teaspoon melted butter and dust with salt. Bake the stuffed potato in a hot oven for about 10–15 minutes. The skin should be crisp and the inside piping hot. Serve at once.

Variations:

Mix the potato with:

    1. 2 teaspoons grated onion in place of the cheese.

    2. Add 1 teaspoon chopped parsley to the basic recipe.

3. Add a little chopped ham to the basic recipe.

4. Add some finely chopped bacon, crisply fried, to the basic recipe.

5. Add $\frac{1}{2}$ clove crushed garlic and 2 teaspoons finely chopped chives to the basic recipe.

6. Substitute sour cream for the milk in the recipe.

Leftover Roast Potatoes

Medium-sized roast potatoes which are not too brown can be cut into thin slices and fried in butter until crisp. Season generously and dust with a little finely-chopped parsley before serving.

Mashed Potatoes as a Topping for Stews and Casseroles

Everyone knows the essential part which mashed potatoes play in the making of a shepherd's or cottage pie. Mashed potatoes can also be used to top stews or casseroles.

Beat the mashed potatoes with a little melted butter and a spoonful of milk or cream; check the seasoning.

Remove any excess liquid from the top of a stew or casserole, spread the potatoes over the surface, brush with a little melted butter, and bake in a hot oven until golden brown.

Crisp Potato Topping for Casseroles and Stews

Cooking time: 10–15 minutes.

Boiled potatoes
Melted butter
salt and pepper

Remove all excess liquid from the surface of a cooked casserole or stew.

Cut the potatoes into thin slices and place them in a layer over the top of the casserole; sprinkle with salt and pepper, and brush with a little melted butter. Return the casserole to a hot oven and bake for 10–15 minutes until the potatoes are golden brown and crisp.

Potato Gnocchi

Gnocchi are one of the many forms of pasta so traditional to Italian cookery. The dough is formed into a long sausage shape, cut into pieces about three quarters of an inch to one inch long, and poached in salted water. The dough is most often made from a mixture of cheese and flour but the potato-base type is also popular and makes an unusual way to serve leftover boiled potatoes.

The gnocchi can be served as a main dish with a meat sauce or as a side dish with melted butter and a sprinkling of grated cheese.

SERVES 4.   Cooking time: 5 minutes.

1 *lb. boiled potatoes*	½ oz. butter
¼ lb. sifted flour	salt and pepper
1 beaten egg	

Rub the potatoes through a fine sieve, mix them into a smooth dough with the flour and beaten egg, season well with salt and pepper.

Roll out the dough into a long sausage shape on a floured board and cut into pieces about one inch long.

Drop the gnocchi into a large pan of boiling salted water and poach for 3–5 minutes until they rise and float on the surface. Lift them out carefully with a perforated spoon and place

them on a warm serving dish; dot with butter and sprinkle
with grated cheese.

Potato Croquettes*

One of the most attractive ways to use up leftover mashed
potatoes. The basic recipe can be used as a model for many
variations on the croquette theme.

SERVES 4. Cooking time: 5–8 minutes for each batch of
croquettes.

1 *lb. mashed potatoes*	dried breadcrumbs
1 beaten egg	flour
salt and pepper	fat for deep frying

Mix the potatoes to a smooth firm consistency with half
the beaten egg; season generously with salt and pepper. With
well-floured hands shape the potato mixture into thick sausage
shapes or round balls, coat each one in beaten egg, and then
roll in breadcrumbs.

Fry the croquettes in very hot deep fat until golden brown.
Drain them on kitchen paper, and arrange on a pre-heated
serving dish.

If you dislike frying in deep fat, the mixture can be shaped
into flat cakes and fried in shallow fat.

Variations:
  1. Add 2 oz. grated cheese to the potato mixture.
  2. Add 1 tablespoon grated onion to the potato mixture.
  3. Add 1 tablespoon finely chopped parsley to the potato
  mixture.
  4. Add 2 oz. minced ham to the potato mixture.

Creole Potatoes

SERVES 4.   Cooking time: 15–20 minutes.

1 *lb. cooked potatoes*	1 teaspoon mustard
1 large onion	1 teaspoon Worcester
1 oz. butter or 1 tablespoon oil	sauce
3 tablespoons tomato ketchup	salt and pepper

Cut the potatoes into thick slices. Finely chop the onion. Combine and mix the tomato ketchup, Worcester sauce and mustard, season with a little salt and pepper.

Heat the butter in a frying pan, add the finely chopped onion, and cook for 3–5 minutes until the onion is soft. Add the potatoes and continue cooking over a medium to high heat until the potatoes and onion are lightly browned. Pour the sauce over and heat through.

This makes a good partner to fried sausages or hamburgers.

Farmhouse Potato Supper

SERVES 4.   Cooking time: 25–35 minutes.

This is a hearty supper dish, complete in itself.

1 *lb. boiled potatoes*	salt and pepper
½ lb. streaky bacon	½ oz. butter
1 onion	4 eggs
1 small green pepper	4 oz. grated cheddar cheese

Dice the potatoes, chop the bacon, and finely chop the onion and pepper.

Fry the bacon, without fat, over a low heat for 2–3 minutes, remove from the pan, and add the potatoes, onion, and green pepper to the fat. Cook over a medium heat until the potatoes are lightly browned. Season with salt and pepper, mix with the bacon, and arrange in a shallow fireproof dish.

Fry the eggs in the butter and arrange them on top of the potato mixture. Sprinkle over the grated cheese and brown quickly under a hot grill. Serve at once.

A layer of thinly-sliced tomatoes can be placed under the fried eggs.

Indian Sauté Potatoes

SERVES 4.   Cooking time: 10–15 minutes.

    1 *lb. boiled potatoes*
    1 heaped tablespoon curry powder
    1 oz. butter

Cut the potatoes into thickish slices, sprinkle each slice with curry powder, and fry them in butter, over a medium to high heat, until they are crisp and browned.

Sauté Potatoes Cooked in the Oven

SERVES 4.   Cooking time: 20–25 minutes.

    1 *lb. boiled potatoes*
    salt and pepper
    ¼ pint olive oil

Dice the potatoes and season them well with salt and pepper.

Pour the olive oil into a fireproof dish and heat in a hot oven (450°F., Reg.7) for 5 minutes. Add the potatoes to the oil, return to the oven, and cook for 15–20 minutes until the potatoes are golden brown. Drain off all the oil and transfer the potatoes to a clean serving dish.

A clove of garlic, finely chopped or put through a garlic press, can be added to the potatoes.

Rich Potato Bake

SERVES 4.   Cooking time: 20–25 minutes.

1 *lb. boiled potatoes*	2 tablespoons milk
4 oz. bacon	salt and pepper
1 onion	2 oz. grated cheese
1 tin condensed mushroom soup	1 oz. dried breadcrumbs

Cut the potatoes into thin slices. Chop the bacon and fry it, without fat, over a medium to high heat until crisp. Finely chop the onion and cook until soft in the bacon fat. Mix the soup with the milk and season with salt and pepper.

Arrange half the potatoes in a greased fireproof dish, cover with bacon and onions and the remainder of the potatoes. Pour the soup mixture over and top with mixed cheese and breadcrumbs. Bake in a hot oven (450°F., Reg. 7) for 15–20 minutes until the top is golden brown.

Pommes Annette

This dish is usually made with raw potatoes, but it can also be made with cooked boiled potatoes and is a delicious accompaniment to any roast meat or stew, or to cold meats.

SERVES 4.   Cooking time: 15–20 minutes.

1 *lb. boiled potatoes*	2 tablespoons cream
1 medium onion	salt and pepper
1½ oz. butter	

Cut the potatoes into thin slices. Peel and finely chop the onion and fry until soft but not brown in ½ oz. butter.

Arrange a layer of potatoes in a buttered baking dish, cover with a little of the softened onions, sprinkle with salt and pepper, and dot with a little butter. Continue the layers of potato and onion, finishing with one of potatoes. Pour over the cream and bake in a moderately hot oven for 15–20 minutes until the top is golden brown.

Potato Pancakes*

Recipes for potato cakes vary from county to county and from country to country. This is one for a thin pancake-like variety, which is ideal to serve for a hearty breakfast or for high tea.

SERVES 4.   Cooking time: 2–3 minutes for each pancake.

½ *lb. boiled potatoes*	1 pint milk
2 eggs	salt and pepper
6 oz. flour	butter or dripping to fry in

Press the potatoes through a coarse sieve. Beat the eggs with the flour and milk, mix in the potatoes, and season with salt and pepper.

Melt a little butter or dripping in a frying pan, put in a generous spoonful of the potato batter, and swirl it round the pan to make a thin cake. Cook for about one minute before turning over and cooking on the other side. Slide the cooked cakes on to a warm serving dish and keep hot whilst the remainder are cooked.

Large Fried Potato Cake

Use an omelette pan or a medium-sized non-stick frying pan.

SERVES 4.   Cooking time: 10 minutes.

1 *lb. boiled potatoes*	1½ gills milk or thin cream
1 onion	salt and pepper
2 tablespoons flour	1½ oz. butter

Cut the potatoes into small dice. Peel and finely chop the onion.

Mix the potatoes and onion with the flour and milk; season with salt and pepper.

Heat the butter, add the potato mixture, press it down to form a flat cake, and fry over a medium to high heat for five minutes. Slide the cake on to a plate, invert, and return to the pan and fry on the other side for a further three minutes. Both sides should be golden brown.

Slide the cake on to a serving dish and serve with fried sausages, eggs or with cold meat.

Large Fried Cheesy Potato Cake

Unlike the previous recipe this potato cake cannot be turned over, as the grated cheese melts during the cooking process and binds the potatoes into a form of flat cake.

SERVES 4.   Cooking time: 10 minutes.

1 *lb. boiled potatoes*	salt and pepper
6 oz. grated cheddar cheese	1 oz. butter

Cut the potatoes into small dice or thin matchstick strips. Combine the potatoes with the cheese and season with salt and pepper.

Melt the butter in an omelette pan or in a non-stick frying pan, add the potato mixture, and cook over medium to high heat for about ten minutes.

Slide the cake on to a serving dish.

The cake can be sprinkled with finely chopped parsley, paprika, or cayenne pepper.

Fried Cooked Potatoes with Cheese and Onion

SERVES 4.   Cooking time: 10–15 minutes.

1 *lb. boiled potatoes*   salt and pepper
1 onion   2 oz. butter
5 oz. cheddar cheese

Cut the potatoes into thin slices. Peel and thinly slice the onion. Cut the cheese into small dice.

Melt the butter in a frying pan, add the potatoes and onion, and cook over a medium to hot heat until the potatoes are lightly brown. Add the diced cheese, season with salt and pepper, and continue to cook for a further 3–5 minutes or until the cheese has almost melted.

Mashed Potato Balls★

mashed potato
beaten egg
salt and pepper

Season beaten egg with salt and pepper. Form mashed potato into small balls, brush with beaten egg, and bake in a moderately hot oven (400°F., Reg. 5) until golden brown.

West Indian Mashed Potatoes

Mixing orange peel with potatoes may sound a rather strange idea, but the subtle flavour of these mashed potatoes makes them a delicious accompaniment to roast poultry or game.

SERVES 4.   Cooking time: 15–20 minutes.

1½ lb. cooked mashed potatoes	grated rind of 1 orange
1 oz. butter	salt and pepper
1 medium onion	

Peel and finely chop the onion. Melt ½ oz. butter and fry the onion until soft but not brown, about 5 minutes. Mix potatoes with the onion and orange peel, and season with salt and pepper. Melt remaining ½ oz. butter.

Pile potatoes in a fireproof serving dish, brush with melted butter, and bake in a hot oven (425°F., Reg. 6) for 10–15 minutes until golden brown and hot through.

Potato Omelette

Cooking time: about 5 minutes.

For each serving:

1 medium boiled potato	1 oz. butter
2 eggs	salt and pepper

Cut the potato into small dice. Beat the eggs and season with salt and pepper.

Melt the butter in an omelette pan, add the potatoes, and cook over a medium heat until they are lightly browned. Pour the eggs over the potatoes, and as the mixture begins to set prick it with a fork to enable uncooked egg from the top to seep through. Slide the omelette on to a warm plate just before the top is completely set.

Serve with a salad or with green vegetables.

Variations:

1. Add 1 small onion, finely chopped, to the potatoes before frying.

2. Add 1 tablespoon grated cheese to the beaten eggs.

Rosti

This is a vegetable dish which I always associate with Switzerland, snow and ski-ing. It is an ideal way to use up leftover potatoes, and can be easily stretched into a main course.

SERVES 4. Cooking time: 10 minutes.

2 fat cloves garlic	14–16 oz. cooked potatoes, sliced
3 tablespoons olive oil	salt and pepper

Peel and finely chop the garlic (or crush through a garlic press). Heat the oil until just smoking in a large shallow pan, add the garlic, and cook for half a minute. Add the sliced potatoes, season generously with salt and pepper, and cook over a high heat until the potatoes are golden brown. If the potatoes stick together, separate them gently with a spatula.

Serve the potatoes with any meat dish, cold ham and salad, or poultry.

To serve the potatoes as a main course add

4 eggs	1 tablespoon finely chopped
4 oz. bacon	parsley

Make the rosti as above. Remove the rind, finely chop the bacon; and fry it until crisp in a second pan. Combine the bacon with the potatoes and the chopped parsley. Arrange in a pre-heated shallow serving dish and top with four fried eggs.

Hot Potato Salad

A variation on the ordinary potato salad and a good one to serve with cold meat on a winter day. It also goes well with fried eggs, sausages, and all fish dishes.

SERVES 4.   Cooking time: 5 minutes.

1 *lb. cooked potatoes*	4 tablespoons chutney
4 tablespoons bottled salad	1 tablespoon vinegar
cream	salt and pepper

Chop the potatoes into small even dice, put them in a saucepan and add the remaining ingredients; season with salt and pepper. Heat gently over a low flame, stirring with a wooden spoon until the mixture is hot through.

Pommes Duchesse★

Potatoes made in this way are usually piped in small mounds on to a greased baking sheet and baked until crisp in a hot oven. They can also be piped in the shape of round, oval or square cases, baked, and filled with vegetables, or they may be served as an hors d'oeuvre, with meat or fish in a cream sauce.

1 *lb. mashed potatoes*	2 egg yolks or 1 egg
1 oz. butter	salt and pepper

Beat the egg yolks, melt the butter. Add the butter and egg to the potatoes and cook over a low heat, beating constantly until thick and smooth. Bring to the boil, remove from the heat, taste for seasoning, and continue beating whilst the mixture cools.

Pipe in mounds on a greased baking sheet and bake in a hot oven until brown.

Pommes Duchesse Cases

Pommes duchesse as above.

Form flat round, square or oval bases on a greased baking sheet. Pipe the rest of the potato to form the sides of the cases.

Bake the cases in a hot oven for 10–15 minutes until golden brown.

Janson's Temptation

Janson's Temptation is a Swedish dish traditionally made with raw potatoes, but leftover potatoes are equally successful. It is one of my favourite dishes because it is both simple and economical, and the result is delicious. I serve it either as an hors d'oeuvre or as a supper dish.

A word of warning: The cooked potatoes need to be firm and whole.

SERVES 4. Cooking time: 20–25 minutes.

1 *lb. boiled potatoes*	2 oz. butter
2 large onions	1 gill cream
1 tin anchovy fillets	pepper

Cut the potatoes into thin strips the size of a matchstick. Peel and thinly slice the onions (break the slices into rings), drain the anchovy fillets and reserve the liquid.

Melt ½ oz. butter and fry the onions over a medium heat until they are soft and transparent.

Arrange half the potatoes in a greased baking dish, cover with the anchovy fillets and the softened onions, and season with pepper. Do not use any salt as the anchovies are salty enough. Add the remaining potatoes, dot with 1½ oz. butter, pour over half the cream and the anchovy oil, season with a little more pepper, and bake in a hot oven (420°F., Reg. 7) for 10 minutes. Pour over the remaining cream and continue baking for a further 10–15 minutes until the top of the dish is golden brown.

Potato and Corned Beef Hash

SERVES 4.   Cooking time: 10 minutes.

½ lb. mashed potatoes
medium tin corned beef
1 medium onion

2 oz. dripping
salt and pepper
1 teaspoon Worcester sauce

Cut the corned beef into small dice. Peel and finely chop the onion. Mix together potatoes, corned beef and onion, season with salt and pepper, and add Worcester sauce.

Heat the dripping, add the hash, pressing it well down into the pan with the back of a spoon. Cook over a medium heat until the mixture is well browned on the underneath and hot through.

Invert the hash on to a warm serving dish, brown side up. The top can be dusted with finely chopped parsley. Serve as a lunch or supper dish with fried eggs.

Potato Salads

The perfectionist will say that all potato salads should be made from potatoes cooked in their skins, peeled whilst they are still hot, and dressed at once with a vinaigrette sauce or mayonnaise. I agree that a potato salad in this way is marginally more delicious than one made with precooked cold vegetables. However, I can think of few better ways of using up cold potatoes, especially if they are new, firm and waxy.

Potato Salad with Mayonnaise

SERVES 4.   No cooking.

1 lb. boiled potatoes
1 tablespoon finely chopped

onion, chives or spring onion

½ tablespoon finely chopped parsley	2 teaspoons vinegar salt and pepper
½ pint mayonnaise	

Chop the potatoes into small dice. Mix potatoes, onions, and parsley together.

Blend the mayonnaise with the vinegar and season quite strongly with salt and pepper. Lightly mix the mayonnaise with the potatoes and onions.

Chill before serving.

Garlic lovers should add to the mayonnaise a clove of garlic finely crushed or put through a garlic press.

Insalata di Patate   (See also p. 42)

An Italian version of the potato salad. It is fairly rich and so goes admirably with the plain cold meats.

SERVES 4.   No cooking.

1 *lb. boiled potatoes*	3 tablespoons olive oil
4 anchovy fillets	1½ tablespoons white wine
4 black olives	vinegar
1 small onion	salt and pepper

Cut the potatoes into small dice. Drain and finely chop the anchovies. Stone and chop the olives. Peel and finely chop the onion.

Combine and mix the olive oil, vinegar and seasoning. Toss all the ingredients lightly together, making sure that the potatoes have a good coating of the dressing.

Chill before serving.

A clove of garlic, crushed or put through a garlic press, and some fresh or dried salad herbs can be added to the dressing.

This salad can also be served as an hors d'oeuvre.

Potato Salad with a Vinaigrette Dressing

SERVES 4.   No cooking.

1 lb. boiled potatoes
1 tablespoon finely chopped
  onion, spring onion, or chives
3 tablespoons olive oil
1½ tablespoons white wine
  vinegar

1 teaspoon dry mustard
salt and pepper
½ tablespoon finely chopped
  parsley

Cut the potatoes into small dice and mix with the onion.

Combine the olive oil, vinegar, and mustard, mix well, and season generously with salt and pepper. Add the chopped parsley and leave to stand for a few minutes.

Pour the dressing over the potatoes and mix gently with a wooden spoon.

Chill well before serving.

A clove of garlic crushed or put through a garlic press may be added to the dressing with the parsley.

Fresh or dried chopped herbs can be added to this salad. Use tarragon, chervil, summer savory, basil, or marjoram.

Curried Potato and Apple Salad

This goes well with cold chicken.

SERVES 4.   No cooking.

½ lb. boiled potatoes
2 crisp eating apples
1 oz. sultanas
½ pint mayonnaise

2 teaspoons curry powder
2 teaspoons lemon juice
1 tablespoon cream
salt and pepper

Cut the potatoes into small dice. Peel, core, and dice the apple. Combine the potatoes, apples and sultanas.

Soften the curry powder over a low heat in the lemon juice, cool and add to the mayonnaise, mix in the cream, and season with salt and pepper.

Gently mix the curry mayonnaise into the potato and apples. Chill before serving.

Eggs, Cheese and Dairy Foods

Eggs

Eggs are still one of the cheapest and most nutritious products on the market. One egg, for example, has a high percentage of vitamins, calcium and iron, and the equivalent protein of 1 oz. lean meat. Yolks, whites and hard-boiled eggs all make a great contribution to the art of producing attractive and flavoursome leftover dishes and have many valuable uses in their own right. Luckily they keep well and can be stored in a refrigerator for 3–4 days or for a few months in the deep freeze (see chapter on 'Storing Leftovers', page 13).

Don't be restricted by those two classic uses for egg whites and yolks, meringues and mayonnaise; they have countless other uses.

Egg Whites

Store egg whites singly or in pairs as one or two are often all that are needed for a specific recipe. If larger numbers of whites are kept together it may be useful to know that each white will measure approximately 1 fluid ounce.

Use unwhipped whites for glazing pastry; for making cake or biscuit icing and as a topping, with a little sugar and nuts, for biscuits.

Whip egg whites (they will greatly increase in bulk if this is done in a copper bowl) and use them for making meringues, meringue topping, and meringue cases; for adding to batters for a lighter consistency; to make sorbets; for adding to soufflés, fruit purées, and mousses; for making light, fluffy jellies and for increasing the bulk of whipped cream.

Recipes using egg whites:

Egg Yolks

Egg yolks add a rich creaminess to many dishes, and a single yolk beaten into cream soups, white sauces, and mashed potatoes can make the difference between a plain and a luxurious dish.

A yolk beaten with a little milk makes a good glaze for sweet and savoury pastry toppings to pies.

The yolks can be poached until hard in a little salted water and then rubbed through a sieve to make an attractive and colourful garnish for cold dishes and soups.

Two yolks, beaten with sugar and added to hot milk, make a good drink for invalids.

Recipes using egg yolks:

Hardboiled Eggs

Hardboiled eggs crop up most often in the summer when one is enjoying picnics and salad dishes. Any eggs left over can be chopped and used to stretch meat, poultry, and fish dishes in a cream sauce. Finely chopped hardboiled eggs can be added to many sandwich fillings, or the whites and yolks can be separated, the whites chopped and the yolks rubbed through a fine sieve to use as a garnish for soups or cold dishes.

Cheese

The heel end of cheeses, when they have gone dry and discoloured, seem to hang around the larder for ever. If you present them amongst a selection of other, fresher, cheeses, they are always ignored and all too often the temptation is to throw them away. Don't! Small pieces of cheese, however dried up or unappetizing to look at, can make great additions to a number of dishes, for although their first bloom has gone their flavour is usually as good as ever.

Grate all hard cheeses, store them in a screw top jar in a dry place, and keep until required. A large piece of Cheddar, Cheshire, or similar cheeses, by the way, will keep fresh far longer if the cut edge is smeared with a thin film of butter each time the cheese is wrapped and put in the refrigerator or larder.

Crumble the remains of blue cheeses, store them in a screw top jar in a cool dry place, and keep until required.

Wrap the remains of soft cheeses such as Brie and Camembert in Saranwrap or tinfoil and keep them in a refrigerator until required.

Closely wrap remains of all cream cheeses in tinfoil and keep in a refrigerator until required.

Hard Cheeses

Add grated cheese to soups, sauces, and soufflés.

Garnish soups with small cubes of hard cheese just before serving.

Finely-grated hard cheese can be added to pastry for a savoury crust and also to a vinaigrette dressing.

Blue Cheeses

A little crumbled blue cheese blended into a vinaigrette dressing will give a very good fillip to any green salad. Small pieces of blue cheese are also very good as an actual ingredient of a green or mixed salad.

Soft Cheeses

Cut the remains of Brie or Camembert into tiny cubes and toss them with a salad.

Cream Cheeses

The remains of cream cheese, softened with a little cream and well flavoured with a few drops of tomato ketchup, Worcester sauce, and some chopped chives, etc., make a good filling for sandwiches or a spread for salted biscuits. Add a little crushed garlic or grated onion and you have a delicious dip for potato crisps, strips of raw carrot, or sprigs of raw cauliflower.

Cheese and Tomato Toast

A good way to use up the tag end of a piece of Cheddar or Cheshire cheese. The toast can be cut into small squares to serve with soup or can be left whole as a snack. I find these make a popular supper dish for younger children.

SERVES 4. Cooking time: about 5 minutes.

4 slices bread
butter
2 large tomatoes

2 oz. *grated cheese*
a pinch of paprika or cayenne
(optional)

Remove crusts from the bread and spread slices generously with softened butter. Cover each slice with thin slices of tomato, sprinkle over the cheese, and dust with paprika or cayenne pepper.

Bake in a hot oven (450°F., Reg. 7) for about 5 minutes until the cheese has melted and is golden brown.

Note: Omit the paprika or cayenne if the toast is for children.

For a sharper flavour a thin layer of mustard can be spread over the butter.

Blue Cheese Dreams

Crisp squares of toasted blue cheese (I use the heel of a piece of stilton) make a good partner to many bland soups. They can also be served as a snack or as a savoury at the end of a meal.

For 4 slices toast. Cooking time: 5 minutes.

2 oz. *grated blue cheese* (it doesn't matter how stale)
½ oz. butter
4 slices bread

Mash together the blue cheese and butter until smooth. Remove crusts from the bread, spread slices with the cheese mixture, and cut into small squares. Bake in a hot oven (425°F., Reg. 6) for about five minutes until golden and bubbling.

Variations:

1. For serving with soup, sprinkle a little paprika or cayenne over the top before baking.

2. As a more substantial snack, cover the bread with a layer of thinly sliced tomatoes before spreading with cheese.

3. For a savoury, add a few drops of Worcester sauce to the cheese mixture.

Milk and Cream

Using up extra milk is no real problem. A pint can make a milk pudding. Half a pint can be used for a white sauce. The odd $\frac{1}{4}$ pint added to enrich vegetable soups.

Recipes using $\frac{1}{2}$ pint of milk or more, can be found in the recipe section under the following headings: –

Sauces, see pages 264–79
Soups, see pages 44–65
Puddings, see pages 241–63

Soured Cream

Cream, whether thick or thin, tends to go off quickly. When you find the remains of a carton of fresh cream lurking in the back of the refrigerator don't turn up your nose with horror and throw it away. Even sour cream has its uses, and can be used to delight both your family and your dinner guests. A $\frac{1}{4}$ pint sour cream is the main ingredient of one of the best hot scone recipes. Besides being popular for tea these scones can also be made in a mini-size and are delicious with soups instead of toast.

A tablespoon or two of sour cream can also be used to thicken stews, rich cream and cheese dishes, or well-flavoured soups.

Scones Made with Sour Milk or Cream

Makes about 12 scones.

Cooking time: 7–10 minutes.

8 oz. plain flour
½ teaspoon salt
1 level teaspoon cream of tartar
1 level teaspoon bicarbonate of
 soda

2 oz. butter
¼ *pint sour milk or sour cream*

Sift flour with salt, cream of tartar, and bicarbonate of soda into a bowl. Mix in the butter using two knives to cut it into small pieces, and rub with fingertips until the mixture resembles coarse breadcrumbs. Blend in the sour milk or cream and knead to a smooth dough.

Roll out the dough to a ¼-inch thickness on a floured board, cut into 1½–2-inch circles with a pastry cutter, brush with milk, and bake in a very hot oven (450°F., Reg. 7) for 7–10 minutes.

Bread, Pastry, Rice and Pasta

Breadcrumbs

White crumbs can be kept in a clean and dry screw-top jar for about four or five days. Golden brown crumbs for coatings and toppings, etc., can be kept in a screw-top jar for two to three weeks.

White Breadcrumbs

Cut the crusts off slices of stale white bread. Grate the bread through a fine grater. Spread crumbs on a flat plate to dry for about half an hour, then store in a jar with a well-fitting screw top.

Use for stuffings, sauces, and puddings.

Brown Breadcrumbs

Remove crusts from slices of stale bread. Put bread in the bottom of a cool oven (250°F., Reg. $\frac{1}{2}$) for 2–3 hours until dry and golden brown. Cool and crush finely on a wooden board by rolling with a rolling pin. Store in a jar with a well fitting screw top.

Use for breadcrumbing, coating, and toppings, etc.

Fried Breadcrumbs

These go well with pheasant or other game and can also be served with roast chicken.

4 oz. breadcrumbs
$\frac{1}{2}$ oz. butter, or bacon fat

Heat butter or fat and fry breadcrumbs over a gentle heat until all the fat has been absorbed and the crumbs are crisp.

Tomato, Cheese, and Breadcrumb Pie

SERVES 4.   Cooking time: 30 minutes.

½ stale white loaf	salt and pepper
8 tomatoes	3 tablespoons brown
4 oz. grated cheese	breadcrumbs
1½ oz. butter	

Discard the crusts and grate bread through a fine grater, or mince finely. Peel and thinly slice tomatoes.

Arrange alternate layers of white crumbs, tomatoes and 3 oz. of the cheese in a greased baking dish. Season the layers with salt and pepper. Top with a layer of brown breadcrumbs, sprinkle with the remaining cheese and dot with the butter.

Bake in a medium hot oven (400°F., Reg. 5) for 25–30 minutes until bubbling and golden brown.

Croustades (baked bread cases)

A useful way to use up a stale loaf, and a good alternative to vol-au-vent cases.

SERVES 4.   Cooking time: about 20 minutes.

1 loaf white bread
2 oz. butter

Cut loaf into 8 1-inch thick slices. Trim off crusts and cut slices into 4 squares. With a sharp knife cut out the centre of the squares to the depth of ¾ inch leaving ¼ inch around the sides. Brush the cases with melted butter and bake them in a hot oven (450°F., Reg. 7) for 5 minutes until crisp and golden.

Fill the cases with one of the following recipes and reheat in a medium oven (375°F., Reg. 4) for 15–20 minutes.

Fillings for Croustades:

Toast Melba

For years I thought there must be some mystical secret about making Melba toast. The only place I ever came across it was on the rare occasions when I was taken for lunch or dinner to one of those classy, expense-account restaurants in London. Then someone came to stay who knew the secret and was generously prepared to share it. Now my dinner parties are graced by those sophisticated swirls of wafer thin toast, made by *me* in a matter of minutes.

If you have some stale, or even fresh, cut bread around, try making some of the toast for your next dinner party. It always seems so popular that I find I have to allow 3 slices per person.

Toast bread slice by slice until lightly browned. As soon as it is toasted remove the crusts and split each slice in half through the middle (this is easy to do when the toast is warm). Bake slices in a hot oven (450°F., Reg. 7) for 1–2 minutes until they curl and are lightly browned throughout. Leave on a wire rack to cool.

Leftover Pancakes

Season pancakes with salt and pepper. Cut pancakes with a knife or scissors into thin strips. Fry the strips until crisp in shallow fat or oil, drain on kitchen paper, and serve with hot soup.

Vol-au-Vent Cases

For 8 cases:

12 oz. puff pastry (I use frozen)
1 beaten egg

Defrost pastry if necessary. Roll out to $\frac{1}{4}$-inch thickness on a well-floured board. Using a floured pastry cutter, cut 8 circles and with a smaller cutter make a second cut, $\frac{3}{4}$ of the way through and about $\frac{1}{4}$-inch in from the outside. Place circles on a damp pastry sheet, brush with well-beaten egg and chill in a refrigerator for 30 minutes.

Bake vol-au-vent cases in a hot oven (400°F., Reg. 5) for about 20 minutes until well risen and golden brown. Slide off the baking sheet and leave to cool on a wire rack.

Carefully remove the cut out centres, keep the tops for lids and scoop out all soft pastry from the middles.

Fill the cases with one of the following recipes and reheat in a moderate oven for about 15–20 minutes.

Suitable fillings for vol-au-vent cases:

Curried Chicken Filling, see page 151
Beef Marikoff, see page 112
Filling for Savoury Pancakes, see page 111 or 134
Chicken in Barbecue Sauce, see page 146
Creamed Fish with Prawns and Peas, see page 72
Fish à la King, see page 78

Large Vol-au-Vent Case

For special occasions one large vol-au-vent case can make an attractive base for a main course. These are made in the same way as the small cases but I should not advise trying to make a large case in a solid fuel stove like an Aga or an Esse. From experience I have found that the solid fuel stoves tend to be more hot at one end than the other, and with sensitive ingredients like puff pastry, uneven heat can lead to the case rising twice as high on one side as it does on the other.

SERVES 4.   Cooking time: 25 minutes.

½ lb. puff pastry (fresh, shop-made, or frozen)
1 well-beaten egg

Roll out pastry to half inch thickness. Using a plate or a saucepan lid about 9 inches in diameter, cut round the edge with a sharp knife, sloping the knife outwards to help the rise of the pastry. Reverse pastry on to a wet baking sheet. Place a smaller plate in the centre of the pastry leaving a 2 inch border and, using a sharp knife, cut half way through. Mark the border with a criss-cross pattern and brush the top with beaten egg, taking care not to let it run down the side of the case. Bake in a hot oven (450°F., Reg. 7) for 20 minutes until well risen and golden brown. Reduce heat to moderate (350°F., Reg. 3) and cook for a further 5 minutes.

Cut around the inner circle of the case and gently lift off the lid. Remove any soft pastry in the centre. Fill the case, replace the lid, and reheat in a moderate or medium hot oven for 20–25 minutes.

Fill the case with one of the mixtures suitable for small vol-au-vent cases, see page 231.

American Muffins

Muffins are something I look forward to whenever I go to America. They are not the same as those once sold by an English 'muffin man', and resemble light cakes rather than scones. Sweet muffins are served at breakfast and the savoury kind are good with any meal. The basic recipe can be varied in a large variety of ways – add *leftover fruit* to sweet muffins and *cooked bacon, ham, smoked sausage*, etc., to savoury muffins.

Basic muffin recipe – makes 12 muffins. Cooking time: 20–25 minutes.

8 oz. flour	2 oz. butter or margarine
pinch salt	1 egg
3 teaspoons baking powder	½ pint milk

Sift together the flour, salt, and baking powder. Mix in the fat with two knives until it is the size of small peas. Beat together the milk and egg and lightly mix them into the flour mixture. Fill well-greased muffin tins two-thirds full, and bake in a medium hot oven (400°F., Reg. 5) for 20–25 minutes until well risen and golden brown. Turn out and serve hot.

Variations:

1. Fruit muffins: Add 3 tablespoons sugar and some *chopped drained fruit* to the basic mixture.

2. Savoury muffins: Add *finely chopped cooked bacon, ham, smoked sausage or tongue*, etc., to the basic mixture.

Savoury Puffs

Made like éclairs or cream puffs these make a delicious casing for many leftovers concocted from minced or finely chopped meat.

SERVES 4.   Cooking time: about 30 minutes.

½ pint water	3 eggs
3 oz. butter	1 beaten egg
¼ teaspoon salt	1 tablespoon milk
5 oz. flour	

Combine water and butter in a saucepan. Add salt, bring to the boil, and cook until butter has all melted. Remove from the heat. Add flour all at once and beat with a wooden spoon until the mixture forms a ball and leaves the sides of the pan. Add the eggs, one by one, beating each one in until the paste is smooth and shiny – about 2 minutes. Drop the paste from a tablespoon on to a greased baking dish. Brush with a mixture of beaten egg and milk. Bake for 15–20 minutes in a medium hot oven (400°F., Reg. 5) until the puffs are golden and dry. Open the oven door and leave them in the oven for a further 8 minutes.

Leave the puffs to cool, then make an insertion with a sharp knife, half way through, to make a hinged lid. Fill the puffs with a suitable filling and reheat for 10 minutes in a moderate oven (350°F., Reg. 3).

Suitable fillings for Savoury Puffs:

Fish à la King, page 78
Creamed Fish with Potatoes, page 77
Creamed Fish with Prawns and Peas, page 72
Savoury Pancake Filling, page 110

Curried Meat, page 99
Savoury Minced Meat, page 102
Creamed Veal or Lamb, page 125
Chicken à la King, page 148

Plain Boiled Rice

Well-cooked rice is delicious and a complement to any food. A dish of leftovers served in a sauce, and surrounded by rice goes further and looks more attractive. Cooking times vary considerably with the quality of the rice, but the main thing to remember is that, for anything except puddings, only patna or long-grained rice should be used.

Here is my basic recipe for cooking rice and the one I use for hot boiled rice, risottos using cooked rice, and cold rice dishes.

SERVES 4.   Cooking time: about 25 minutes.

½ lb. rice
water
¼ oz. butter

Put rice into a fairly large, thick-bottomed saucepan and cover with water until there is a clear 1-inch above the rice. Add the butter, bring to the boil, stir, and boil until the water is absorbed. Cover with a lid and leave, over the lowest possible heat, without stirring, for 12 minutes. The rice should then be tender and fluffy but not sticky.

The rice can be rinsed in cold water to remove excess starch (for weight watchers) before being dried in a warm oven and served.

Re-heating cooked rice

There is a wide variety of things that can be done with cooked rice, in fact I would count it as one of the most versatile of leftovers. If however you have sufficient rice to serve by itself and merely want to re-heat it, this can be done satisfactorily in 3 ways.

1. Toss cooked rice in some melted butter over a low heat until hot through.
2. Mix the rice with melted butter, cover with foil or grease-proof paper, and heat in a low oven until hot through.
3. Steam the rice over hot, not boiling, water until it is heated right through.

Rice and Vegetables

Often there are not enough leftover vegetables to justify trying to serve them again for another meal, but small quantities of peas, beans, carrots, etc., can be successfully combined with boiled rice to make a good vegetable dish to serve with any creamed main course, a casserole, or a stew.

SERVES 4.   Cooking time: about 30 minutes.

½ lb. rice	½ oz. butter
leftover vegetables	salt and pepper

Cook the rice according to the instructions on page 235. Drain it well and mix it with the cooked vegetables which should be chopped, if necessary, into very small dice.

Melt the butter in a large saucepan, add vegetables and rice, and toss over a low heat until warmed through. Season with plenty of salt and pepper.

To cook Spaghetti or Pasta

It is really impossible to give a definite time for the cooking of
pasta as this will vary according to the type, quality, and
freshness of the ingredients. Packet spaghetti, for instance,
especially if it is British- rather than Italian-made, will take
much longer to cook than fresh pasta which one can buy from
some of the Italian shops in Soho.

As a rough guide I would say that spaghetti takes between
10 and 20 minutes to cook in plenty of boiling salted water.
Smaller varieties of pasta will take less time and larger varieties,
more. Tasting is the only reliable guide.

The water should always be boiling fast when you add the
pasta and the addition of a knob of butter will both add to the
flavour and prevent the liquid from boiling over the top of the
saucepan.

Drain pasta as soon as it has cooked, and if you cannot use
it immediately, keep it in the top of a steamer, over hot water.

To re-heat cooked spaghetti or other pasta, toss it in some
melted butter over a low heat; heat in a colander or steamer
over hot water; or mix well with melted butter and re-heat
in a low oven, covered with foil or greaseproof paper.

Leftover Pastry Trimmings

However carefully you try to judge the amount of pastry you
are likely to need for making a flan case or pie top there are
invariably trimmings and little bits and pieces left over. In
my house they usually get pounced on by my ten-year-old
daughter and are turned into grubby looking dough men with
currants for eyes and a strip of angelica for a mouth, but these

leftover pastry pieces *can* be used in a number of rather more constructive ways.

Both rich sweetened shortcrust pastry and ordinary shortcrust or flan pastry trimmings can be pressed into a ball, wrapped in a damp cloth or in a polythene bag and stored for up to five days in a cold place. All pastry can be sealed in polythene bags and deep-frozen.

Rich Sweet Shortcrust Pastry

1. As garnish for hot stewed or puréed fruit

   rich shortcrust pastry trimmings
   white of egg
   castor sugar

   Roll out pastry trimmings to about ¼ inch thick, brush with white of egg and sprinkle with castor sugar. Cut into triangles, crescents or star shapes and bake in a moderately hot oven (400°F., Reg. 5) until golden brown.

2. Small fruit tarts

Roll pastry out thinly, cut into circles with a pastry cutter, and line small patty tins. Prick the bases with a fork, cover with a small circle of greaseproof paper, fill with dried peas to stop the pastry rising, and bake 'blind' in a moderately hot oven (400°F., Reg. 5) for 8–10 minutes until golden brown. Cool pastry cases, remove paper and peas, and fill with fresh fruit glazed with a little melted apricot or redcurrant jelly.

Shortcrust Pastry

1. As a garnish for stews or casseroles, etc.

   shortcrust pastry trimmings
   milk or beaten egg

   Roll out pastry trimmings to about ¼ inch thick, cut into small triangle or crescent shapes, brush with milk or beaten egg and bake in a moderately hot oven (400°F., Reg. 5) until golden brown. Use to garnish the top of stews or casseroles, etc.

2. Cheese Straws

shortcrust pastry trimmings
beaten egg

grated parmesan cheese
paprika

Roll out pastry trimmings to about $\frac{1}{4}$ inch thick and cut into $\frac{1}{4}$ inch by 2 inch lengths. Brush with beaten egg, dust with grated parmesan, sprinkle with a little paprika, and bake in a moderately hot oven (400°F., Reg. 5) until the straws are golden brown. Serve hot or cold with soups or with cocktails.

3. Savoury pastry cases

Roll pastry out thinly, cut into circles with a pastry cutter and line small patty tins. Prick bases with a fork, cover with a small circle of greaseproof paper, fill with dried peas, to stop the pastry rising, and bake 'blind' in a moderately hot oven (400°F., Reg. 5) for 8–10 minutes until light golden brown. Cool cases and fill with one of the following mixtures: –

As an accompaniment to a main dish: Fill cases with cooked vegetables cut into small dice and mixed with a white sauce.
As a first course: Fill cases with flaked cooked fish (cod, haddock, smoked salmon, tinned fish, etc.) mixed with a rich cheese sauce.
As a savoury: Fill cases with thinly sliced mushrooms or chopped chicken's liver cooked in butter.

Heat cases and fillings through before serving.

Puff Pastry

1. To serve with puddings

puff pastry trimmings
white of egg

castor sugar
chopped shelled walnuts

Roll out pastry trimmings to about $\frac{1}{4}$ inch thick, cut into rectangles about finger size, brush with white of egg, sprinkle with sugar and chopped nuts, and bake for 8–10 minutes in a hot oven. Leave to cool and serve with ice cream or cold puddings.

2. To serve with casseroles or stews

Roll out pastry to about $\frac{1}{4}$ inch thick, cut into small triangles or crescents, brush with milk, and bake for a few minutes in a hot oven (425°F., Reg. 5). Use to decorate stews, casseroles or hot fish dishes.

Puddings

The appearance of a pudding is always important, and though the remains of a lemon or chocolate mousse may taste delicious one will be put off by its looks if the sweet has spent some time in the larder or refrigerator. Turn the remains of soft puddings such as mousses, trifles and jellies into a clean dish and mask them with some whipped cream and a garnish of roasted chopped nuts.

Steamed or cooked puddings can often be repacked in a smaller bowl, gently re-heated, and served with a new sauce, melted jam, or hot syrup.

Stewed fruit and fruit salad can be put to good use by incorporating it with other ingredients to make an entirely new sweet.

Custard

Like mayonnaise, home made custard provides a useful way to use up leftover egg yolks and can be served as a pleasant sweet by itself or as a sauce for other puddings.

For ½ pint custard.   Cooking time: 10 minutes.

2 *egg yolks*	¼ pint milk
½ oz. sugar	3–4 drops vanilla essence

Beat egg yolks with the milk until the mixture is smooth. Strain into a saucepan through a fine sieve. Add sugar and heat gently, stirring constantly until the custard is thickened and smooth – this takes about 8–10 minutes. Beat in vanilla essence and serve either hot or cold.

Chocolate custard

Leave out the sugar and add 2 tablespoons sweetened chocolate powder to the custard before heating.

Bread and Butter Pudding

This is a pudding to make on those occasions when a tea party or picnic leaves you with a mound of buttered bread.

SERVES 4–6.   Cooking time: 30 minutes.

4–8 *slices buttered bread*	1 pint milk
2 oz. sultanas	2 eggs
grated rind of 1 lemon	2 tablespoons sugar

Remove crusts and cut buttered bread into small squares. Place half the bread in a greased baking dish, sprinkle with half the sultanas and lemon rind, and cover with remaining bread. Sprinkle surface with remaining sultanas and rind.

Beat eggs with the milk and sugar. Pour custard mixture over the bread and leave to stand for 30 minutes. Place the pudding in a tin of hot water and bake in a medium oven (375°F., Reg.4) for 30 minutes until golden brown and set.

Queen of Puddings

I wouldn't be surprised if this recipe wasn't originally invented with the sole purpose of using up stale bread. It succeeds into turning that mundane dreary ingredient into the most delicious of nursery puddings.

SERVES 4.   Cooking time: 1 hour.

4 *slices bread*   1 oz. sugar
2 eggs   3 tablespoons raspberry jam
½ pint milk   2 oz. castor sugar
grated rind of 1 lemon

Remove crusts from the bread and cut into small cubes.
Separate the eggs. Heat milk and beat with the egg yolks. Mix
bread cubes, lemon rind and sugar with the custard and pour
the mixture into a lightly greased baking dish. Bake in a warm
oven (325°F., Reg.3) for 45 minutes.

Spread the jam on the pudding and top with meringue
made by whisking the egg whites until stiff and folding in
2 oz. castor sugar. Return to a moderate oven (350°F., Reg.4)
for 15 minutes until the meringue is slightly golden and crisp.

Christmas Pudding

The headache of what to do with the remains of the Christmas pudding always seems to me a worse problem than what to
do with the remains of the turkey. These two recipes are my
most satisfactory solution.

Fried Christmas Pudding

Christmas Pudding
butter
castor sugar

Cut pudding into thin slices. Cook slices in hot butter for
2 minutes on each side. Sprinkle at once with castor sugar and
serve hot or cold.

Iced Christmas Pudding

Christmas pudding
brandy or rum butter

Cut pudding into thin slices. Spread each slice with brandy butter and sandwich firmly together one on top of another. Wrap in foil or greaseproof paper and freeze in the freezing compartment of the refrigerator for at least half an hour. Cut into thick fingers, sprinkle with a little sugar and serve ice-cold.

Tipsy Trifle

SERVES 4.   Cooking time: about 10 minutes.

slices stale sponge cake
4 tablespoons sherry, Madeira or rum
2 tablespoons custard powder
2 tablespoons sugar
¾ pint milk
fresh or tinned fruit (raspberries, strawberries, mandarines,
    pineapple, peaches, etc.)
¼ pint double cream

Soak the sponge cake in the sherry and arrange the slices in the bottom of a glass bowl or serving dish.

Use a little cold milk to make a smooth paste with the custard powder and sugar. Bring remaining milk to the boil, beat it into the custard paste and stir until smooth. Heat the custard over a low heat and stir constantly until thick and smooth, about 5 minutes. Leave to cool a little.

Cover the soaked sponge with fruit, pour over the custard, and chill in a refrigerator or cold place. Whip the cream and spread it over the top of the trifle before serving.

Note: Raspberry or strawberry jam can be used in place of fruit.

Fruit Cake Fudge

What can be done with the dried-up remains of some fruit cake? You might think it impossible to use it for anything, but fruit cake combined with golden syrup and cocoa can be made into the most delicious fudge which is an out-and-out winner with any child I've ever met.

Cooking time: about 10 minutes.

4 oz. fruit cake
1 oz. butter
1½ tablespoons golden syrup
1 oz. cocoa
1 oz. brown sugar

Heat butter with the golden syrup until melted. Add brown sugar and cook for a few minutes to melt the sugar. Add crumbled fruit cake and cocoa, mix well and cook for 2 minutes. Spread the mixture on a lightly greased baking sheet and chill for at least ½ hour in a refrigerator. Cut into neat squares.

Note: Fruit cake remains can also be used in the following recipe for Hot Cake and Vanilla Sauce.

Hot Cake and Vanilla Sauce

Stale or dried-out sponge cake or fruit cake can be turned into a very good pudding if it is heated with orange juice and served with a vanilla sauce.

SERVES 4.   Cooking time: 20 minutes.

4 slices sponge or fruit cake
¼ pint orange juice (I use canned or frozen juice)
2 oz. castor sugar
1 tablespoon cornflour
pinch salt
2 egg yolks
¾ pint single cream
1 teaspoon vanilla essence

Arrange cake slices in a fireproof serving dish. Pour over the orange juice and heat through in a medium oven (375°F., Reg.4) for about ten minutes. Keep warm.

Combine sugar, cornflour, and a pinch salt in a heavy-bottomed pan. Beat the egg yolks and cream together, and beat them into the cornflour mixture, over a low heat, until the sauce is smooth. Whisk over a low heat, without boiling, for 2–3 minutes until the sauce is thick. Beat in vanilla essence, pour over the cake slices and serve at once.

Note: This sauce is also delicious cold.

Apple Trifle

A really simple dish but nevertheless a delicious one. Make it from leftovers of cake, stewed apple, custard, or all three.

SERVES 4.   No cooking.

2–4 oz. sponge cake
8 oz. sweet stewed apple
½ pint sweet custard

chopped blanched almonds or
  desiccated coconut

Cut the cake into small cubes and put into the bottom of a glass bowl or serving dish.

Beat the stewed apple until smooth and check sweetness. Cover the cake with apple purée.

Pour over the custard and sprinkle with toasted almonds or desiccated coconut. Chill before serving.

Frozen Orange Cream

SERVES 4.   No cooking.

2 6-oz. cans frozen orange juice
1½ tablespoons brandy

½ pint double cream
2–4 slices stale sponge cake

Leave orange juice to thaw for 3 minutes. Whip cream until stiff. Cut sponge cake into small cubes.

Mix brandy with orange juice. Fold in the whipped cream and sponge cake. Turn into a serving dish or 4 glasses, and chill well before serving.

Chocolate Cake Mousse*

SERVES 4–6.   Cooking time: about 5 minutes.

2–4 *slices stale chocolate cake*
3 oz. cooking chocolate
3 eggs
3 oz. castor sugar
2 tablespoons concentrated orange juice, tinned or frozen
¼ pint double cream

Cut cake into small cubes. Melt chocolate until runny in a bowl over hot water. Separate eggs and beat yolks with sugar until pale yellow and fluffy. Beat in melted chocolate and orange juice and fold in cake pieces.

Whip egg whites until stiff but not dry. Whip cream until thick. Fold cream and egg whites into chocolate mixture, turn into a serving bowl or glass dishes, and chill for at least an hour.

Rice Pudding Réchauffé

Leftover rice pudding is not one of the most inspiring sights in the world but it *can* be made into a new and appetizing pudding without too much trouble.

Cooking time: 15–20 minutes.

cooked rice pudding
3 tablespoons double cream
tinned fruit cocktail or chopped fruit

Remove any skin from the surface of the pudding. Drain

fruit and chop if necessary. Combine pudding, cream, and fruit and turn into a lightly buttered serving dish. Bake in a medium hot oven (400°F., Reg.5) for 15–20 minutes.

Serve with a little extra cream.

Rice Pudding Moulds

Remove any skin from the pudding and pack the rice, whilst still warm if possible, into some dampened individual moulds. Leave to set in a refrigerator or cold place for at least 2 hours, turn out, and serve with fresh, stewed, or tinned fruit.

Jelly

Small amounts of jelly often sit around in the refrigerator for days. Even these have their uses.

Cut jelly into cubes, or break up with a fork, and combine in layers, in glass dishes, with a little fruit salad, ice cream and whipped cream. Top with a sprinkling of chopped nuts and serve at once.

Break jelly up with a fork and use to decorate the tops of cold mousses, trifles, etc.

Melt the jelly over a low heat and use to glaze the tops of fruit tarts or flans.

Fluffy Jelly

SERVES 4. No cooking.

1 packet fruit jelly
¾ pint water
1–2 *egg whites*

Heat ¼ pint water and mix it with the jelly cubes until they are dissolved. Add remaining water and leave in a cool place until the jelly is beginning to thicken and set. Whip egg white until stiff, fold it into the jelly and leave to set for at least $1\frac{1}{2}$ hours.

Serve the jelly with fruit and cream.

Fruit Jelly

An attractive way to use up the remains of a fruit salad or some tinned fruit.

SERVES 4.   No cooking.

1 packet jelly
fresh fruit salad or tinned fruit

Add enough water to the jelly to dissolve it. Make the liquid up to $\frac{3}{4}$ pint using fruit juice and more water, and leave in a cool place until the jelly begins to set.

Pour enough jelly into a mould to cover the bottom and leave to set firm. Cover with the well-drained fruit, and pour over remaining jelly. Leave to set firm and unmould before serving.

Note: For a more sophisticated pudding, mask the unmoulded jelly with sweetened whipped cream and decorate with roasted almonds.

Bananas with Fruit Sauce

SERVES 4.   Cooking time: 30 minutes.

8 bananas	1 tablespoon lemon juice
small amount tinned or stewed	$1\frac{1}{2}$ tablespoons brown sugar
fruit with juice	2 oz. chopped almonds

Cut bananas in half lengthwise and chop fruit into small pieces.

Arrange banana slices in a lightly buttered baking dish, cover with fruit, and pour over fruit juice and lemon juice. Sprinkle over the brown sugar and the chopped almonds. Bake in a moderately hot oven (375°F., Reg. 5) for 30 minutes.

Serve hot or cold with cream.

Red- or Blackcurrant Water Ice, using Egg Whites*

SERVES 4.   Cooking time: 5 minutes.

1 lb. fresh currants	2 tablespoons orange juice
½ pint boiling water	2 egg whites
8 oz. sugar	

Add currants to boiling water and cook for 5 minutes. Force fruit through a fine sieve, cool, and add sugar and orange juice. Pour into refrigerator trays and freeze until crystals begin to form.

Beat egg whites until stiff. Stir fruit mixture to a mush, fold in egg whites, and return to the freezer. Freeze for at least 2 hours before serving.

Meringues

The obvious recipe for using up leftover egg whites. A stiffer more adaptable mixture is obtained if the whites are between three and six days old. Allow 2 oz. castor sugar for each egg white.

For 24 small meringues. Cooking time: 2–3 hours.

2 egg whites
4 oz. castor sugar

Whip egg whites until stiff but not dry. Add half the sugar and whisk it well into the whites. Lightly fold in the remaining sugar with a fork.

Prepare a baking sheet by covering it with a tight layer of greaseproof paper well spread with olive oil.

Pipe the meringue mixture with a forcing bag and a half inch nozzle into rounds, allowing a good ¾ inch between each one. Alternatively the meringues can be dropped in rounds from a spoon dipped in cold water.

Bake meringues in a very cool oven (225°F., Reg. ¼) for 2–3 hours until they are firm on the outside and underneath. Leave to cool for a few minutes, then slide from the greased paper on to a wire rack to dry.

Variations:

Almond Meringues. Add a few drops almond essence to the meringue mixture.

Vanilla Meringues. Add a few drops vanilla essence to the meringue mixture.

Chocolate or coffee Meringues. Add 2 teaspoons cocoa or a teaspoon coffee essence to the meringue mixture.

Fillings for Meringues

1. Plain whipped cream.
2. Crème Chantilly: Flavour whipped cream with a little castor sugar and a drop or two of vanilla essence.
3. Plain or flavoured ice cream.

Meringue Pyramid Pudding

SERVES 6.   No cooking.

12 medium meringues
½ pint thick cream
1 teaspoon castor sugar

2 drops vanilla essence
2 oz. cooking chocolate

Whip cream until thick and flavour with the sugar and 2 drops vanilla essence.

Melt chocolate on a saucer over a pan of hot water, leave to cool but not set.

Arrange a layer of meringues on a serving dish, spread with some of the whipped cream and dribble over a little of the melted chocolate. Continue building up the layers to form a pyramid and chill before serving.

Variations:
Sprinkle over some chopped walnuts or lightly roasted chopped almonds before serving.

Meringue Cake

SERVES 6. No cooking.

½ pint double cream	4–8 meringues
1 tablespoon castor sugar	½–1 tablespoon kirsch

Whip cream until stiff. Break up meringues into small pieces. Oil a cake tin, with a removable bottom, with some pure olive oil.

Blend the kirsch into the cream, sweeten with sugar, and fold in the meringue pieces. Pack the mixture in the cake tin, and freeze in the freezing compartment of a refrigerator until solid, at least 2½ hours. Turn out and serve, cut into wedges, with fresh, stewed, or tinned fruit.

Meringue Topping for Puddings and Pies

The odd *egg white* or two left over from making something like mayonnaise can be made into a delicious topping for puddings or pies.

Allow 1½ oz. castor sugar for each egg white. Two egg

whites will make a satisfactory topping for a pudding or pie which will serve four.

Whisk egg whites until stiff but not dry. Beat in sugar a small amount at a time. Spoon the meringue over pies or puddings and bake in a medium oven (350°F., Reg.4) for 15–20 minutes until meringue is light gold on the top.

This kind of topping can be used on pies and puddings which are to be served either hot or cold.

Meringue Pie Shell

A pie shell made from meringue makes an attractive container for fresh soft fruit, such as strawberries and raspberries. The shell must be baked firm or it will be impossible to remove from the dish.

For a 9-inch pie shell.   Cooking time: 40 minutes.

3 *egg whites*
pinch salt
¼ teaspoon cream of tartar

6 oz. castor sugar
3 drops vanilla essence

Beat egg whites until white and foamy. Beat in cream of tartar and gradually add sugar, whisking all the time until all the sugar has been used and the mixture is really stiff. Beat in vanilla essence.

Well grease a 9-inch pie dish with olive oil. Spread meringue over the bottom and pile it up around the sides of the dish. Bake in a warm oven (300°F., Reg.2) for 30–40 minutes until the case is firm and just slightly golden.

Carefully loosen the shell from the sides and bottom of the dish with a spatula, leave to cool, and remove from the dish to fill.

Note: Unfilled cases can be kept for up to a week in an airtight tin.

This mixture can also be spread in squares on a baking sheet lined with oiled greaseproof paper. The squares can be sandwiched together with fruit and whipped cream.

Zabaglione

SERVES 4. Cooking time: 15 minutes.

   6 egg yolks
   6 oz. sugar
   1½ gills Marsala

Whisk yolks, sugar, and Marsala until well mixed. Put the bowl over hot, not boiling, water and continue whisking until the mixture is thick and light – about 12–15 minutes. Pour into four glasses and serve at once.

Iced Zabaglione

SERVES 4. Cooking time: about 25 minutes.

Follow the recipe for Zabaglione. When the mixture is thick place the bowl over a large basin filled with ice cubes and continue whisking until the mixture is quite cold, about ten minutes. Pour into four glasses and refrigerate until required.

Fruit Salad

For some reason I always find it impossible to gauge the exact amount of fruit salad to make for one meal. Inevitably I end up with too much and as a result I've become adept at finding ways in which to make the fruit stretch for another meal.

One of the most simple ways is to use the salad as a base and increase the pudding by adding more fruit and syrup. This can be done by adding fresh chopped or sliced fruit with some sugar syrup, or by adding tinned fruit cocktail.

Whatever you decide to do with the remains of a fruit salad, remember to remove any banana before putting the fruit in a refrigerator or cool larder. Banana quickly turns brown, discolouring the juice and making the dish look unattractive.

For other ways to use up fruit salad, see:

Coupe à la Vanille, page 257
Fruit and Rice Mould, page 260
Fruit Jelly, page 249
Rice Pudding Réchauffé, page 247

Leftover fruit salad can be given a lift by being served in individual glass goblets, flavoured with a dash of kirsch and topped with a sprinkling of chopped walnuts, chopped lightly roasted almonds or chopped glacé cherries.

Fruit Upside-down Cake*

SERVES 6.   Cooking time: 30 minutes.

6–8 oz. tinned fruit (pineapple, peaches, apricots, etc.)	2 oz. self raising flour
	1 egg
2 oz. butter or margarine	½ pint custard or double cream
2 oz. castor sugar	

Drain fruit and arrange in the bottom of a well-greased 7-inch sandwich tin brushed with castor sugar. Beat butter or margarine with sugar until light yellow and creamy. Add egg and beat well. Lightly fold in the flour.

Pour cake mixture over the fruit and bake in a medium oven (350°F., Reg.4) for 30 minutes until cake is cooked. Turn out and serve hot or cold with custard or cream.

Fruit Fool

Here is a way of using up cooked or puréed fruit as well as the custard that went with it.

SERVES 4.   No cooking.

1 *lb. cooked fruit (apples,*	¼ *pint custard*
rhubarb, currants,	sugar
gooseberries, etc.)	¼ pint double cream

Purée the fruit through a fine sieve, through a food mill or in an electric blender. Remove any skin from the custard and mix it with the fruit. Sweeten with sugar if necessary. Whip the cream and sweeten with a little sugar. Pour the fruit fool into a glass bowl or four glasses and decorate with the whipped cream.

Serve with sweet biscuits.

Cream Feather Pancakes

SERVES 6.   Cooking time: about 2 minutes for each pancake.

1 oz. flour	4 *beaten egg yolks*
½ oz. castor sugar	2 *egg whites, stiffly beaten*
grated rind of 1 lemon	butter
2 tablespoons milk	½ *pint fruit purée (apple, apricot,*
½ pint cream	*blackcurrant, etc.)*

Mix flour, sugar, and lemon rind to a smooth paste with the milk. Stir in egg yolks and cream, fold in stiffly beaten egg whites, and use at once.

Melt a little butter in an omelette pan, pour in enough batter to cover the surface and cook, turning once, until the pancake is golden on both sides.

Spread each pancake with fruit purée, roll up, arrange in a shallow dish and keep warm.

I usually make these with a purée made from the remains of stewed or tinned fruit, but I have also filled the pancakes with leftover fruit mousse or soufflé and found that very popular too.

Iced Fruit Pudding*

The proportion of fruit in this pudding can vary enormously, so it provides a useful method for using up the odd remains of tinned fruit.

SERVES 4.   No cooking.

tinned pineapple, apricots, fruit
   cocktail, etc.
6 tablespoons strawberry or
   raspberry jam

½ pint double cream
2 oz. macaroons or meringues
few drops vanilla essence
1 tablespoon castor sugar

Drain the fruit well. Whip cream until stiff but not dry, and add the jam, a little vanilla essence, sugar, and the macaroons or meringues crushed into small pieces. Fold in most of the fruit (chopped if necessary), turn the mixture into a mould and freeze for at least 3 hours.

Turn out the pudding and decorate with the remaining fruit before serving.

Coupe à la Vanille

SERVES 4.   No cooking.

1 block vanilla ice cream
tinned fruit or fruit salad

¼ pint cream, whipped
1 tablespoon chopped almonds

Drain tinned fruit or fresh fruit salad and chop fruit if necessary into small pieces. Arrange alternate layers of ice cream and fruit in glass dishes, and top with whipped cream and a sprinkling of chopped almonds or other nuts.

Fruit Tarts

short pastry (see page 238)
stewed apples, plums, rhubarb, or other fruit
sugar

Purée the fruit in an electric liquidizer, through a food mill or through a sieve, and sweeten with sugar if necessary.

Line patty tins with shortcrust pastry, prick the bottoms lightly with a fork, and half fill with fruit purée.

Bake the tarts in a hot oven (425°F., Reg. 6) for 10–15 minutes.

The tarts can be served cold for tea or they can be re-heated and served with cream as a pudding.

Fruit Foolishness

SERVES 4. No cooking.

½ *pint stewed apples, plums, rhubarb, or other fruit*	sugar
	½ pint thick cream
½ pint thick custard	½ oz. split, blanched almonds

Purée the fruit in an electric liquidizer, through a food mill or through a sieve.

Make the custard according to directions on the tin or packet, leave to cool, mix with the fruit purée, and add enough sugar to sweeten. Pour the mixture into a glass bowl and chill well.

Whip the cream until stiff and sweeten with a little castor sugar. Spread cream over the fruit custard and decorate with the split almonds which can be lightly roasted in a hot oven.

Serve well chilled.

Biscuit Pie Crust

The biscuit crust is, I think, an American invention and makes a good change from the more usual pastry case. It is quick to make and can be a useful way to use up that jumble of broken biscuits which stays at the bottom of the tin.

Use any plain, sweet biscuits; ginger nuts are particularly good.
No cooking.

8 oz. *biscuits*
6 oz. unsalted butter
1 teaspoon lemon peel, grated ⎫
1 teaspoon ground cinnamon ⎭ optional

Crush the biscuits with a rolling pin until they look like fine breadcrumbs.

Heat the butter until melted, pour it over the crumbs, and stir until well blended. Add lemon peel and cinnamon for a more spicy crust.

Press the crumb mixture into a flan case making sure that it is evenly distributed. Chill in a refrigerator for at least an hour before filling.

Some Suggestions for Quick Fillings for Biscuit Crust Pies

1. *Peach filling*

1 tin drained peaches, or six fresh peaches skinned and halved
3 tablespoons raspberry jam

¼ pint cream
2 teaspoons sugar
2 tablespoons split roasted almonds

Whip the cream until stiff and mix in the sugar.

Arrange the peach halves in the pie cases, top with raspberry jam and cover with whipped, sweetened cream. Decorate the pie with roasted almonds and chill before serving.

2. *Banana Custard Filling*

1 tablespoon custard powder	2 drops vanilla essence
2 tablespoons sugar	2 bananas
½ pint milk	2 tablespoons shredded coconut

Mix the custard powder with a little milk until smooth. Heat the rest of the milk with the sugar until almost boiling. Add the milk to the custard with the vanilla essence, mix well, return to the saucepan and cook, stirring constantly, over a low heat until the custard is thick and smooth. Leave to cool.

Slice the bananas and add them to the cooled custard. Spoon this mixture into the biscuit crust. Roast the coconut in a hot oven until golden brown, leave to cool, and sprinkle over the banana filling. Chill before serving.

Fruit and Rice Mould

SERVES 4.   Cooking time: about 40 minutes.

small quantity of fresh or tinned fruit	1 pint milk
	2 tablespoons sugar
2 oz. pudding rice	rind of 1 lemon, finely grated

Cook the rice with the milk, sugar and lemon rind over a very low heat until rice is tender and the milk has all been absorbed, about 40 minutes. Cool, stir in fruit, chopped if necessary, and pour into a dampened mould. Leave to set in a cool place, turn out, and decorate with orange segments or other fresh fruit.

Fruit Purée Pudding*

SERVES 4. No cooking.

A quick way of using up any remains of stewed or fresh fruit.

1 *pint fruit purée*   1 tablespoon gelatine
sugar if necessary   2 *egg whites*

Sweeten the purée with a little castor sugar if necessary.

Dissolve the gelatine in a little water or lemon juice over a low heat, add it to the fruit purée, and leave until the mixture thickens and begins to set.

Whip the egg whites until stiff and fold them lightly into the fruit mixture. Turn into a damp mould and leave to set in a cold place.

Turn the pudding on to a serving dish and decorate with whipped cream or fruit.

Bavarian Cream

SERVES 4. Cooking time: about 5 minutes.

½ *pint fruit juice or syrup from*   1 tablespoon gelatine
  fresh, frozen, stewed, or tinned   ¼ pint whipped cream
  fruit   sugar if necessary

Dissolve gelatine in a little of the fruit juice over a low heat, add it to the rest of the fruit juice, mix well, and leave until it begins to thicken and set. Sweeten if necessary.

Fold the whipped cream into the thickened jelly mixture and pour into a damp mould.

To serve, turn out the mould and decorate with fresh fruit or a little extra sweetened whipped cream.

Apple Peelings

I had been peeling apples by the score one day, making apple purée to put in the deep freeze, when it occurred to me that there must be something one could do with the skins and cores.

After some experimenting I came up with this recipe which produces a really delicious apple syrup, which I found I could keep successfully in the refrigerator for at least a week. The syrup was popular as a drink or could be used instead of a straight sugar syrup for cooking other fruit; it also provided the base of a simple but attractive pudding.

Apple Syrup, using tart cooking apples

For each pound of apple peelings and cores add 6 oz. sugar, juice and rind of one lemon, and 1 pint water. Put all the ingredients in a heavy pan, bring to the boil, lower the heat and simmer gently for 40 minutes. Strain the syrup through muslin or through a fine sieve.

Orange Slices in Apple Syrup

SERVES 4.   Cooking time: about 25 minutes.

  1½ pints apple syrup
  4 oranges, large
  2 tablespoons Grand Marnier or brandy

Peel the oranges, remove all pith and membrane and cut them into wafer thin slices, discarding any pips. Remove all the white pith from inside the skins of two of the oranges and cut the skin into really thin Julienne strips. Blanch the skin in boiling water for three minutes to remove any bitterness.

Bring the apple syrup to the boil, add the orange skin, and

PUDDINGS 263

simmer for 20 minutes or until the skin is soft and glazed.
Pour the syrup and skin over the orange slices and leave to
cool. Add the Grand Marnier or brandy to the oranges and
chill well before serving.

Apple Syrup Pudding

SERVES 4.   Cooking time: about 5 minutes.

2 pints apple syrup
juice of half a lemon
2 tablespoons gelatine
2 oz. blanched almonds

1½ gills cream
2 tablespoons castor sugar
½ teaspoon vanilla essence

Soften the gelatine in the lemon juice and a little water, add
to the apple syrup, pour into a circular mould, and leave to set.

Cut the blanched almonds into thin strips and roast in a hot
oven for 2–3 minutes until golden brown (almonds brown
very quickly so take care they don't get burnt). Leave to cool.

Whip the cream until soft, fold in the sugar and the vanilla
essence.

Turn out the jelly, mask with the flavoured cream and
sprinkle over the roasted almonds. Serve chilled.

Sauces to Serve with Leftovers

One of the greatest aids to cookery of all kinds is the ability to make a good sauce, and in the cooking of leftovers this is particularly important. Even the most dreary slab of cooked meat or fish can be turned into something really exciting if it is livened up with a well-flavoured, succulent sauce, and in this section you will find a number of ideas for both hot and cold sauces to serve with re-heated or salad dishes.

Since all cooked foods tend to lose colour and flavour, once they have been cooked and cooled, it is important that the sauces served with them should replace any lost taste. Be generous with seasonings, and make sure that your sauce has an attractive colour and appearance. In hot sauces a little tomato purée, a stock cube, a touch of Worcester sauce, Tabasco or mushroom ketchup will all help to give a necessary lift when needed.

Leftover sauces

The quarter of a pint or so of a sauce which remains after a meal may not look worth hanging on to, but even small quantities of cold sauces, like mayonnaise and its offshoots, can usually be increased by the addition of more olive oil, vinegar and seasonings to serve at another meal. Leftover hot sauces can give an extra zing to soups, stews and casseroles.

Mayonnaise

Mayonnaise is one of the most useful and versatile of the cold sauces, and one that can be adapted to make any leftover seem like a party dish. It is also an ideal way to use up *spare egg yolks*.

If you have time, make double quantities as the sauce will keep at least a week if stored in a screw-topped jar and kept in a cool place (not a refrigerator).

Leftover mayonnaise can be increased merely by adding more oil and a little lemon juice or vinegar, but remember that the oil *must* be added slowly.

In the following recipes using mayonnaise as a base, you will find ideas for some of the ways you can adapt the sauce to suit cold meat, fish, pasta or vegetables, but of course there are a hundred other variations and one can have a lot of fun experimenting with them.

To make ½ pint Mayonnaise

2 *egg yolks*
½ pint olive oil
2 teaspoons lemon juice or white wine vinegar
    salt and pepper

Place yolks in a clean bowl and beat them well with a wooden spoon. Gradually beat the oil into the egg yolks adding only a drop at a time and never adding more oil until the preceding drop has become absorbed into the yolks. When the sauce becomes thick, a pale yellow and the consistency of glue, the oil may be added in a thin stream.

When all oil has been used, blend in the lemon juice or vinegar and season with salt and pepper.

For a sauce that has a slightly stronger taste, add 1 teaspoon of dry or Dijon mustard to the egg yolks before adding the oil.

Note: If the mayonnaise should curdle (this happens if you add the oil too fast, if oil and eggs are at a different tempera-ture, and sometimes if the weather is thundery) beat a third egg yolk in a clean bowl and gradually add the curdled mixture drop by drop.

Variations:

Tarragon Mayonnaise

Soak 2 teaspoons chopped dried tarragon in the lemon juice or vinegar before adding it to the mayonnaise and leave the sauce to stand for at least 15 minutes before serving.

Seafood Sauce to serve with fish, shellfish, and fish cocktails

½ pint mayonnaise	few drops Tabasco sauce
2 tablespoons tomato ketchup	1 teaspoon lemon juice
2 tablespoons cream	salt and pepper
few drops Worcester sauce	

Combine all the ingredients and season with salt and pepper if necessary.

Sauce Tartare to serve with fish

½ pint mayonnaise	2 tablespoons capers
2 teaspoons Dijon mustard	1 tablespoon gherkins

Mix mustard with the mayonnaise. Finely chop or mince the capers and gherkins and fold them into the sauce.

Anchovy Mayonnaise to serve with fish or vegetables

¼ pint mayonnaise	2 tablespoons finely chopped
3 tablespoons sour cream	parsley or chives
8 anchovy fillets	1 clove garlic

Drain and finely chop anchovy fillets, crush and chop garlic (or pass through a garlic press). Blend sour cream with the mayonnaise and fold in anchovies, parsley or chives, and garlic.

Garlic Mayonnaise or Aioli to serve with fish or with cooked or raw vegetables

Pound 3 cloves garlic in a pestle and mortar until they are creamy and add them to the egg yolks before beating in the oil.

Curried Mayonnaise to serve with cold fish, shellfish, chicken, and eggs

½ oz. butter
1 small onion
1 tablespoon curry powder
1 teaspoon flour
4 tomatoes
¼ pint chicken stock (this can be made with water and a stock cube)

½ teaspoon sugar
2 tablespoons cream
¼–½ pint mayonnaise
salt and pepper
1 teaspoon lemon juice

Peel and chop the onion. Chop the tomatoes.

Melt the butter in a saucepan, add the onion and cook over medium heat until it is soft and transparent but not brown. Add chopped tomatoes, stir in the curry powder and flour, and mix well. Add stock and sugar, bring to the boil and simmer for 20 minutes. Strain the mixture through a fine sieve and leave to cool. Add the curry mixture to the mayonnaise and blend in the cream. Mix well and season with salt, pepper, and lemon juice.

Pink Pimento Sauce

This is a pretty variety of mayonnaise and goes well with fish and white meat such as chicken.

Add 3 tablespoons finely chopped tinned red pimento to ½ pint mayonnaise.

Green Mayonnaise to serve with vegetables

    ½ pint mayonnaise
    2 handfuls raw spinach
    1 tablespoon Dijon mustard

Wash spinach, remove stems, and plunge leaves into boiling salted water. Cook for 3 minutes, drain well, and squeeze out any remaining liquid from the leaves into a bowl. Chop spinach very finely and add it to the mayonnaise with the mustard and enough spinach juice to colour the sauce to a delicate green.

Piquant Tomato Mayonnaise to serve with fish or shellfish

½ pint mayonnaise	1 teaspoon lemon juice
1 tablespoon tomato chutney	1 tablespoon chopped pimento
1 teaspoon Worcester sauce	salt and pepper

Combine mayonnaise with the other ingredients and season if necessary with salt and pepper.

Herb Mayonnaise to serve with vegetables, pasta or white meat

Soak 2 teaspoons mixed finely chopped chives, parsley, chervil and tarragon in the lemon juice or vinegar before adding it to the mayonnaise.

Celeste Sauce to serve with cold fish, chicken etc.

¼–½ pint mayonnaise
2 anchovy fillets
1 teaspoon finely chopped
  parsley
2 teaspoons capers
pepper

Finely chop anchovy fillets and capers. Mix all the ingredients into the mayonnaise and season with pepper.

Red Devil Sauce to serve with leftover cold white fish or with shellfish

3 tablespoons finely chopped
  red pimento
½ teaspoon chili powder
few drops Tabasco sauce
½ pint mayonnaise
1 teaspoon lemon juice
salt and pepper

Mix the chopped pimento, chili powder, and Tabasco sauce with the mayonnaise, add the lemon juice, and season to taste with salt and pepper.

Black Devil Sauce to serve with leftover cold fish: sole, plaice, cod, hake, etc.

10 pickled walnuts
¼ pint yoghurt
½ pint mayonnaise
freshly ground black pepper

Finely chop the walnuts and mix them with the yoghurt and mayonnaise. Season the sauce with freshly ground black pepper and spoon it over the fish. Chill before serving.

Hollandaise Sauce

Hollandaise is one of the greatest of all sauces: poured over re-heated vegetables it can make them into something really special.

4 *egg yolks*	1 tablespoon lemon juice
6 oz. softened unsalted butter	salt and white pepper
3 tablespoons boiling water	

Place egg yolks in the top of a double boiler over hot, but not boiling, water. Whisk them with one tablespoon of the water for 3 minutes. Gradually whisk in the softened butter a teaspoon at a time allowing the butter and egg yolks to thicken and emulsify (without letting them become like scrambled eggs) before each addition of more butter. When all the butter has been absorbed, add the remaining water and the lemon juice. Season with salt and white pepper.

Like mayonnaise, hollandaise sauce has a tendency to curdle. If this happens add a teaspoon of boiling water to the curdled sauce and whisk vigorously until it becomes thick and smooth.

Note: Hollandaise should be served as soon as it is made, but if you should have to keep it, cover the sauce with a lid and leave standing over warm water.

White Sauce

1½ oz. butter	½ pint milk
2 tablespoons flour	salt and pepper

Melt the butter in a saucepan. Add flour and mix well until butter and flour form a ball and leave the sides of the pan – do not allow to brown. Gradually blend in the milk, stirring constantly over a medium heat until the sauce becomes thick and smooth. Bring to the boil and cook for 1–2 minutes. Season with salt and pepper. If the milk is first infused with a slice of onion, a blade of mace, a bay leaf and 6 peppercorns, this becomes a Béchamel sauce.

Rich White Sauce

½ pint white sauce
1 egg yolk
2 tablespoons cream

Make white sauce as above. Beat egg yolk with the cream and blend into the sauce – do not allow to boil.

Parsley Sauce

½ pint white sauce
2 tablespoons finely chopped parsley

Make white sauce as above (or rich white sauce if preferred), add the finely chopped parsley and cook for a further 2 minutes.

Cooked fish or chicken can be added to this sauce, heated through and used as a filling for vol-au-vents, etc.

White Sauce using Fish Stock

2 oz. butter
2 oz. flour

1 pint fish stock
salt and pepper

Melt the butter in a saucepan, add the flour, mix well until the flour and butter form a ball and leave the sides of the pan, and then gradually blend in the stock stirring constantly until the sauce comes to the boil and is thick and smooth. Season with salt and pepper.

Variations:

1. Add a teaspoon of mustard and two chopped hardboiled eggs.

2. Add two tablespoons finely chopped parsley.

3. Add 2 oz. chopped mushrooms lightly cooked in a little butter.

4. Add 1–1½ teaspoons dried tarragon softened in a little lemon juice.

5. Add 1 tablespoon tomato purée or tomato chutney.

6. Add 2 teaspoons dried dill softened in a little lemon juice.

7. Add 1 tablespoon dry sherry or vermouth to the basic sauce or to any of the above variations.

Egg and Mustard Sauce

½ pint white sauce or rich white sauce
3 hardboiled eggs
1 teaspoon English mustard

Make white sauce (or rich white sauce) as above. Finely chop the hardboiled eggs and add them to the sauce with the mustard. Mix well and heat through.

Cooked fish or cooked chopped vegetables can be added to this sauce, heated through and used as a filling for vol-au-vents, savoury pancakes, etc.

Mushroom Sauce

½ pint white sauce or rich white sauce
¼ lb. mushrooms
½ oz. butter

Make white sauce (or rich white sauce) as above. Thinly

slice the mushrooms, cook them gently in melted butter until soft – about 4 minutes – add to the sauce, and heat through.

Diced chicken or lamb, flaked cooked fish, or chopped cooked vegetables can be added to this sauce, heated through and used as a filling for vol-au-vents, savoury pancakes, etc.

Horseradish Sauce

Good greengrocers should keep fresh horseradish in stock and the best sauce is made from the freshly grated root.

3 tablespoons freshly grated horseradish	2 teaspoons castor sugar
¼ teaspoon dry mustard	1 tablespoon white wine vinegar
salt and pepper	¼ pint double cream

Combine horseradish, mustard, castor sugar and vinegar, season with a little salt and pepper, and leave to stand for five minutes.

Whip cream lightly and fold in the horseradish mixture.

Quick Horseradish Sauce

4 tablespoons bottle creamed horseradish sauce	¼ pint double cream
1 teaspoon white wine vinegar	salt and pepper

Mix vinegar with horseradish sauce, season well with salt and pepper, and leave to stand for a few minutes. Whip cream lightly and fold it into the horseradish.

Cumberland Sauce

A useful quickly made sauce which makes all the difference to cold tongue and ham.

¼ pint port

1 teaspoon lemon juice

2½ tablespoons redcurrant jelly

salt and pepper

juice and rind of one orange

Thinly pare the rind from the orange, cut off any white membrane from the inside of the skin, cut into very thin strips and blanch for 3 minutes in boiling water. Drain well.

Combine all the ingredients in a saucepan and heat gently until the redcurrant jelly has dissolved. Cool before serving.

Note: For a more piquant sauce, add 1 teaspoon made mustard.

Sauce Vinaigrette

This is another of those classic French sauces which can be varied in countless ways. It provides the basis for many of the best meat, fish and vegetable salads and can happily pep up the most mundane of leftovers.

Basic Vinaigrette

3 tablespoons olive oil

1 tablespoon vinegar

salt and freshly ground black pepper

Combine all the ingredients and mix well by stirring, whisking or shaking in a screw-top jar.

Variations:

Vinaigrette with Mustard

The basic sauce is made sharper and more piquant by the addition of 2 teaspoons Dijon mustard or 1 teaspoon dry English mustard. Add a pinch of sugar to this mixture as well.

Curried Vinaigrette Dressing

Add ½ teaspoon grated onion and 1 teaspoon curry paste or powder to the basic dressing.

Onion Dressing

Add 2–4 teaspoons minced or grated onion to the basic recipe.

Garlic Dressing

Add a crushed garlic clove to the basic recipe.

Blue Cheese Dressing

Blend 1 oz. soft blue cheese to the basic recipe. This is good with vegetable salads.

Cream Cheese Dressing

Add 1 oz. cream cheese, 1 tablespoon chopped chives and a pinch paprika to the basic recipe and mix until blended.

Herb Dressing

Add 2 teaspoons finely chopped mixed chives, tarragon and chervil or parsley to the basic recipe.

Sharp Vinaigrette Dressing

Add 1 tablespoon finely chopped parsley, 1 tablespoon finely chopped chives and ½ tablespoon finely chopped capers to the basic recipe.

Mint Sauce

Serve with cold lamb or mutton.

1 handful (about 4 heads) mint	3 tablespoons white wine
1 tablespoon sugar	vinegar
2 tablespoons boiling water	small pinch salt

Remove stalks from mint leaves and chop leaves very finely. Combine mint and sugar and pour over the boiling water. Leave for 1 minute and mix in vinegar and salt. Allow the mint sauce to stand for at least an hour before using.

Chicken Giblet Sauce

chicken liver, heart and gizzard	few drops Worcester sauce
1 small onion	pepper
½ oz. butter	½ oz. butter
¾ pint water	½ tablespoon flour
1 chicken stock cube	

Chop the chicken liver and the heart, mince the gizzard, having removed all the surrounding fat. Peel and finely chop the onion.

Melt the butter in a saucepan, add the onion and fry over a high heat until golden brown, add the liver, heart, and minced gizzard, and cook until well browned. Pour over the water, add chicken stock cube, and a few drops of Worcester sauce, and season with a little pepper. Bring to the boil, lower the heat, and simmer for 20 minutes.

Beat ½ oz. butter with ½ tablespoon flour until smooth. Add this to the sauce and stir well, over a medium heat, until the sauce is thick.

Use as a piquant sauce for re-heating thin slices of cooked poultry or meat.

Mustard—Dill Sauce

A Swedish sauce and one which is delicious to serve with any fish salad or with cold sliced veal or thinly sliced cold beef. Fresh dill is difficult to get in this country but if you have a small patch in the garden, dill plants grow easily and make an attractive addition to an herbaceous border. Dried dill can be used in the place of fresh, but should be well soaked, drained and lightly dried before being added to the sauce.

4 tablespoons French mustard
1 teaspoon dried English mustard
2 tablespoons castor sugar
2 tablespoons white wine vinegar
6 tablespoons olive oil
3–4 tablespoons finely chopped fresh dill
salt and pepper

Mix together the mustards and sugar until they form a smooth paste. Beat in the oil, drop by drop, with a wire whisk until the mixture forms a thick emulsion, like mayonnaise. Gradually mix in vinegar. Blend in the dill and season with a little salt and pepper.

Quick Tomato Sauce*

1 medium onion
1 clove garlic
1 tablespoon olive oil
1 medium tin tomatoes (14 oz.)
1 tablespoon finely chopped parsley
1 heaped teaspoon dried chopped bell peppers
   (or 1 tablespoon finely chopped red pepper) } optional
pinch dried sage
salt and pepper

Peel and finely chop the onion, crush the garlic or put it through a garlic press.

Heat the olive oil in a saucepan, add the onion and garlic, and cook over a medium heat for 3–5 minutes until the onion is soft. Add the remaining ingredients, season with salt and pepper, bring to the boil, cover and simmer for fifteen minutes. *Note:* Some tinned tomatoes tend to have a rather sharp taste; if this is the case add a teaspoon of sugar to the sauce.

Serve the sauce with vegetables, meat or vegetable fritters, croquettes, patties, etc.

Italian Tomato Sauce*

2 tablespoons olive oil
2 rashers bacon
1 clove garlic
1 onion
1 medium tin tomatoes

1 tablespoon tomato purée
½ teaspoon sugar
pinch of sage and thyme
salt and freshly ground black pepper

Remove bacon rinds and finely chop the rashers. Crush and finely chop the garlic. Peel and finely chop the onion.

Heat the oil, add the garlic, onion and bacon, and cook over a medium heat for 5 minutes. Add the tomatoes, purée, sugar, and herbs. Season with salt and pepper, mix well, cover, and simmer for 15 minutes.

Apple Sauce*

We tend to think of apple sauce as being served only with roast pork or with roast goose but in fact it goes well with a great many other dishes. When you happen to have some cooked apple left over from a dessert try serving it with sausages and crisply fried bacon, with boiled ham, or with hamburgers and potato pancakes.

1–1½ gills *stewed apple or apple
  purée*
a knob of butter the size of a
  walnut

2 teaspoons lemon juice
salt and pepper

If the apples have been stewed in slices or rings press them through a fine sieve, purée them through a food mill or in an electric blender.

Heat the apple purée in a saucepan over a medium heat with the butter and lemon juice, season well with salt and pepper, and serve hot.

Caramel Sauce

This is a useful sauce which you can make in a few minutes and serve hot or cold over yesterday's lemon mousse, leftover ice-cream or those crushed meringues which happened to break as you tried to lever them off the baking tray.

8 oz. sugar
½ gill water
juice ½ lemon

Put sugar in a heavy-bottomed saucepan and cook, without stirring, over a medium heat until it melts and turns a dark brown. This should take about 5 minutes. Add the water, taking care that the sugar doesn't splutter and burn your hand. Stir over the heat until smooth and add the lemon juice.

Accompaniments

Whilst the main course is obviously the most important part of a meal, carefully thought-out accompaniments can give a plain dish an extra special touch. Try croûtons served with soup, crescents of pastry added to a stew or casserole, a plate of Melba toast with almost anything.

Pâté

Bought pâté used to be something of a luxury food, now it is possible to buy many delicious brands for only just over a shilling a ¼ lb. Try using small amounts of leftover pâté in any of the following ways:
1. Spread a little on circles of toast and serve under cooked steaks or hamburgers.
2. Spread pâté thinly on bread with the crusts removed. Cut bread into small squares and cook until crisp in a hot oven. Serve with soups.
3. Use in sandwiches.
4. Mix with a little cream cheese, season well with salt, pepper and paprika or cayenne, and use to stuff 2 inch lengths of cleaned crisp celery. Serve with salads or with drinks.

Frosted Grapes

These make an attractive table decoration or a garnish for a cake or pudding. They also make good use of a leftover egg white.

1 *egg white*
small green or red grapes
icing sugar

Lightly beat egg white until it is broken up but not fluffy.
Dip grapes, in small bunches, into the egg white and then dust
well with icing sugar. Place dipped grapes on a wire tray and
chill in a refrigerator for several hours.

Aspic Jelly

I am basically a lazy person, and admit that I usually make
aspic from packet crystals or by adding gelatine and a little
sherry to tinned consommé. If you feel like making the real
thing yourself, then here's how to do it.

1¾ pints good, well-coloured stock, made from meat, chicken, or fish	½ gill sherry
	2 oz. gelatine
	2 *egg whites, lightly beaten*
½ gill white wine	

The stock must be well skimmed and free from any grease.
Choose a large pan, preferably of thick enamel, and rinse
it out with boiling water. Scald a wire whisk in boiling water
together with a muslin cloth. Wring out the cloth and spread
it over the top of a bowl.

Dissolve gelatine in the wine and sherry. Put the cold stock
into the pan, add egg whites beaten to a light froth, and whisk
whites into the stock over a low heat. When the stock is hot,
add the gelatine mixture, and continue whisking until the
liquid comes to the boil. Remove the whisk and boil for 1
minute. Draw carefully aside and leave to settle for 5 minutes.
Return the pan to the heat and bring rapidly to the boil, then
set aside again and leave to settle for a further 5 minutes.
Repeat boiling and settling process once more and then pour
the aspic through the muslin. Lift up the cloth carefully and

set over another clean bowl and re-strain the aspic through the filter. If the aspic is not clear, strain it a third time.

To line a mould with Aspic Jelly

Chill a bowl or mould in the refrigerator until it is icy cold. Pour in some aspic jelly which is on the point of setting. Place the mould on a bed of ice cubes and swirl the jelly around until it forms a thin coating around the sides and bottom. Add more aspic if necessary. Decorate with thin slices of tomato, mushrooms (dipped in lemon juice), hardboiled egg or cooked vegetables, all brushed with a little aspic to keep them in place. Finish with another thin layer of the jelly before filling the mould.

Moulds can be filled with alternate layers of meat, or fish, and cooked vegetables and in this case each layer should be left to set before the next is arranged.

Chopped Aspic Jelly for decoration

Set the jelly in a shallow dish about $\frac{1}{2}$ inch thick. When set firm, turn the jelly out on to a piece of dampened greaseproof paper and chop, cut into strips, or into neat cubes. Keep the jelly in a refrigerator until the last minute before using it.

Making Aspic Jelly from packet crystals

Follow the directions for making the jelly but substitute 1 or 2 tablespoons of water with an equal amount of sherry.

Making Aspic Jelly from tinned consommé

Add 1 or 2 tablespoons sherry to the consommé together with 1 teaspoon gelatine per $\frac{1}{2}$ pint of liquid. Dissolve the gelatine in a small amount of hot consommé.

Quick Tomato Aspic

This is a jelly with a lot of flavour. It can be made in just a few minutes and goes well with many egg, fish, and vegetable recipes.

For 1 pint aspic:

1 pint tomato juice	1 teaspoon lemon juice
1 chicken stock cube	pinch celery salt
1 tablespoon gelatine	pinch paprika pepper

Heat the tomato juice, add stock cube, and stir until dissolved. Soften the gelatine in lemon juice, add to tomato juice, mix well, season with celery salt and paprika.

Chill the tomato aspic in a refrigerator until set.

Accompaniments for Soup

Most soups are improved by a garnish. Here are a few ideas to give even the most plain of soups a lift.

Sprinkle the surface of soup with:

Finely chopped parsley, chopped chives, or a little finely chopped lettuce.

Add to the soup at the last minute:

a spoonful of sour cream for each serving (this can be made by adding lemon juice, salt and pepper, to fresh cream)
a little finely shredded ham, tongue, or cooked meat
cheese cut into very small dice
raw mushrooms cut into wafer thin slices and dipped in seasoned lemon juice

Serve on the side:

 a bowl of grated cheese
 croûtons – tiny cubes of bread fried until golden brown in
   butter, dripping or bacon fat
 chopped or crumbled bacon, crisply fried
 cheese straws
 garlic bread or toast

Accompaniments for Curries

Someone once said to me: 'It doesn't matter much what a
curry tastes like, it's the trimmings that go with it which
count!' I have a sneaking feeling that this is right and now I
tend to fuss more with the bits and pieces which go with a
curry than with the dish itself.

Traditionally, of course, these dishes are designed either to
sharpen the taste of the curry itself or to soothe a burned
mouth after each mouthful – therefore they should be a good
cross-section of the piquant and the bland.

Bland accompaniments or side dishes for curries

1. Thin slices of banana sprinkled with fresh lemon juice.
2. Peeled and grated cucumber in sour cream or yoghurt,
seasoned with salt and pepper.
3. Desiccated coconut, lightly roasted in a hot oven for a few
minutes.
3. Popadums – paper thin pancakes of a pasta-like substance,
which can be bought from most good delicatessen stores and
which should be fried in very hot oil until they double in size.
Drain popadums to remove all the oil before serving and allow
one per person.

Sharp accompaniments or side dishes for curries

Serve a selection of at least four different chutneys (mango, tomato, sharp pickles, etc.) in small dishes.

Orange Salad

An essential accompaniment for cold roast duck or wild duck and many other cold meat and poultry dishes.

SERVES 4. No cooking.

4 oranges
1 bunch watercress
2 tablespoons olive oil
1 tablespoon white wine
  vinegar

1 teaspoon sugar
salt and pepper
1 tablespoon brandy (optional)
½ teaspoon chopped tarragon
  (optional)

Peel the oranges, remove all the white pith and membranes, and cut into thin slices discarding any pips.

Chop the watercress and arrange it on a flat serving dish. Cover with slices of orange and sprinkle with chopped tarragon.

Combine olive oil, vinegar, sugar, salt, pepper and brandy, mix well, and pour over the oranges.

Chill the salad before serving.

Potato Stuffing for Poultry

Stuffing a chicken is a job I hate, and so tend to ignore whenever I can. This is silly, because a stuffing does help to keep the bird moist as it cooks and also a spoonful of stuffing on each plate helps to make the meat go much further. Leftover mashed potatoes make a good and unusual stuffing for a chicken, duck or goose.

Cooking time for stuffing before roasting: 3–5 minutes.

½ lb. *mashed potatoes*	pinch thyme
chicken (duck or goose) liver	½ oz. butter
1 onion	½ tablespoon cream
½ teaspoon dried sage	salt and pepper

Finely chop the chicken liver. Peel and finely chop the onion. Melt the butter in a frying pan, add the liver and onion, and cook over a medium heat until the onion is soft and transparent, 3–5 minutes.

Mix all the ingredients together and season with salt and pepper. Fill the chicken with the stuffing and roast as usual.

Amount of leftover ingredient	Other main ingredients	Serves	Recipe
COOKED FISH			
ANY WHITE FISH			
4 oz.	prawns, mushrooms, double cream	4	Fish Filling for Savoury Pancakes, page 67
		4	Thick Fish Soup, page 50
6 oz.	mushrooms, prawns, scallops, cooked potatoes	4	Captain's Pie, page 75
6–8 oz.	mayonnaise, lettuce heart	4	Fish Cocktail, page 33
	tomatoes, sour cream	4	Fish Tart, page 66
	puff pastry	4	Cheesy Fish Puff, page 76
7–8 oz.	mushrooms, green pepper	4	Fish à la King, page 78
8 oz.	cooked potatoes	4	Fish Cakes, page 72
	beetroot	4	Fish with Beetroot, page 73
	cooked peas, cooked potatoes	4	Fisherman's Pie, page 74
	anchovies	4	Fish and Anchovy Ramekins, page 35
		4	Fish Soup, page 49
	green pepper, black olives, tomato, lettuce	4	Salad Niçoise, page 164
8–10 oz.	cooked potatoes	4	Danish Fish au Gratin, page 70

Amount of leftover ingredient	Other main ingredients	Serves	Recipe
COOKED FISH – *cont.*			
8–10 oz.	cooked potatoes, mushrooms	4	Creamed Fish with Potatoes, page 77
		4	Goujons of Cooked Fish, page 79
	avocados	4	Fish Salad with Avocado Sauce, page 35
8–12 oz.	cooked potatoes, tomatoes	4	Savoury Fish Pudding, page 69
	tin pimentos, peas, lettuce	4	Fish and Pimento Salad, page 165
10–14 oz.		4	Fish Croquettes, page 71
	prawns and cooked peas	4	Creamed Fish with Prawns and Peas, page 72
1 lb.	eggs	4	Fish Soufflé, page 68
1¼ lb.	frozen spinach, tomato	4	Fish Florentine, page 36
SALMON			
4 oz.	mushrooms, prawns, scallops, cooked potatoes	4	Thick Fish Soup, page 50
6 oz.		4	Captain's Pie, page 75
6–8 oz.	mayonnaise, lettuce heart	4	Fish Cocktail, page 33
	puff pastry	4	Cheesy Fish Puff, page 76
	tomatoes, sour cream	4	Fish Tart, page 66

Amount of leftover ingredient	Other main ingredients	Serves	Recipes
SALMON – *cont.*			
8 oz.		4	Potted Salmon, page 33
		4	Fish Soup, page 49
	cooked peas, cooked potatoes	4	Fisherman's Pie, page 74
	cooked potatoes	4	Fish Cakes, page 72
	green pepper, black olives, tomato, lettuce	4	Salad Niçoise, page 104
	mushrooms, cooked potatoes	4	Creamed Fish with Potatoes, page 77
8–10 oz.	prawns	4 (6)	Salmon and Prawn Mousse, page 162
	cooked potatoes, tomatoes	4	Savoury Fish Pudding, page 69
8–12 oz.	fish stock or cream	4	Fish Croquettes, page 71
10–14 oz.	prawns, peas	4	Creamed Fish with Prawns and Peas, page 72
1 lb.		4	Salmon Mould, page 163
	eggs	4	Fish Soufflé, page 68
SEA TROUT			
8 oz.		4	Potted Salmon (or Sea Trout), page 33
1 lb.	eggs	4	Fish Soufflé, page 68

Amount of leftover ingredient	Other main ingredients	Serves	Recipe
SHELLFISH			
6–8 oz.	anchovies	4	Fish and Anchovy Ramekins, page 35
8 oz.	mayonnaise, lettuce heart	4	Fish Cocktail, page 33
8–10 oz.	avocados	4	Fish Salad with Avocado Sauce, page 35
SMOKED FISH			
6–8 oz.	puff pastry	4	Cheesy Fish Puff, page 76
8 oz.	tomatoes, eggs	4	Scrambled Eggs with Haddock, page 80
8 oz.	green pepper, black olives, tomato, lettuce	4	Salad Niçoise, page 164
8–12 oz.	cooked potatoes, tomatoes	4	Savoury Fish Pudding, page 69
CHICKEN			
2 oz.	2 avocados, double cream	4	Avocados with Chicken, page 37

Amount of leftover ingredient	Other main ingredients	Serves	Recipe
CHICKEN – *cont.*			
2 oz.	mushrooms	4	Cream of Chicken Soup, page 50
	red or green pepper	1	Stuffed Green or Red Pepper, page 94
2 oz. or more		4	Curried Chicken or Veal Soup, page 51
2–4 oz.	chicken liver	4	Chicken Pâté, page 38
4 oz.	eggs, mushrooms	4	Chicken or Turkey Cocottes, page 39
	aubergines, tin tomatoes	4	Stuffed Aubergines, page 95
	eggs	4	Ham Mimosa, page 127
	ham	4	Ham and Chicken Savouries, page 134
	cooked peas, green pepper, rice	4	Chicken or Ham and Rice Salad, page 173
4–6 oz.	red or green peppers	4	Stuffed Peppers II, page 94
6 tablespoons	eggs, mayonnaise	4	Savoury Stuffed Eggs, page 31
wing or leg		1	Devilled Chicken Bones, page 145
6 oz.	cooked french beans, tomatoes, black olives, cucumber	4	Mediterranean Chicken or Ham Salad, page 41

Amount of leftover ingredient	Other main ingredients	Serves	Recipes
CHICKEN – cont.			
6 oz.	tuna fish, frozen peas or cooked vegetables	4	Chicken Robbelin, page 147
		4	Gelda's Fancy, page 152
	green pepper	4	Chicken Fritters Maryland, page 149
8 oz.	cooked ham	4	Chicken and Ham Velouté, page 176
	green pepper, salted almonds	4	Chicken Pilaff with Salted Almonds, page 143
		4	Creamy Chicken Pie, page 144
	mushrooms, almonds, pineapple	4	Curried Chicken and Rice Salad, page 177
8–10 oz.	cooked potatoes	4	Scalloped Meat with Potatoes, page 89
8–12 oz.	mushrooms	4	Risotto Milanese, page 86
		4	Basic Curry, page 98
	mushrooms	4	Meat or Chicken Pilaff, page 86
8 thin slices	cooked cauliflower, carrots or broccoli spears	4	Mr T's Chicken or Turkey Toasts, page 153

Amount of leftover ingredient	Other main ingredients	Serves	Recipe
CHICKEN – cont.			
8–12 slices		4	Chicken or Turkey à l'Estragon, page 142
	aspic jelly, red pimento	4	Chaudfroid of Chicken or Turkey, page 179
	pâté, red pimento, aspic jelly	4	Chicken and Pâté in Aspic, page 178
10 oz.	cooked vegetables	4	Cooked Meat Pasties, page 151
10–12 oz.		4	Potted Chicken, page 39
	double cream	4	Chicken Mousse, page 179
	vol-au-vent cases	4	Curried Chicken Filling for Vol-au-Vents, page 151
	mushrooms, green pepper, celery	4	Chicken à la King, page 148
	pancakes	4	Stuffed Savoury Filling, page 111
	aspic jelly, double cream	4	Chicken Mousse II, page 180
12 oz.	ham or bacon, prawns, cod, peas, tin red pimento	4	Paella, page 141
	celery, leftover vegetables	4	Maidenwell Special, page 150
	tomato juice	4	Chicken and Tomato Ring, page 177

Amount of leftover ingredient	Other main ingredients	Serves	Recipe
CHICKEN – cont.			
12 oz.	pineapple, green pepper, tomatoes	4	Special Chicken and Pineapple Salad, page 181
	celery, oranges, almonds	4	Chicken and Almond Salad, page 181
4 joints or 12 oz.	oranges, honey, almonds	4	Madders' Chicken Morocco, page 147
12–15 oz.	mushrooms	4	Turkey (or Chicken) Porjarski, page 156
1 lb.	mushrooms	4	Creamed Veal or Lamb (or Chicken), page 125
1½ lb.	celery, green pepper	4	Turkey or Chicken Rasputin, page 158
		4	Curried Meat, page 99
carcase			Stock, page 46
CHICKEN LIVERS			
1	cooked or frozen peas	4	Chicken Liver Soup, page 52
	tins consommé	4	Quick Chicken Liver Soup, page 52
Other suggestions for 1 chicken liver on page 154			

Amount of leftover ingredient	Other main ingredients	Serves	Recipe
CHICKEN GIBLETS			
Chicken liver,	carrots, onion, celery	4	Chicken Giblet Soup, page 53
Heart and gizzard			Chicken Giblet Sauce, page 276
TURKEY			
4 oz.	eggs, mushrooms	4	Turkey or Chicken Cocottes, page 39
6 tablespoons	eggs, mayonnaise	4	Savoury Stuffed Eggs, page 31
Wing or leg		1	Devilled Chicken Bones, page 145
8 thin slices	wine	4	Turkey Slices in Wine Sauce, page 158
8 slices		4	Devilled Turkey, page 157
8 thin slices	cooked cauliflower, carrots or broccoli spears	4	Mr T's Chicken or Turkey Toasts, page 153
8–12 thin slices	aspic jelly, red pimento	4	Chaudfroid of Chicken or Turkey, page 179
8–10 oz.		4	Basic Curry, page 98
12 oz.	mayonnaise	4	Turkey Mayonnaise, page 182

Amount of leftover ingredient	Other main ingredients	Serves	Recipes
TURKEY – cont.			
12–16 oz.	mushrooms	4	Turkey Pojarski, page 156
¾–1 lb.	tin mushrooms	4	Turkey Tetrazzini, page 159
1 lb.	celery, green pepper	4	Turkey or Chicken Rasputin, page 158
DUCK			
3–4 oz. per serving	tin pineapple, preserved ginger, ginger syrup	1	Duck with Ginger and Pineapple Sauce, page 161
8 thin slices	tuna fish	4	Duck with Tuna Fish Sauce, page 160
8–12 oz.	bacon	4	Duck Pilaff, page 159
GOOSE OR DUCK GIBLETS			
	carrots, onion, celery	4	Goose or Duck Giblet Soup, page 54
STUFFED GOOSE NECK			
1 neck	1 goose liver, eggs	4	Stuffed Goose Neck, page 155

Amount of leftover ingredient	Other main ingredients	Serves	Recipe
GAME			
4 oz.	game stock	4	Game Soup, page 55
carcase			Game Stock, page 46
2 oz.	red or green pepper, mushrooms	1	Stuffed Green or Red Pepper, page 94
COOKED MEATS			
2 oz. or more			
4 oz.	aubergines, tomatoes	4	Stuffed Aubergines, page 95
	sausage meat, mushrooms	4	Mini Meat Patties, page 128
	green or red peppers	4	Stuffed Peppers II, page 94
4–6 oz.	large onions	4	Stuffed Onions, page 96
4–8 oz.	mushrooms, bacon	4	Stuffed Bacon Rolls, page 96
6 oz.	marrow, tomatoes	4	Stuffed Marrow Rings, page 93
	eggs	4	Shepherd's Omelette, page 105
	noodles	4	Noodles with Meat Sauce, page 108
8 oz.	tomatoes	4	Minced Meat and Tomato Patties, page 103

Amount of leftover ingredient	Other main ingredients	Serves	Recipe
COOKED MEATS – cont.			
8 oz.	mushrooms	4	Mushroom and Minced Meat Patties, page 104
	mushrooms, celery, tomatoes	4	Meat, Mushroom and Herb Sauce for Spaghetti or Pasta, page 109
8 slices		4	Sliced Meat in Bagatelle Sauce, page 106
		4	Cold Meat Diable, page 85
8–10 oz.	potatoes	4	Scalloped Meat with Potatoes, page 89
	cabbage	4	Meat and Cabbage Casserole, page 102
8–12 oz.	mushrooms	4	Risotto Milanese, page 86
8–12 oz.	aubergines, tomatoes	4	Basic Curry, page 98
	mushrooms	4	Meat Provençale, page 87
		4	Meat or Chicken Pilaff, page 86
10 oz.	lasagne, mushrooms, tin tomatoes	4	Lasagne with Meat and Tomato Sauce, page 107
		4–6	Savoury Meat Pie, page 84

Amount of leftover ingredient	Other main ingredients	Serves	Recipe
COOKED MEATS – contd.			
10 oz.		4	Meat Sauce for Spaghetti, page 108
10–12 oz.	mashed potatoes	4	Meat and Potato Croquettes, page 104
	pancakes	4	Savoury Pancakes Stuffed with Cooked Meat or Poultry, page 111
12 oz.	mushrooms, tomato, marrow	4	Stuffed Baked Marrow, page 92
	potatoes	4	Cottage Pie, page 91
1 lb.	mushrooms, tin tomatoes, potatoes	4	Savoury Minced Meat, page 102
	tomatoes	4	Mary's Minced Meat Casserole, page 101
	aubergines, tomato	4	Moussaka, page 100
		4	Leftover No. 162, page 97
	cooked potatoes	4	Shepherd's Pie, page 90
	cooked potatoes, tomatoes	4	Continental Shepherd's Pie, page 91
		4	Petty i Panna, page 88
	tomatoes	4	Cold Meat in Fresh Tomato Sauce, page 166
	bananas	4	Caribbean Meat Patties, page 106
1½ lb.		4	Curried Meat, page 99

Amount of leftover ingredient	Other main ingredients	Serves	Recipe
BEEF			
2 oz. or more	horseradish	1	Beef and Horseradish Rolls, page 113
2 thin slices	ham, tongue, mushrooms, cooked vegetables	4	Mixed Meat Salad with Mayonnaise, page 167
4 oz.	cooked potatoes	4	Ham or Beef and Potato Salad, page 172
6 oz.	ham, mushrooms	4	Beef Olives, page 112
8 thin slices (undercooked)	macaroni, green pepper, tomatoes	4	Macaroni and Beef Pie, page 115
8–10 oz.	cooked peas and carrots, aspic jelly	4	Beef and Vegetables in Aspic, page 169
8–12 oz.		4	Potted Beef, page 37
10–12 oz.	cooked potatoes	4	Cheesy Beef Pie, page 115
	black olives, mushrooms, sour cream	4	Beef Stroganoff Salad, page 170
	cooked potatoes	4	Beef Salad, page 168
12–15 oz. (sirloin or fillet)		4	Cold Beef at its best, page 168
14–16 oz.		4	Beef Marikoff, page 112
1 lb.		4	Miroton of Beef, page 114

Amount of leftover ingredient	Other main ingredients	Serves	Recipe
SALT BEEF, BRISKET OR CORNED BEEF			
8 oz.			Red-Flannel Hash, page 116
8 slices	beetroot	4	Piquant Salt Beef, page 116
LAMB			
4 oz.	ham, tongue, mushrooms, cooked vegetables	4	Mixed Meat Salad with Mayonnaise, page 167
4–6 oz.		4	A Kind of Scotch Broth, page 56
8–10 oz.	cooked vegetables	4	Cardinham Special (Spiced Lamb Loaf), page 120
8–12 oz.		4	Lamb Pilaff, page 119
12 oz. or 8 slices	mushrooms	4	Lamb with Mushrooms, page 118
10–12 oz.	mushrooms, orange	4	Lamb in Rich Orange Sauce, page 118
1 lb.	mushrooms	4	Creamed Veal or Lamb, page 125
1–1½ lb.		4	Réchauffé of Lamb or Mutton, page 117

Amount of leftover ingredient	Serves	Recipe	Other main ingredients
MUTTON			
4–6 oz.	4	A Kind of Scotch Broth, page 56	cooked vegetables
1–1½ lb.	4	Réchauffé of Lamb or Mutton, page 117	
VEAL			
2–4 oz.	4	Curried Chicken or Veal Soup, page 51	
8 oz.	4	Cannelloni Toscana, page 125	cooked spinach, cannelloni
8 thin slices	4	Veal with Tuna Fish Sauce, page 124	tuna fish
8–10 thin slices	4	Veal Paprika, page 124	sour cream
1 lb.	4	Creamed Veal or Lamb, page 125	mushrooms
PORK			
8 slices	4	Cold Pork with Horseradish and Apple Sauce, page 170	apple purée, horseradish
8 thin slices	4	Pork, Apple and Vegetable Bake, page 121	cooking apples

Amount of leftover ingredient	Other main ingredients	Serves	Recipe
PORK – cont.			
8–12 oz.	bean sprouts or celery	4	Pork with Sweet and Sour Sauce, page 122
	bean sprouts, celery	4	Pork Chow Mein, page 123
10 oz.	tin tomatoes, cooked potatoes	4	Savoury Pork Shepherd's Pie, page 122
LIVER			
10–12 oz.		4	Potted Liver, page 42
LUNCHEON MEAT, SPAM			
10 oz.	cooked vegetables	4	Cooked Meat Pasties, page 151
TONGUE			
2 slices		1	Devilled Tongue, page 135
4 oz.	beef or lamb, ham, mushrooms cooked vegetables	4	Mixed Meat Salad with Mayonnaise, page 167
8 slices	mushrooms	4	Tongue Véronique, page 136
10–12 oz.	cooked potatoes	4	Tangy Tongue Salad, page 175

Amount of leftover ingredient	Other main ingredients	Serves	Recipe
COOKED HAM			
2 oz.	green or red peppers, mushrooms	1	Stuffed Green or Red Peppers, page 94
2 oz. ham or bacon	cooked chicken, prawns, cod, peas, tin red pimento	4	Paella, page 141
2 oz. or more			
2–4 oz.	tin tomatoes	4	Macaroni con Pomidori, page 128
	eggs	4	Egg and Ham Cocottes, page 32
4 oz.	aubergines, tin tomatoes, aubergines	4	Stuffed Aubergines, page 95
	eggs	4	Ham Mimosa, page 127
	chicken	4	Ham and Chicken Savouries, page 134
	cooked vegetables	4	Cooked Vegetables with Ham in a Mornay Sauce, page 186
	beef or lamb, tongue, mushrooms, cooked vegetables	4	Mixed Meat Salad with Mayonnaise, page 167
	cooked peas, green pepper, rice	4	Ham or Chicken and Rice Salad, page 173
	eggs, mayonnaise	4	Omelette à la Paysanne, page 132

Amount of leftover ingredient	Other main ingredients	Serves	Recipe
COOKED HAM – cont.			
4 oz.	sausage meat, mushrooms	4	Mini Meat Patties, page 128
	mushrooms	4	Ham and Mushroom Custard, page 40
	eggs, cheese	4	Ham and Cheese Soufflé, page 130
4–6 oz.	green or red peppers	4	Stuffed Peppers II, page 94
	cooked potatoes	4	Autumn Ham Salad, page 174
6 tablespoons	eggs	4	Savoury Stuffed Eggs, page 31
2 thin slices	cooked asparagus spears, lettuce	4	Ham Rolls with Asparagus, page 175
6 oz.	cooked french beans, cucumber, tomatoes, black olives, anchovies	4	Mediterranean Chicken or Ham Salad, page 41
	mushrooms, bacon	4	Stuffed Bacon Rolls, page 96
		4	Gelda's Fancy, page 152
	mushrooms	4	Ham Filling for Savoury Pancakes, page 134
	cooked potatoes	4	Ham or Beef and Potato Salad, page 172
8 oz.	eggs	4	Ham Omelette, page 131
	cooked chicken	4	Chicken and Ham Velouté, page 176

Amount of leftover ingredient	Other main ingredients	Serves	Recipe
COOKED HAM – cont.			
	mayonnaise, double cream	4	Ham Mousse I, page 171
	double cream	4	Ham Mousse II, page 172
	mushrooms	4	Creamed Ham and Mushrooms on Toast, page 135
8–10 oz.	cooked potatoes	4	Scalloped Meat with Potatoes, page 89
8 thin slices	button mushrooms, double cream	4	Ham and Mushroom Rolls, page 132
	mixed cooked vegetables	4	Curried Ham Rolls, page 174
	undercooked roast beef, mushrooms	4	Beef Olives, page 112
10 oz.	cooked vegetables	4	Cooked Meat Pasties, page 151
10–12 oz.		4	Potted Ham, page 41
	pancakes	4	Stuffed Savoury Pancakes, page 111
12 oz.		4	Rich Ham Quiche, page 130

EGGS – See Chapter on Eggs, page 221

EGG WHITES

EGG YOLKS

Amount of leftover ingredient	Other main ingredients	Serves	Recipe
HARDBOILED EGGS			To stretch meat and poultry and fish dishes in cream sauce sandwich fillings, garnish.
COOKED VEGETABLES – Cabbage, cauliflower, carrots, peas, etc., or a mixture			
From 2 oz.	tins consommé	4	Consommé Julienne, page 65
		4	Minestrone, page 62
3 oz.	cooked lamb or mutton	4	A Kind of Scotch Broth, page 56
4 oz.	cooked beef or lamb, ham, tongue, mushrooms	4	Mixed Meat Salad with Mayonnaise, page 167
	cooked chicken	4	Chicken Robbelin, page 147
	cooked chicken	4	Maidenwell Special, page 150
4–6 oz. or more		4	Thick Vegetable soup, page 57
4–8 oz.		4	Vegetable and Macaroni Cheese, page 192

Amount of leftover ingredient	Other main ingredients	Serves	Recipe
COOKED VEGETABLES – cont.			
From 4 oz.	rice	4	Mixed Rice with Vegetables, page 236
6 oz.	cheese	6	Cheese and Vegetable Quiche, page 198
8 oz.	mashed potatoes	4	Vegetable Patties, page 191
		4	Vegetable Pie, page 191
	sausages	4	Creamed Vegetables with Sausages, page 193
	ham	4	Curried Ham Rolls, page 174
	cooked chicken or turkey	4	Mr T's Chicken or Turkey Toasts, page 153
12–16 oz.	cooked bacon or ham	4	Cooked Vegetables with Ham in a Mornay Sauce, page 186
1 lb.		4	Purée of Vegetable Soup, page 58
		4	Russian Salad, page 200
		4	Cooked Vegetables in a Vinaigrette Dressing, page 200
1 lb. (green)	eggs	4	Green Omelette, page 199
1½ lb.		4	Vegetables in a Jellied Mould, page 201

Amount of leftover ingredient	Other main ingredients	Serves	Recipe
BROCCOLI			
8–10 oz.		4	Cauliflower, Broccoli, or Brussels Sprouts Soup, page 60
1 lb.	eggs	4	Green Omelette, page 199
BRUSSELS SPROUTS			
8–10 oz.		4	Cauliflower, Broccoli or Brussels Sprouts Soup, page 60
CABBAGE			
4 oz.		4	Cabbage Soup with Rice and Bacon, page 57
6 oz.	rice	4	Fried Cabbage and Rice, page 190

Amount of leftover ingredient	Other main ingredients	Serves	Recipe
CABBAGE – cont.			
8 oz.	cooked potatoes	4	Colcannon, page 198
		4	Cabbage with Egg and Cheese Sauce, page 187
10 oz.		4	Cabbage Soup, page 56
12–16 oz.		4	Hot Cabbage Salad, page 189
	tin tomatoes	4	Spiced Cabbage, page 189
		4	Cabbage with Sweet and Sour Sauce, page 188
1 lb. (or spring greens)	eggs	4	Green Omelette, page 199
CARROTS			
8 oz.	cooked beef and peas, aspic jelly	4	Beef and Vegetables in Aspic, page 169
	cooked potatoes, cooked cauliflower, lettuce, petits pois, frozen beans	4	Spring Vegetable Loaf, page 195
12–16 oz.		4	Cabbage with Sweet and Sour Sauce, page 188

Amount of leftover ingredient	Other main ingredients	Serves	Recipe
CARROTS – *cont.*			
1 lb.		4	Carrot Soup, page 58
1–1½ lb.		4	Vichy Carrots, page 196
CAULIFLOWER			
8 oz.	cooked potatoes, young carrots, lettuce, petits pois, frozen beans	4	Spring Vegetable Loaf, page 195
8–10 oz.		4	Cauliflower, Broccoli or Brussels Sprouts Soup, page 60
leaves of 1 large or 2 small	melted butter, or sauce Hollandaise	4	Poor Man's Asparagus, page 185
FRENCH BEANS			
6 oz.	cooked chicken or ham, cucumber, tomatoes, black olives, anchovies	4	Mediterranean Chicken or Ham Salad, page 41

Amount of leftover ingredient	Other main ingredients	Serves	Recipe
LEEKS			
8 oz.	cooked potatoes, tomatoes	4	Spanish Vegetable Flan, page 194
1 lb.		4	Scalloped Leeks, page 190
LETTUCE			
outside leaves of 2 large lettuces		4	Lettuce Soup, page 59
PEAS			
4 oz.	cooked beef, cooked carrots, aspic jelly	4	Beef and Vegetables in Aspic, page 169
	cooked ham or chicken, green pepper	4	Ham or Chicken and Rice Salad, page 173
	cooked fish, prawns	4	Creamed Fish with Prawns and Peas, page 72
	cooked fish, potatoes	4	Fisherman's Pie, page 74

Amount of leftover ingredient	Other main ingredients	Serves	Recipe
PEAS – *cont.*			
8 oz.	lettuce	4	French Peas, page 186
8–10 oz.	lettuce	4	Cream of Pea Soup, page 63
SPINACH			
4 oz.	cooked veal, cannelloni	4	Cannelloni Toscana, page 126
8–10 oz.		4	Spinach Salad, page 202
1 lb.	eggs	4	Green Omelette, page 199
POTATOES			
Baked Potatoes – see Using Leftover Baked Potatoes, page 203			
Roast Potatoes – see Leftover Roast Potatoes, page 204			
Boiled			
1 potato		2	Potato Omelette, page 213
4 oz.	cooked beef	4	Beef Salad, page 168
8 oz.	eating apples	4	Curried Potato and Apple Salad, page 219

Amount of leftover ingredient	Other main ingredients	Serves	Recipe
POTATOES – cont.			
	cooked leeks, tomatoes	4	Spanish Vegetable Flan, page 194
		4	Potato Pancakes, page 210
8 oz. (new)	cooked young carrots, cooked cauliflower, lettuce, petits pois, packet frozen beans	4	Spring Vegetable Loaf, page 195
8–12 oz.	pimento, black olives, tomatoes	4	Insalata di Patate, page 42
14–16 oz.		4	Rosti, page 214
1 lb.	cheese	4	Large Fried Cheesy Potato Cake, page 211
		4	Large Fried Potato Cake, page 210
	cheese	4	Fried Cooked Potatoes with Cheese and Onion, page 212
		4	Hot Potato Salad, page 214
	ham, eating apples, celery, chicory mayonnaise	4	Autumn Ham Salad, page 174
	black olives	4	Insalate di Patate, page 218
		4	Potato Salad with a Vinaigrette Dressing, page 219

Amount of leftover ingredient	Other main ingredients	Serves	Recipe
POTATOES – *cont.*			
	leeks	4	Vichyssoise, page 60
		4	Potato Soup, page 61
		4	Janson's Temptation, page 216
		4	Potato Gnocchi, page 205
		4	Creole Potatoes, page 207
Boiled			
1 lb.	green pepper	4	Farmhouse Potato Supper, page 207
		4	Indian Sauté Potatoes, page 208
		4	Sauté Potatoes Cooked in the Oven, page 208
	tin condensed mushroom soup	4	Rich Potato Bake, page 209
		4	Pommes Annette, page 209
1½ lb.		4	Pan Haggerty, page 195
Mashed			Toppings for Stews and Casseroles, page 204
			Mashed Potato Balls, page 212

Amount of leftover ingredient	Other main ingredients	Serves	Recipes
POTATOES – *cont.*			
8 oz.	cooked vegetables	4	Vegetable Pie, page 191
8 oz.	tin corned beef	4	Potato and Corned Beef Hash, page 217
	chicken (duck or goose) liver		Potato Stuffing for Poultry, page 285
12 oz.	cooked meat	4	Meat and Potato Croquettes, page 104
1 lb.	cooked cabbage	4	Colcannon, page 198
		4	Bubble and Squeak, page 197
		4	Potato Croquettes, page 206
		4	Pommes Duchesse, page 215
1½ lb.	orange	4	West Indian Mashed Potatoes, page 212
RICE			
2 oz.	ham	1	Ham Roll Stuffed with Rice, page 133
3 oz.	tin consommé, tomato purée	4	Consommé with Rice and Tomato, page 64
4 oz.	cooked cabbage	4	Fried Cabbage and Rice, page 190
8 oz.	cooked chicken, mushrooms	4	Curried Chicken and Rice Salad, page 177

Amount of leftover ingredient	Other main ingredients	Serves	Recipe
PÂTÉ – see Pâté, page 280			
4 slices	cooked chicken, red pimento, aspic jelly	4	Chicken and Pâté in Aspic, page 178
SAUSAGES AND SAUSAGE MEAT – see Sausages, page 138			
2 sausages	cooked carrots	4	Carrot Soup, page 58
4 oz.	eggs, cooked potatoes	4	Omelette à la Paysanne, page 132
BISCUITS			
8 oz.			Biscuit Pie Crust, page 259
BREAD			
4 slices		4	Queen of Puddings, page 242
4–8 slices		4–6	Bread and Butter Pudding, page 242

Amount of leftover ingredient	Other main ingredients	Serves	Recipe
BREAD – *cont.*			
½ stale loaf	tomatoes, cheese	4	Tomato, Cheese and Breadcrumb Pie, page 229
1 loaf		4	Croustades, page 229
CHEESE – see Cheese, page 223			
2 oz.	tomatoes	4	Cheese and Tomato Toast, page 224
2 oz. (blue cheese)		4	Blue Cheese Dreams, page 225
MACARONI			
6 oz.	red or green pepper, celery	4	Macaroni Salad, page 183
MILK – see Milk, page 226			
¼ pint sour milk or sour cream			Scones made with sour milk or cream, page 227

Amount of leftover ingredient	Other main ingredients	Serves	Recipe
PASTRY – see Leftover Pastry, page 237			
CHRISTMAS PUDDING			
			Fried Christmas Pudding, page 243
			Iced Christmas Pudding, page 243
CUSTARD			
¼ pint	cooked fruit, cream	4	Fruit Fool, page 256
½ pint	tinned fruit	4	Fruit Upside-down Cake, page 255
	fruit, cream, almonds	4	Fruit Foolishness, page 258
	cake, apple	4	Apple Trifle, page 246
FRUIT and FRUIT SALAD			
small amount of bananas, chopped almonds tinned or fresh		4	Bananas with Fruit Sauce (hot), page 249
6–8 oz. tinned	custard	4	Fruit Upside-down Cake, page 255

Amount of leftover ingredient	Other main ingredients	Serves	Recipes
FRUIT AND FRUIT SALAD – *cont.*			
fruit salad			Fruit Salad, page 254
tinned fruit	cream	4	Iced Fruit Pudding, page 257
tinned fruit or fruit salad	ice cream	4	Coupe à la Vanille, page 257
fruit salad	jelly	4	Fruit Jelly, page 249
fresh or tinned fruit	rice pudding	4	Fruit and Rice Mould, page 260
1 lb.	custard, cream	4	Fruit Fool, page 256
½ pint	cream, almonds, custard	4	Fruit Foolishness, page 258
stewed fruit			Fruit Tarts, page 258
8 oz. apple	cake, custard	4	Apple Trifle, page 246
½ pint purée	pancakes	4	Cream Feather Pancakes, page 256
1 pint purée	egg whites	4	Fruit Purée Pudding, page 261
½ pint juice or syrup	cream	4	Bavarian Cream, page 261

Amount of leftover ingredient	Other main ingredients	Serves	Recipe
JELLY – see Jellies, page 248			
RICE PUDDING			
	tinned fruit, cream		Rice Pudding Réchauffé, page 247
			Rice Pudding Moulds, page 248
CAKE			
2–4 oz. (sponge)	apple, custard	4	Apple Trifle, page 246
2–4 slices (sponge)	frozen orange juice, double cream	4	Frozen Orange Cream, page 246
2–4 slices (chocolate)	orange juice, double cream, chocolate	4	Chocolate Cake Mousse, page 247
4 slices (sponge or fruit)	fruit, double cream	4	Tipsy Trifle, page 244
	orange juice, egg yolks	4	Hot Cake and Vanilla Sauce, page 245
4 oz. (fruit)			Fruit Cake Fudge, page 245

Index